ARISTOTLE AND HIS SCHOOL

ARISTOTLE AND HIS SCHOOL

An Inquiry into the History
of the Peripatos
With a Commentary on
Metaphysics Z, H, Λ and Θ

Felix Grayeff

BOOKS
10 East 53d St., New York 10022
(a division of Harper & Row Publishers, Inc.)

Published in the U.S.A. 1974 by
Harper & Row Publishers, Inc.
Barnes & Noble Import Division

© 1974 by Felix Grayeff

ISBN 06 492531 5

Printed in Great Britain

CONTENTS

PREFACE

It gives me great pleasure to record my gratitude to Professor D. J. Allan who read the manuscript of this book and was good enough to send me some critical notes on various aspects of it. His suggestions have been most valuable to me and they have led me, in several instances, to modify my text or add to it.

I further wish to express my thanks to Mr Simon Marks for his efficient help in preparing the manuscript for the press; to Mrs Janet Rayner of Watford for her much appreciated assistance, especially with regard to the first chapter; and to my daughter Leonie who in reading the proofs suggested several stylistic improvements and also compiled the two indexes.

ABBREVIATIONS

An. Post.	*Analytica Posteriora*
An. Pr.	*Analytica Priora*
Cat.	*Categoriae*
Eth. Eud.	*Ethica Eudemia*
Eth. Nic.	*Ethica Nicomachea*
Gen. Corr.	*De Generatione et Corruptione*
Hist. An.	*Historia Animalium*
De Interpr.	*De Interpretatione*
Mag. Mor.	*Magna Moralia*
Metaph.	*Metaphysica*
Mete.	*Meteorologica*
Part. An.	*De Partibus Animalium*
Inc. An.	*De Incessu Animalium*
Phys.	*Physica*
Phygn.	*Physiognomonica*
Pol.	*Politica*
Rhet.	*Rhetorica*
Soph. El.	*De Sophisticis Elenchis*
Top.	*Topica*

INTRODUCTION

This book on Aristotle and the Peripatos aims at elucidating the origin and growth of the Aristotelian treatises and it poses the question whether the treatises are the work of Aristotle himself, or of some of the outstanding members of his school.

It had been assumed for many centuries that the work of Aristotle formed a unitary system to be understood as a whole, but as early as the beginning of the nineteenth century critics became increasingly aware of the difficulties inherent in this assumption. As they devoted their attention to a detailed study of the text they discovered inconsistencies, variants, repetitions and doublets, interrupted arguments and excursions, references to passages that could not be found, even manifest contradictions. It became the objective of Aristotelian scholarship to open a way to the understanding of Aristotelian thought by removing or at least explaining the inadequacies which had been detected. On the one hand, scholars tried to cure the flaws of the text, sometimes by altering or deleting words or clauses, often by transposing passages in an effort to establish a satisfactory reading, that is, one showing a consistent flow of thought. On the other hand, there were critics even in the nineteenth century who suspected a deeper cause of the deficiencies encountered. E. Zeller spoke of a 'basic dualism' in Aristotle's philosophy—an antinomy between idealism and realism. The English philosophers J. Cook Wilson and R. Shute were the first to call Aristotle's authorship of the treatises into doubt.[1] Then, in the early decades of our own century, W. Jaeger[2] proposed that the

[1] See J. Cook Wilson, *Aristotelian Studies* I, Oxford 1879, and 'On the structure of book VII of the *Nicomachean Ethics*, chapters I–IX', *Göttinger Gelehrter Anzeiger* 1880 (I); R. Shute, *A History of Aristotelian Writings*, Oxford 1888. Both these authors came to the conclusion that the text of the Corpus Aristotelicum as we read it was compiled by later Peripatetics and contains little of Aristotle's own words.

[2] W. Jaeger, *Studien zur Entstehungsgeschichte der Metaphysik des Aristoteles*, Berlin 1912, and *Aristoteles. Grundlegung einer Geschichte seiner Entwicklung*, Berlin 1923. Jaeger's *Aristoteles* has been translated into English by R. Robinson under the title *Aristotle: Fundamental: of the History of his Development*, Oxford 1948, 2nd ed. (quoted in this book). T. Case is another early exponent of the view that the Aristotelian philosophy developed gradually. See his article on Aristotle in *Ency. Brit.*, 14th ed.

Aristotelian text with its inherent difficulties should on the whole be accepted, and its conflicting statements understood as the varying expressions of the philosopher's gradually developing thought, maturing from Platonic idealism to his own realism. At first much acclaimed, this thesis has since met with growing opposition.[1] It was felt that the progress of Aristotle's thought could not have been as simple and straightforward as that envisaged by Jaeger. More particularly, it has been pointed out that several of the treatises expressing eidetic views are, by clear criteria, later than some of those showing a realistic tendency. Still, it is Jaeger's merit to have shown a way by which to free Aristotelian scholarship from the vain search for system. In this he has been followed—Aristotle's development in its various stages is still a much-debated question—though, lately, the study of Aristotle has to some extent reverted to the methods of the earlier scholars.

In making this new attempt at explaining the Aristotelian contradictions I intend to analyse the structure of *Metaphysics* Z, H, Θ and Λ—a task greatly facilitated by W. D. Ross's commentary on Aristotle's works. The analysis, which forms the main part of this book, is preceded by an introductory section on Aristotle's life and the history of the Peripatos after Aristotle's death, and on the history of the school library, especially after the closure of the school. Both sections of the book are designed to throw light on the genesis of the treatises, which must not be read as though they had been composed in a void, but as lectures delivered before often critical audiences of students, in the consciousness of changing trends of thought.

---

[1] See H. von Arnim, 'Die Entwicklung der aristotelischen Gotteslehre', in *Sitzungsberichte der Akad. d. Wissensch. in Wien* 212, 5 (1931); G. R. G. Mure, *Aristotle*, London 1932; W. K. C. Guthrie, 'The development of Aristotle's theology', in *Classical Quarterly* 27 (1933) and 28 (1934). More recently: F. Dirlmeier, 'Zum gegenwärtigen Stand der Aristoteles-Forschung', *Wiener Studien* 76 (1963), pp. 52 ff. and G. E. L. Owen, 'The Platonism of Aristotle', British Academy Lecture 1965.

Part One

CHAPTER ONE

Life of Aristotle

Considering the evidence that has been preserved, one may doubt whether it is possible at all to relate the life of Aristotle. The extant 'lives' are without exception late; they were written, or rather compiled, many centuries after Aristotle's death, in the late Roman period; their sources are uncertain and, at best, even these go back to late Hellenistic times. Hermippus of Smyrna (*c.* 200 B.C.) is generally regarded as the authority for the most important biographies, in particular that of Diogenes Laertius.[1] What the 'lives' tell us is often unimportant, in many cases unreliable, indeed fictitious, full of stereotyped anecdotes often recounted of other philosophers as well. They say almost nothing about what we should most like to hear: the genesis of the works, their order and their relation to the life of the author. And yet, disappointing though it may be that we cannot paint a colourful picture of the personality and the fortunes of Aristotle, some essential facts emerge, some principal features of his character and his career stand out clearly. Hence, the basic pattern of Aristotle's life can be reconstructed with near certainty. Beyond this, some important details can be established, with a high degree of probability, by inference.

*   *   *

It is a remarkable fact that the life of Aristotle, whose work appears as the very embodiment of contemplative thought and disinterested learning, was determined and formed, more perhaps than that of any other philosopher, by the events of the day, by intrigues and political upheavals. His home was Chalcidice in northern Greece, which about three centuries previously had been colonized by Ionic Greeks, chiefly from Chalcis and Andros. It bordered in the south-west on Thessaly, in the north-east on Thrace, in the north on Macedonia; to the east, beyond the Aegean-Thracian sea, it faced towards Asia and Persia. One can hardly name another district of

[1] See I. Düring, *Aristotle in the Ancient Biographical Tradition*, Göteborg 1957.

Greece that was as contested as Chalcidice. Athenians, Spartans and Corinthians claimed rights over its various cities. During Xerxes's campaign Potidaea was besieged and Olynthus destroyed. The great war between Athens and Sparta, the Peloponnesian War, began here, with the siege of Potidaea. Later there was a bitter struggle for the largest town of Chalcidice, Amphipolis, and the last decisive battle of this war, the battle of Aegospotami, was fought not far from here, in the Dardanelles. The Peloponnesian War was also a conflict of ideologies; every change in the political balance was reflected in the areas affected by the war. Whenever Sparta won, this meant that democratic town councils were banished and the government taken over by oligarchs. As soon as Athens regained the ascendancy, the oligarchs were expelled and the *dêmos* achieved power once more. And long after the end of the war between Athens and Sparta, Chalcidice again became a disputed country, when Macedonia grew in strength. The Athenian orator Demosthenes summoned Greece to the defence of Amphipolis and Olynthus against Philip of Macedon, who wished to subjugate Chalcidice.

Here, then, in the medium-sized or small town of Stagira, Aristotle was born, according to reliable calculation in the year 384/3 B.C., the son of the physician Nicomachus and his wife Phaestis;[1] he had a brother and a sister. Whether his father was born in Chalcidice or whether he moved there cannot be said; certainly his mother came from Chalcis in Euboea, where she possessed a house which remained the property of the family throughout Aristotle's lifetime. The aged philosopher fled to this house after his banishment from Athens, and in it he ended his life.

No doubt the young Aristotle was at first destined for the medical profession. The doctors of that time formed a sacred guild, or rather a single clan; they all claimed to be the descendants of the god of healing, Asclepius. So the art was a scrupulously guarded secret, into which father initiated son. Only the descendants of Asclepius were to practise the profession. These moved about freely; they met, learnt from one another and studied together while observing sacred ceremonies. Writings were produced among them in the course of time; one of the greatest of them,

---

[1] According to the *Vita Marciana* Phaestis, too, was of Asclepiad descent. See Düring, p. 107.

Hippocrates of Cos, was later regarded as their sole author. The education of the future doctor, who had at the same time to be an apothecary, no doubt began early. And so one may surmise (with Wilamowitz) that the boy Aristotle learned to crush herbs and roll pills.

The Asclepiads were travelling doctors; they wandered through towns and villages where the sick waited for their arrival. Normally, they would move within a limited area. It appears, however, that Aristotle's father found the conditions of life in Chalcidice unsatisfactory, and that in the course of his travels he crossed the border to Macedonia. Here prospects were more favourable, and here he was successful. Perhaps he attracted the attention of court circles through his industry, or he carried letters of introduction; in any case, he was appointed personal physician to the Macedonian king, Amyntas II (III), at a time when Aristotle was still a child. This was a highly significant turning-point, not only for Nicomachus himself, but also for the whole future of his son. For Nicomachus succeeded in laying the foundation of an intimate relationship between the Macedonian dynasty and his own family. Still, times were troubled. Amyntas was seldom able to reside in his capital. The country was not yet united under the throne and the king had continually to lead campaigns against rebellious princes, the heads of important families. His doctor had to accompany him on his campaigns, but unfortunately Nicomachus could fulfil his obligations only for a few years. The hard camp life was obviously too much for him; he died relatively young, when his son was only about ten years old.

It is nowhere recorded whether Nicomachus took his family with him to Macedonia or left them in Stagira.[1] This is a serious gap in the tradition (which here perhaps deliberately conceals an important circumstance). It may, however, be considered highly probable that Aristotle accompanied his father and so spent several years of his childhood and early youth in Macedonia, in the capital, Pella, at court. This is a natural assumption. It is confirmed by the fact that throughout his life Aristotle enjoyed close relations with the Macedonian government. It cannot after all be assumed that a connection with a royal court devolves from father to son without the latter being personally known at the court in question. Moreover,

[1] According to Diog. L. v, 14, Nicomachus owned a house in Stagira, but the passage has been called into doubt,

Aristotle later found in Philip II, Amyntas's youngest son, a patron and sponsor. As the two were of exactly the same age it is likely that they already knew each other as boys.

In the early development of Aristotle there were two deciding factors: the premature death of his father—and probably also of his mother; and later a new civil war and fierce feuds at the Macedonian court. The loss of his father meant the end of his intended career, for his father had also been his teacher of medicine. It may be that he, too, was to be trained as the king's personal physician. Now a relative, Proxenus of Atarneus, was appointed his guardian, to whom Aristotle was deeply grateful all his life (as his will demonstrates). Proxenus gave his ward's upbringing a new direction. He had him instructed in Greek rhetoric and poetry. In Macedonia this was nothing unusual. For some time it had been the custom for the Macedonian upper classes to try to acquire Greek refinement and culture. This is shown, among other things, by the fact that Euripides stayed in Macedonia for some time as the guest of King Archelaus. One can assume that at the very least there were at this time Greek teachers in Macedonia capable of giving excellent instruction. Aristotle would never have been able to write the fine Attic, which was universally admired, if he had not learnt it as a boy. Generally, Greeks and Macedonians regarded one another with a mixture of contempt and respect. The Macedonians were considered almost barbarians in Greece; their accent and their imitation of Hellenic customs were laughed at, though the wealth of their princes and the country's potential strength were known and respected; while on the other side the Macedonians, however much they tried to assimilate the Greek way of life, nevertheless despised the Sophists' playing on words and were conscious of the superiority of their own kingdom over the Greek city States, weakening each other by their everlasting disputes.

A new phase in Aristotle's life began in 367/6 when, at the age of seventeen, he went to Athens to join the Academy as a pupil. The moment at which he moved is perhaps not without significance. It coincided with a period of civil wars and bloody strife for the throne of Macedonia. For after the death of Amyntas in 370, his widow Eurydice allied herself with a noble of the country against her son, the new king. In the course of the war, the rebellious noble slew the legitimate ruler, whereupon the Queen-dowager married the successful rebel—the murderer of her son—and made

him Regent. So conditions at the Macedonian court were un-
favourable, even threatening, for a youth of Greek birth and a
favourite of the toppled royal house at that. It is therefore possible
that Aristotle's premature journey to Athens (for he was still a
minor) was partially due to the unrest in Macedonia.

It can be assumed that Aristotle joined the Academy as soon as he
arrived in Athens, doubtless in accordance with the wishes of his
guardian. The choice of the Academy was not a matter of course.
At that time there was another famous school, that of Isocrates,
which engaged in keen rivalry with the Academy.[1] Both schools, as
institutions, were something new, at least in Athens. There had, it
is true, long been travelling teachers or Sophists; Socrates, too, had
collected a circle around himself and held discussions with strangers
and friends in the streets and in the market-place. But the establishment of schools (*thiasoi*), sacred fraternities, with their own land
and temples was a development—an epoch-making one!—of that
period only. When Aristotle became a member, the Academy had
been in existence for about twenty years. Besides philosophical
dialectic, mathematics and science were taught there. And yet, what
characterized it in this early phase, was a desire not so much to
spread knowledge as to inquire into thought itself and explore its
power. Indeed one may say that a new awareness of the power of
thought had provided the stimulus to found the Academy. For
while previously it had been generally accepted that poets and sages
were the teachers of the Greeks, now it was felt that only those
practised in thinking—methodically trained philosophers—were
capable of guiding their fellow men; that they alone—if anyone at
all—would be able to solve the problems of mankind, those of the
individual and those of the community. For it was thought that if one
knew and could define justice, courage and piety, one would be
able to realize virtue both in oneself and in one's State, and make a
happy life (*eudaimonia*), possible. One must appreciate what great
enthusiasm, even euphoria, filled the Academy in its early period,
and that, as is only natural with a new discovery, excessive hopes
for the future were pinned on it. And just as Aristotle arrived in
Athens, such expectations had reached their zenith. The master
himself, the head of the school, Plato, had travelled to Sicily in
order to find, through philosophy, a successful solution to an
extremely difficult situation.

[1] See Isocrates, *Antidosis* 84; 261 ff.; 267 ff.

2

Plato had already been called upon once or twice before to give new laws to cities plagued with unrest, that is to say, to act as a political leader.[1] Until now, he had declined such tasks, but he was unable to refuse the invitation to Sicily. So, just as Aristotle joined it, the Academy was beginning to play a political role. However, it soon became apparent to Plato and his friends that many obstacles had to be overcome before philosophy could be made the basis of legislation, even in a monarchic State. An unexpected development occurred: philosophy itself was drawn into the turmoil of conflicting interests and party strife—an unfortunate turn symbolic for all future history. And yet Plato's Sicilian journey was the beginning of the Academy's political activities which continued for several decades. This is an aspect of the history of the Academy that has not yet been fully appreciated: no monograph on it has yet been written. Still, the political involvement of the schools was not unusual. Isocrates, the successor of the Sophists, was after all not only a teacher but also a political writer and consequently a politician, with pan-Hellenic tendencies. The Academy, on the other hand, as far as we can tell, always supported Athenian interests, at least as long as these were compatible with those of Sparta (at this time Athens and Sparta were usually allies). Thus the Academy achieved considerable consequence in Athens, and the *dêmos* of Athens could not but take a lively interest, particularly in Plato's Sicilian venture. For it was after all not so long ago that Athens had tried to conquer Sicily and incorporate it into the Attic maritime empire.

This, then, was the position of the Academy at the time of Aristotle's arrival in Athens. Plato himself was absent; in his place the mathematician Eudoxus of Cnidos was temporarily in charge of the school. We do not know which teachers first instructed Aristotle. It may be assumed that Plato's nephew and subsequent successor Speusippus (born about 407) was already lecturing, as was Xenocrates of Chalcedon, Plato's second successor as principal of the school (born about 396); it appears that later he and Aristotle were, for some time, friends. We know of other members of the Academy through Diogenes Laertius (Diog. L. III, 46), but none of them is named as Aristotle's teacher. It is however recorded that Aristotle received instruction from a pupil of Isocrates,

[1] Plato had been invited to legislate for the people of Megalopolis; Diog. L. III, 23.

the orator and tragic poet, Theodectes of Chios—that is, outside the Academy. Aristotle did not meet Plato himself until after Plato's return from Sicily. Plato, it is said, respected and praised the diligence and talent of the younger philosopher. He called him 'reader' and 'reason' (*nous*), as an anecdote has it.

Aristotle belonged to the Academy for twenty years, first as pupil, then as teacher and author. However fundamental this period must have been in his development, one must accept the fact that very little about it can be established with certainty. All we learn from Diogenes Laertius is that he held classes in dialectic and taught rhetoric (Diog. L. v, 3). It is impossible to say whether this was the sum total of his work as a teacher. Rather more can be deduced about his literary work, though even here much remains obscure. The works of Aristotle are, of course, divided into two groups: the esoteric, which were not published in the philosopher's lifetime, and the exoteric, i.e. books or pamphlets intended for a wider public, which Aristotle brought out himself. The former are preserved for us in the 'Corpus Aristotelicum'; of the latter, on which Aristotle's fame as an outstanding writer of the Platonic school rested in antiquity, only fragments survive.[1] These can be divided into philosophical, rhetorical and political writings.

Several unresolved questions arise in connection with the fragments. (1) In many cases it is uncertain whether a fragment really belongs to the published writings and not to the lectures.[2] In particular, many of the fragments collected together under the title *On Ideas* are quite close to the Corpus in style and content. (2) Moreover, a work's date of origin can never be determined with certainty. While it has often been assumed that the *ekdota* all belong to Aristotle's early period, there is no evidence for this assumption; in fact it is untenable. For example, *The Statesman* is addressed to Alexander, so must be late (about 330). And as *On Ideas*, whether genuine fragments of an *ekdoton* under this title are preserved or not, contained a critique of Plato's theory of ideas—and indeed in that form which Speusippus gave to it—this work is in all probability also late. So, no firm conclusions can be drawn from these *ekdota* about the early Aristotle.

---

[1] See *Fragmenta Selecta*, (ed.) Ross, Oxford 1955.
[2] No generally agreed conclusions have been obtained from the fragments, although many scholars have analysed them. See the bibliography in Ross's translation of select fragments, in *The Works of Aristotle*, vol. XII, Oxford 1952

On the other hand, we have fragments of works written entirely in the spirit of Plato and the Academy. The best preserved of these, including the *Protrepticus*, were obviously meant to win students for the Academy and arouse interest in philosophy. One may assume that Aristotle was respected within the Academy on account of these writings, in which his much-praised 'golden' style is discernible. Two things should be noted about the works of this group: (1) while they show the influence of Plato, they do not, as far as we can see, penetrate to the depths of Platonic philosophy; and (2) hardly anything in them points to a future Peripatetic philosophy. On the contrary, they occasionally contradict the views contained in the Corpus or at least have very little in common with them. For example, the discussion of the problem of the soul in *Eudemus* (the immortality of the soul is here the chief topic) is far removed from the epistemological standpoint and the close reasoning of *De Anima*. The *ekdota* of this group reflect the enthusiasm prevalent in the early days of the Academy, and they are addressed to a wide public. Aristotle wants all educated people to understand that even in practical life contemplative thought is highly useful.[1]

Over and above his propagandist writings, Aristotle published, as did other members of the Academy, a considerable number of books or pamphlets on popular subjects, mostly in the form of dialogues; these too could not but enhance further the Academy's reputation. He wrote about rhetoric and poets; about love and drunkenness, riches and nobility of birth; about Sophists and philosophers. All these writings, it seems, contained historic parts— stories or anecdotes about well-known figures of the past. In the work *On Poets*, for instance, he tells an amusing tale about the descent and birth of Homer; he also discusses Orpheus's right to be called a poet. Another point may be mentioned. At some time, perhaps during the last decade of Plato's life (357–347), religious concepts and ideas originating in the Orient aroused great interest in Athens. Oriental prophets and sages—Zoroaster and the Persian Magi—became well known there and the Persian gods Ahuramazda and Ahriman were equated with Zeus and Hades.[2] This contemporary mood is reflected in Aristotle's popular writings, where both the worship of the starry heavens and the veneration of a

[1] See *Protrepticus*; Ross, *Fragm.* pp. 47 ff.
[2] See Jaeger, pp. 132 ff.

creator who had produced earth and heaven found eloquent expression, in words that occasionally recall the verses of the psalms and the prophetic books.[1]

We can say, then, with some certainty that in the years when he belonged to the Academy Aristotle already displayed a literary versatility on which rested both his contemporary reputation and his fame during several centuries. On the other hand there is no clear evidence from which to conclude that, already in his Academic period, Aristotle was beginning to go his own way as a philosopher, as it were secretly or with a few intimates, or that he freed himself inwardly from Plato, starting his own independent philosophic development. It is true, one can hardly expect to hear about such profound aspects from the writers of the 'lives' which have come down to us. What is more important is that the surviving fragments of the undoubted *ekdota* hardly contain anything which would indicate a new, germinating Peripatetic philosophy. For as far as the criticism of the theory of ideas is concerned, this can date at the earliest from the period immediately after Aristotle's withdrawal from the Academy in 347 (as Jaeger assumes) or, far more probably, from the time of the founding of the Peripatetic school, after 335.

*   *   *

There can be no doubt that in the first decades of its existence the Academy consciously aspired to wield intellectual and political power in Greece. It succeeded in both, at least temporarily, despite some setbacks. For many of those educated at the Academy travelled abroad. They were particularly welcome at the courts of princes, where they acted as advisers and orators, as librarians and tutors; they spread Greek culture (as the Peripatetic philosophers did later), and wherever possible worked for Athens. Still, the greatest of the Academy's political enterprises was its first: the intervention in

---

[1] From the *ekdoton*, *On Philosophy*; Ross, *Fragm.* pp. 75 and 81 ff. B. Effe, in a well-argued recent study, has advanced the view that the doctrines of *On Philosophy* are entirely those of the mature Aristotle; see 'Studien zur Kosmologie und Theologie der aristotelischen Schrift "Ueber die Philosophie"', *Zetemata* 50, Munich 1970. But the new fragments which he would like to add to those usually attributed to *On Philosophy*, and on which his view is mainly based, are more likely to have come from esoteric than from exoteric writings; indeed, several of them are directly taken from the Corpus.

the affairs of Sicily. Plato went there twice,[1] and what happened in Sicily was of great significance both for Greek history and for the Academy.

Let us briefly outline the situation in which Plato was summoned. The tyrant Dionysius I, who had founded the dynasty, had been succeeded by his son, Dionysius II, in 367. The first tyrant had created a Sicilian empire with overseas possessions, in constant conflict with the Carthaginians, who occupied western Sicily. The eastern towns of Sicily, however much they would have preferred to be free, saw that they were protected by the tyrant from the Carthaginian invaders. So the monarchy had a firm foundation: it rested above all on its military strength, an army of mercenaries, a fleet and fortresses. It was still strong enough under Dionysius II to make its laws and decrees respected; it was still the best guarantee of order, and neither the old nor the young tyrant was personally unpopular. And yet there was discontent, which was probably, as always, caused by economic hardship, the ambition of individuals, the power of the factions and the mutual jealousy of the cities. Dionysius I had used his intimate knowledge of the country and its personalities to keep down all opposition through cunning or force. Now such measures seemed outdated. Something new was required. A reform party had arisen, the leadership of which was assumed by a powerful noble, Dion, a statesman related twice over by marriage to the tyrant's family, who was at the same time a friend or pupil of Plato.

Through Dion, Dionysius II was, shortly after his accession, referred to Plato. The young tyrant no doubt had a receptive mind: he was a child of the new era. Now it was explained to him that contemplative thought could lead far; that by setting high standards, he could establish a harmonious community life for all, instead of merely imposing unity by force. Plato was summoned and the Athenians urged him to go; what political goal Plato had in view is not recorded. Probably he wanted in the course of reforms to transfer the leadership in the towns to the new progressives, 'the best ones', so that they could then voluntarily form a Greek-

---

[1] See Plato, *Epistles*, especially VII; Plutarch, *Dion*. A new argument to prove the genuineness of the *Seventh Epistle* is contained in Professor K. von Fritz's recent, fine study on Plato in Sicily; see *Platon in Sizilien und das Problem der Philosophenherrschaft*, Berlin 1968. See also K. von Fritz's discussion of the philosophical part of the *Seventh Epistle*, in *Phronesis* XI (1966), pp. 117–53.

Sicilian alliance under the king of Syracuse. It is certain that Plato's intended constitution had monarchic as well as paternalistic and aristocratic features. But Plato's very first task was to win over the young Dionysius. He must make him understand the value of philosophy. But this he could only achieve by teaching him to think. In short, Dionysius was to become a pupil of the Academy, a Platonist—not in any dogmatic sense (as in our day a Marxist)—but in that he himself would philosophize. For only if he himself learned to argue in the Platonic manner would he be won over and remain convinced, and be able to renew his conviction whenever it seemed shaken. So Dionysius's instruction by Plato began. At once, however, all opponents of reform joined together. Whether they regarded Plato's intervention as dangerous for the peace of Sicily, or whether they saw themselves threatened in their privileges, they acted by summoning to the country a 'counter-philosopher', the historian and admiral, Philistus, who was to prove the superiority of the existing order over that visualized by Plato. The tyrant, faced with the choice between two contradictory doctrines, became unsure. At the same time suspicions arose as to Plato's intentions. He had come, it was said, to work not for Sicily but for Athens, for Dion. The parties opposed one another sharply. Plato was now no longer regarded as the king's philosopher; he had become the ally of the reform party. Completely under the influence of his friends at court, Dionysius then struck a blow not against Plato but against the reform party. He banished its leader Dion, and confiscated his entire property. Plato had to recognize that his enterprise had failed. He wanted to go home. The tyrant detained him for a long while. Eventually he was given permission to leave.

But, unsuccessful as Plato's first visit to Sicily had been, neither he nor the Academy gave up their plans for Sicily. Dion now lived in Athens, in close association with Plato's nephew Speusippus, honoured as a prince. He visited the large cities of Greece, including Sparta, soliciting support. From outside he brought influence to bear on the powers in Sicily. At last the tyrant saw himself obliged to restore Dion's property. A considerable success had been achieved; the reform party in Sicily grew in strength once more. Dionysius now thought that he would be able to maintain himself in power only through a reconciliation with Dion. So he summoned Plato for the second time, apparently as a mediator. A Sicilian State trireme came to Athens to fetch the philosopher ceremoniously;

equally formally, with the highest honours, he was welcomed to Sicily. The *Seventh Epistle* describes in detail what happened then. At first it seemed as though this time Plato's plan was to succeed. Then there occurred a kind of coup d'état, in which the king's bodyguard played an important part. Plato was taken prisoner and held in the castle; he seemed to be in danger of his life. All over Greece people began to show concern for his fate; so the philosopher and his school became known everywhere. At last, freed from his Sicilian captivity through the intervention of Archytas, a statesman of southern Italy, Plato could return home to Athens for the second time.

Yet even this was by no means the end. Plato himself, one may assume, now retired from political activity, in order to write his last great dialogues. But the Academy continued the battle against the Sicilian monarchy. As the last attempt at reconciliation had failed, Dion recruited troops in Greece. With these he landed in Sicily, accompanied by friends from the Academy. He managed to drive out the tyrant and take over the government. But he could not carry through his further plans and his reign was short-lived and unhappy. Barely a year after his landing he was murdered by a member of the Academy, Callippus, who now succeeded Dion, but could assert himself just as little.

The Academy could not have been more deeply involved in the struggle for Sicily. Although it had not succeeded in pacifying the island (this was only to be achieved ten years later by Timoleon) it had overthrown the tyrant and given the word for the unification of the Sicilian Greeks against the Carthaginians. Moreover, its intervention in Sicily was by no means an isolated action. On several other occasions the Academy took a hand in shaping events to the advantage of Athens, or at least roused others to action. Men connected with the Academy killed the Thracian tyrant Cotys[1] as well as a tyrant in Pontus. The murderers of the former, who escaped, were celebrated in Athens as heroes and freedom fighters. The memory of the murderers of the Pontine tyrant, who were caught and crucified, was long honoured in the Academy. Later, the Academy was to participate in the most determined way in the struggle between Athens and Macedonia.

There is no direct information about Aristotle's attitude at this time; his name is nowhere mentioned in connection with Plato's

[1] On Cotys, see *Politics* 1311^{b}22.

voyages to Sicily. Still, he could not have stood aside as a mere spectator; indeed he supported the Academy's enterprise vigorously through his propagandist writings. It is remarkable that parts of the *Protrepticus* bear a great resemblance to parts of Plato's *Seventh Epistle* (which indicates that the *Protrepticus* was written in these years).[1] And on the whole, even if he did not in other respects participate actively in the Sicilian undertaking, the events associated with it must have had a profound influence on his development and on the formation of his character and personality. They fell, after all, in the first fourteen years of his membership of the Academy, where no doubt they provided a constant topic of conversation and occupied everyone's thoughts. During this whole period Aristotle was able to sympathize with the Academy's view. He, like the others, must have wished for the victory of the Greeks over the Carthaginians, and in the matter of the internal Greek quarrels, his views were not incompatible with those of the rest of the Academy. Several Chalcidian towns belonged to the second Athenian maritime confederation (which had been founded in 378), and as long as Thebes and not Sparta was the rival of Athens in the struggle for the possession of Chalcidice, Aristotle, like the Academy, was on the Athenian side. But his position within the Academy and in Athens in general was bound to undergo a fundamental change when, after the fall of Thebes, Macedonia became her chief opponent. That great turning-point of history, the rise of Macedonia, also represented a landmark in Aristotle's fortunes. Here it is necessary to describe briefly the Macedonian kingdom and its changing relations with the Greek city States, particularly Athens.

For about a decade, as intimated, Macedonia had been crippled by internal disturbances and external wars. A party supporting the murdered king's brother was formed to oppose the Regent, Queen Eurydice's lover; the former was backed by Athens, the latter sought help from Thebes. Athens proved itself superior; the Regent was overthrown and killed. But the new king did not rule long either and fell in battle against the Illyrians. Then an epoch-making change occurred. The next ruler, Philip II, the youngest son of Amyntas and Eurydice, Aristotle's contemporary, not only

---

[1] Ross, *Fragm.* pp. 49–52 (*Protrepticus*). Compare Plato, *Epistles* VII, 328D ff. and 334D ff. In both the *Seventh Epistle* and the *Protrepticus* virtue is extolled as against pleasure; the philosopher is compared with the physician and is described as the only good legislator, while a unique role is assigned to philosophy.

freed Macedonia from external intervention, but also began to exploit the internal Greek disputes to his own advantage, and in this was so successful that by the end of his reign he was master of all Greece. The Macedonians were a warlike people, lacking only discipline and organization; Philip gave them both, and soon his army had become invincible. At the beginning of his reign it was Philip's intention not to allow any enmity between himself and Athens to arise while he still feared her power. The Athenians' leading statesman at this time was Eubulus, under whom trade and commerce flourished, and it seems there was general prosperity. Eubulus, it is true, also endeavoured to check the expansion of Macedonian power, but his chief aim was the preservation of peace, through a policy of coming to terms with Philip. However, voices were soon raised in opposition; a passionately patriotic party formed under the leadership of Demosthenes, which called for open war against Philip, not only in Athens, but also in the rest of Greece. Again, it was over the possession of Chalcidice that a quarrel flared up. Philip's first success was the capture of Amphipolis, which made him master of the Pangaeic gold-mines. As a result, the Attic maritime confederation collapsed, and Isocrates, who supported Eubulus, advised the Athenians to accept the dissolution of their empire. The moderates were still trying to pursue their policy of peace. But when Philip began to besiege Olynthus, the capital of the Chalcidian federation, and this city sent an embassy to Athens to ask for help, Eubulus lost the power and influence he had long enjoyed and the party of Demosthenes became dominant. It was decided to send an Athenian army to Chalcidice—too late. Olynthus fell (348) and the majority of the Chalcidian towns surrendered. Stagira, Aristotle's birth-place, resisted, but was subdued and had to swear the oath of allegiance to Philip.

In the same year (347), Aristotle left Athens. A violently anti-Macedonian atmosphere was prevalent there. Whether Aristotle's position had already become difficult during the immediately preceding years cannot be determined. Disturbances now broke out, directed against the friends of Macedonia. According to an ancient source, an accusation was made against Aristotle himself,[1] and although the source is unreliable (its story might refer to 323), there may well be a grain of truth in it. For if at that time even

---

[1] See Düring, p. 59; also Chroust in *Historia* 15, 2 (1966), pp. 185 ff. and *Greece and Rome* 14, 1 (1967), pp. 39-43.

Athenians came under suspicion of being corrupted by Philip, how much more likely was suspicion to turn against a metic, in particular against someone who had grown up at the Macedonian court, and who was a native of Chalcidice, which had just become a Macedonian province? Moreover, Aristotle, it seems, had taken no action during the siege of Stagira, while he might have been expected to help in the defence of his native city. A few years later, the Academician Cleon resolutely held Byzantium against Philip (Plut. *Phokion*, 14).

Still, it is conceivable that it was not political reasons which caused Aristotle to leave Athens at this time, but the internal affairs of the Academy. It so happened that, in the same year in which Stagira fell, Plato died, and his nephew Speusippus became head of the school. Diogenes Laertius says in one place (Diog. L. v, 2) that Aristotle had broken away from the Academy even in Plato's lifetime, but in another (Diog. L. v, 9) that he did not leave Athens until after Plato's death. No doubt it would have been disagreeable for Aristotle to work at the Academy under Speusippus, whose philosophy he rejected; it was the theory of ideas in its Speusippean form that later became the chief target of Peripatetic criticism. But, however much one may suspect that Aristotle left Athens because he no longer wanted to stay at the Academy, it is clear, from the destination of the journey on which he now set out, that the political motive was the deciding one; and furthermore, that not only was he acting on Macedonian instructions but that he had in all probability been in contact with emissaries from Philip for some time. For he now set out for the court of the tyrant Hermias, who ruled Assos in Asia Minor (in the Troad), an outpost of Greece, a district bordering on Persia and of great significance for all Philip's military plans against the Persian empire. And here—it must also be emphasized—Aristotle was received with unusual honours.

*   *   *

Assos in the Troad faces the island of Lesbos; it had been colonized by Greeks and belonged to Mysia. The population consisted mostly of Mysian peasants, day-labourers and slaves; to these was added a Greek, mainly Ionic, upper class. To all appearances an independent monarchy (*tyrannis*), Assos was in reality dependent on the Persian king. A few facts have been recorded about the ruler of this period, Hermias.[1] He was, it is said, of Bithynian origin (as was Xeno-crates), without doubt a Greek. According to a hostile tradition he was a eunuch and began as a slave, becoming the confidant of his predecessor, the tyrant Eubulus, after whose violent death he seized power. For more than twenty years he had kept his throne, doubtless by managing to keep in favour with the Persians without alienating his Greek subjects. He was rich enough to support an army of mercenaries. His court possessed a certain glamour, and he established, here on colonial soil, a centre of Greek culture. Two philosophers from the Troad who had been trained at the Academy, Erastus and Coriscus, worked here.[2] He therefore fostered cultural relations with Athens, which, since it no longer feared her, the Persian government tolerated and even favoured.

Now, however, after Philip's victories in Chalcidice, the overall political situation began to change. It was no longer the ancient Greek cities but Macedonia which appeared as the champion of pan-Hellenic aspirations. Assos gained in importance as a strong point, a bridge-head for a possible Greek attack on Persia. Athens too recognized this; out of hatred for Philip, Demosthenes warned the Persians of Macedonian intentions against Asia Minor and even tried to form an alliance with Persia to protect Assos against Philip. Much depended on the attitude of the ruler of Assos, Hermias. For many years he had tacked skilfully, reconciling Persians and Greeks with one another. But now—just as Aristotle arrived in Assos—he changed course sharply. He went over to Philip's side and made a secret military treaty with him. And about the same time he bestowed honours on Aristotle, indeed, took him into his family by marrying him to his niece, or adopted daughter, Pythias.

Aristotle's close relationship with Hermias was taken much amiss in Academic circles.[3] This and a great deal of other evidence supports the view that Aristotle went to Assos on Philip's behalf. Obviously Hermias saw Macedonia as the rising power, through whose goodwill alone he would be able to secure his throne, and

---

[1] See D. E. W. Wormell, 'The literary tradition concerning Hermias of Atarneus', in *Yale Classical Studies* 5 (1928); Demosth. *Oratio* x, 31 with scholia. Compare Jaeger, p. 119.

[2] See Plato, *Epistles*, VI.

[3] See Diog. L. v, 11.

with whom he wanted to ally himself closely. If, then, he made Aristotle his son-in-law, he must have regarded him as Philip's favoured representative and ambassador, almost as a member of the Macedonian court. Only this can explain his action. Although there exists no special study of the matrimonial policy of the Greek tyrants, a glance at the history of Cylon, of Pisistratus and of Dionysius and his son shows—as might be expected—that the tyrants entered into or arranged marriages in order to achieve power or to maintain themselves in it. For Aristotle too this marriage meant many and great advantages. Through it he rose almost to the rank of prince, and acquired a fortune befitting his new position.[1] He never forgot what he owed to his marriage with Hermias's daughter. He always treated his wife with reverence as a princess, and when she died, after ten years of marriage, he raised a shrine to her in his house, at which he offered her sacrifices as though to a goddess removed to heaven. He had a daughter by her, who bore her mother's name, Pythias. Nor did he marry again after his wife's death. It is true that in later years he enjoyed a happy relationship with a woman from his home town of Stagira, Herpyllis, who gave him a son, Nicomachus, but he never made this second companion his legal wife.

Let us now see what happened in Assos while Aristotle resided there. Hermias, after ruling for twenty years with Persian support, was preparing to defect openly from Persia. It may be that Demosthenes denounced him, or that his own subjects betrayed him; in any event the Persian government became suspicious of his designs and after some hesitation decided on military intervention. A Persian army was sent to Assos. Soon Hermias found himself besieged in his citadel in Atarneus. In which year the campaign took place (certainly after 347, and before 341) or how long the siege dragged on, we do not know. At last the Persian commander managed to defeat Hermias by trickery. He invited him to a conference. Hermias accepted, but hardly had he left his castle when he was declared a prisoner and taken to Persia in chains. Put on trial in Susa, he was subjected to torture, but even so did not betray his Macedonian friends. Although he admitted nothing, he was found guilty and executed by crucifixion. Aristotle, however, with his wife and probably his servants, as well as the other philosophers who had belonged to Hermias's court, had managed to

[1] Aelianus, *Var. Hist.* IV, 19; Athenaeus IX, 398[e]. See Düring, pp. 298 ff.

escape; a ship lying ready in the harbour had taken them to the neighbouring island of Lesbos (Strabo XIII, 1, 57).[1]

Aristotle had spent about three years in Assos (from 347 to 344/3) and—as his later career allows us to infer—he had here proved himself in the eyes of the Macedonian government. Hermias had been overthrown, but he had advanced Philip's plans and he had revealed no secrets to the Persians. Grateful to his memory, Aristotle dedicated a hymn to him, in which he praised the dead man for his loyalty and courage (*aretê*) and compared him to Hercules and Ajax. And when a statue and a cenotaph were dedicated to Hermias in Delphi, Aristotle is supposed to have written the epitaph (Diog. L. v, 6). But even this pious gesture was harshly criticized by the Athenians, as an epigram by Theocritus of Chios shows. 'The empty-headed Aristotle,' it says, 'has given the slave Hermias an empty grave—Aristotle, who out of insatiable greed had preferred the murky waters of Assos to the ⟨pure spring of the⟩ Academy' (Diog. L. v, 11).

In Athens, then, they thought little of the school in Assos. Nevertheless, useful work was probably done there. A circle of philosophers had been at the court for many years. When Aristotle arrived, straight from the Academy, famous as an author and supported by Hermias, the leadership naturally fell to him. So he would have had at his disposal a staff of assistants; perhaps Xenocrates too belonged to it for a time, for it is said that he left Athens with Aristotle, but did not stay long in Assos. One can, therefore, assume that here, for the first time, Aristotle organized the joint work of several scholars and scientists, a prelude to a greater achievement in later years. In particular, biological studies were pursued in this circle, as had been done before in the Academy, which in this respect too served as a model for Aristotle; for in the *Historia Animalium* many observations are recorded which refer to places situated in the vicinity of Assos and Lesbos.[2]

*   *   *

[1] Jaeger, pp. 115–17, Wormell (see p. 28 n.) and Düring, p. 279 doubt that Aristotle had to flee from Assos. But Strabo XIII, 1, 57 reports Aristotle's flight and it is hard to imagine why Aristotle should have gone to Lesbos—just opposite the coast of Assos—if he had had a choice.

[2] This was first noted by D. W. Thompson in *The Works of Aristotle Translated*, vol. 4, Oxford 1910, p. vii.

The island of Lesbos, to which Aristotle had fled from Assos, was only intended by him as a temporary refuge. Here he waited until he could continue his journey to Macedonia. The opportunity for this arose quite soon; he probably remained in Lesbos little more than a year. Although we have no direct information about his stay, the *Historia Animalium* (see above) does show that the biological and zoological studies begun in Assos were continued here on a larger scale, from which it may be deduced that in Lesbos too Aristotle directed the joint work of many, stimulating his collaborators to carry the work further after he had left. For these studies, which demanded a large number of assistants such as hunters, fishermen etc., must have extended over many years. Besides, it is known that for this undertaking ample Macedonian funds were placed at Aristotle's disposal—eight hundred talents, according to Athenaeus (Ath. IX, 398ᵉ). At first, his scientific assistants were probably the same ones who had gathered around him in Assos, but it is not improbable that Theophrastus, who himself came from Lesbos (Eresus), now joined him there. About fifteen years younger than Aristotle and later, of course, his successor as head of the Peripatetic school, Theophrastus too may originally have been a pupil of Plato; afterwards, however, he proved to be one of Aristotle's most important and loyal assistants; certainly he was already at Aristotle's side during his subsequent stay in Macedonia.[1]

We must now look again at the general situation. The years following Aristotle's departure from Athens were marked by the continued rise of Macedonia. In 346 Philip had made an advantageous peace with Athens. He used this to conduct new campaigns in the west and north. Epirus on the Ionic sea, the home of his wife Olympias, had rebelled against him; he invaded Epirus and subjugated it again. Then he turned against the half-barbarian Thracians, whose territory bordered on Macedonia in the northeast and had been fought over by Greeks and Persians for over a century, and in a few years accomplished what Athens, Sparta and Thebes had never achieved: he wrested Thrace from the Persians and, after eliminating the influence of Athens, made it a Macedonian protectorate. Thus he secured his position in the north. A new phase of his activities could begin; he could again turn his attention to Greece. From Thrace he returned to his capital, Pella (342/1).

[1] See Jaeger, p. 115 n.

At about this time, as far as we know, Aristotle too arrived in Macedonia.

It was a different Macedonia from that which Aristotle had left as a youth twenty-five years before. Then civil wars had torn the country, now it was united under Philip. Order had been achieved, and that joyful consciousness of strength which accompanies or precedes great national deeds permeated all classes of the population, the princes in command of the army as well as those who fought in the ranks of the phalanx. Philip himself was revered as hardly a king of the Greek world had been before him. Nor was he satisfied with anything less than limitless flattery, from his own courtiers as well as from strangers. Below the surface, the intrigues at the Macedonian court probably never ceased, but openly nobody dared speak of Philip without comparing him if not to the gods, at least to Hercules.

Whether Aristotle came on Philip's invitation or of his own accord, chancing his luck, as it were, cannot be said. It is likely that he travelled through Chalcidice and that there he visited his native town of Stagira, which had been half-destroyed by Philip. For according to Plutarch (*Alex.* VII) he prevailed on the Macedonian kings to rebuild the town and allow its banished inhabitants to return. One may guess that he was asked by the exiles to intercede on their behalf and that this request served him as a pretext for his journey to Macedonia. Of course, Plutarch also tells us that Aristotle was summoned to Macedonia as Alexander's tutor, but, by all accounts, this famous story can only be a legend which originated much later. For Plutarch himself, reporting the story in the seventh chapter of his biography of Alexander, where he draws on a Stoically moralizing source, informs us in the fifth chapter—as a historian—that naturally Alexander had a large number of tutors and teachers; that the official director of his studies was a prince, his maternal uncle Leonidas, while the actual director was a philosopher or orator from Acarnania, Lysimachus. At this time, moreover, as Jaeger has pointed out,[1] Aristotle was by no means the outstanding philosopher that Plutarch knew of. In fact, the legend cannot have arisen earlier than towards the end of the first century B.C., at which time not only was Alexander famous as the greatest conqueror, but Aristotle was famous as one of the foremost thinkers. At best, then, Aristotle was among those who lectured occasionally to the young

[1] See Jaeger, p. 120.

Alexander, especially as in any case it was one of the tasks of a philosopher or Sophist resident at court that he should play his part in the education of the younger generation. In short, the true purpose of Aristotle's stay in Macedonia, which lasted about seven years, must be sought elsewhere, in the realm of politics and, in particular, in connection with Philip's plans to unite all Greece under his leadership.

The most influential of the Greek cities was still, or once more, Athens. This city could be Philip's most dangerous opponent or his most valuable ally. With Athens on his side he could dominate Greece. Therefore Philip's policy after his return from Thrace was almost exclusively directed at winning over Athens, by peaceful means if possible. There is no need to discuss here the economic and diplomatic measures he took for this purpose. The role of cultural policy in his calculations is, however, important for us. The school of Isocrates in Athens was in sympathy with his efforts; it had Hellenic and cosmopolitan tendencies, and Isocrates himself saw in Philip the champion of Greece, who would bring Greek enlightenment to a barbarian world. The Academy, however, supported Athenian and patriotic policies; it inclined towards the party of Demosthenes, which fought Philip bitterly. Its head at this time, Plato's nephew Speusippus, was without doubt an opponent of Macedonia (despite the conclusions recent commentators have drawn from the spurious thirtieth Sophist epistle).[1] When Philip besieged Byzantium (340), an Academician, Cleon, went to the city and, rousing the fighting spirit of the inhabitants (as Gylippus had done in Syracuse), he triumphantly succeeded in holding Byzantium against Philip. So if the Academy's attitude were to change, if it were directed by a man whom Philip could trust, this would be of inestimable value to the king. Athens was *Hellados Hellas*, 'Greece's Greece'. Aristotle had been a member of the Academy for twenty years; he had worked there with the other *hetairoi*, and he knew Athens. Speusippus was old; the question of his successor was bound soon to become acute. No doubt Aristotle was welcome at the Macedonian court and received help in every way because it was hoped that, when the time came, he would, as scholarch, take charge of the Academy in Athens.

This, then, was the purpose of Aristotle's stay in Macedonia and the task for which he was preparing himself. As is to be expected,

[1] See Bickermann and J. Sykutris in *Ber. Leipz. Ges.* 80 (1927), p. 2.

no particulars of how he went about the latter are found in our records, least of all details about his intellectual development at this time. Since, however, we learn that, when he arrived in Athens some seven years later, he brought with him an extensive library, as well as abundant other teaching material, and since he was doubtless accompanied by assistants, we may deduce that Aristotle collected material and books in Macedonia and that within his circle of helpers he undertook or directed research. One may well ask what kind of studies these were. First, it is certain that the biological studies which had been begun earlier were continued in Lesbos for many years, but were not taken up in Macedonia; the evidence for this is the absence in the *Historia Animalium* of place-names relating to Macedonia. So Aristotle's studies now lay in other fields, and it may be presumed that their range was now much wider and that he began to collect, or to have collected, data on the history of philosophy and science, on early poetry and poets, perhaps even on the history of cities and their constitutions. And since, according to Diogenes Laertius, Aristotle himself as a lecturer had already held classes in dialectic, he no doubt assembled further material for use in such classes—arguments, proofs, refutations of fallacies. This material, it seems, is preserved in *Topics* books II–VII, which do not presuppose the discovery of the syllogism and seem to be borrowed from, or stimulated by, the Academy.[1] Callisthenes, Aristotle's nephew, was certainly one of his assistants; he later accompanied Alexander to Asia, but he fell into disgrace and was executed for attempted regicide. That Theophrastus was probably his assistant in Macedonia has been mentioned above. It is likely that during his stay in Macedonia Aristotle also wrote and published new works, on poetry, wealth, and concerning the duties of kings. In one of the latter he toned down— apparently in accordance with, or perhaps shaping, Macedonian views—one of Plato's famous sayings. The world would not recover its health, Plato had said, until philosophers were kings and kings philosophers. Kings, Aristotle declared, should not themselves be philosophers, this would produce grave disadvantages; but they should have philosophers as advisers.[2]

Whether he was already beginning to formulate his criticism of

[1] See Ross, *Aristotle*, London 1923, p. 56; Jaeger too holds the *Topica* to be early (p. 84).

[2] Them. *Or.* 107^(c-d); Ross, *Fragm.* p. 62.

the Academy's theory of ideas, it is difficult to say. It was in any case necessary for him gradually to free himself from the spirit of the Platonic school. For if the Academy was to alter its political attitude and behaviour towards Philip, its philosophy too must undergo a change. Aristotle must have considered what direction this change might take in Macedonia, but his thoughts and intentions become clear only later, when they began to be realized after the foundation of the Peripatetic school (see below).

In 340/39 relations between Macedonia and Athens entered a new phase. Philip's proposals for a peaceful settlement were rejected. Demosthenes controlled the assembly; he managed to create an alliance between Athens and Thebes against Philip. War was imminent. Just at this time (339) Plato's successor, Speusippus, died. At once the members of the Academy gathered to elect a new leader of the school. Aristotle was proposed for the office but not elected, on the grounds, it is recorded, that he lived in Macedonia. Xenocrates was appointed; he was only about fifteen years older than Aristotle, so the post of scholarch, which Philip wished to fill with one of his supporters, was no longer available, probably for some considerable time to come. Xenocrates was as little an Athenian as Aristotle, but his home, Chalcedon in Bithynia, unlike Chalcidice, was independent and inclined rather towards Athens; it had resisted Philip. Subsequent events proved that the choice of Xenocrates was well-considered. Important both as a philosopher and a scholar—like Speusippus before him he carried on Plato's work—Xenocrates was also a wise administrator with statesman-like qualities. He maintained the Academy against its opponents, and at a later stage was able to perform invaluable services as a mediator between Athens and Macedonia in a most difficult situation.

It is well known that Aristotle, who rejected Speusippus's philosophy, criticized that of Xenocrates with equal severity (more precisely, the Platonic theory of ideas in the altered forms which first Speusippus and then Xenocrates gave it). There is no doubt that his failure in the election for the headship of the Academy meant a serious setback for his plans; he might well fear that he would now sink into total oblivion. Indeed, it appears that Philip did lose interest in him as may be deduced from his further behaviour towards Aristotle. One might even suggest that from now on Philip excluded not only the Academy but also philosophy in general from his political calculations. In any case Philip, it seems, tended to favour orators and the education provided by the rhetorical schools. For a long time rhetoricians and philosophers had competed sharply with one another at his court, much as in Athens itself, where the Academy and the school of Isocrates violently opposed each other. Of the orators around Philip, Theopompus of Chios, a pupil of Isocrates, was the foremost. Famous as a historian, he was a furious opponent of the Platonic school and certainly also an adversary of Aristotle. Theopompus wrote a work on contemporary history, in which he praised Philip as the greatest of all mortals, past and present. It seems that Philip now wished to lean on men of this type; through them he hoped to change the mood of the Greeks in his favour.

However, even if Aristotle had lost Philip's favour, he was not without friends in Macedonia. He managed to win the trust of other powerful personages, not the least of them being Antipater, a general at court and later viceroy of Macedonia. Moreover, as once before, the court was threatened by dangerous intrigues. The royal family was split into two camps, that of the king and that of Olympias and Alexander. Aristotle joined the party of the latter, as subsequent developments prove: Alexander promoted him and steadfastly favoured him throughout his life. We also hear from Plutarch that, as heir to the throne, Alexander held court in the fortress Mieza, and that Aristotle was staying there with him (Plut. *Alex.* VII and VIII). But for this very reason, that he now belonged to the circle of Olympias and Alexander, Aristotle was passed over by Philip at every turn. In 338 Philip won a decisive victory over the allied Greek cities at Chaironea, as a result of which Demosthenes forfeited his influence in Athens. A party favourable to Philip came to power, under Demades. At once Philip resumed his policy of reconciliation.[1] While he treated Thebes harshly, he sent all Athenian prisoners back home without a ransom. Thereupon a statue was erected to him in the Agora and the friendliest relations were established between him and Athens. For Aristotle, however, who nine years previously had been expelled from the city by a patriotic party, and who had been preparing for the moment of change ever since, the victory was barren; even now, he was assigned no task in Athens.

As Commander-in-Chief of all the Greeks, Philip returned to

[1] It appears that Philip tried to win over Xenocrates; see Diog. L. IV, 8 ff.

Macedonia, but he was not destined to achieve new triumphs. The quarrels at his court now broke out openly. At enmity with his son Alexander, Philip had divorced Olympias and at once married again, this time the daughter of a Macedonian noble. If his new wife gave him a son, he was to be the heir to Macedonia. But the discord in the royal family began to endanger the throne itself; a rebellion threatened in Epirus, Olympias's home country. Philip therefore decided to confirm Alexander as his successor, pacifying Olympias. But it was too late; the hatred that had been aroused was too deeply rooted. At a festive procession intended to symbolize the reconciliation, Philip was murdered.

Alexander ascended the throne, acclaimed throughout Macedonia. At the head of his army he quelled revolts that broke out against him in Greece. Within a year, Athens lay at his feet, as it had at his father's before him. Without delay he resumed Philip's policy of friendship. The Macedonian influence was to penetrate Athens peaceably. The Academy was to be spared all interference in its teaching and administration; Xenocrates was to continue as its head. Still, teachers of philosophy whom he could trust should work in Athens. So Aristotle was sent to Athens, not for the purpose of reshaping the Academy, but of opening a new school of his own, whose achievements would if possible surpass those of the Academy.

*   *   *

Aristotle's return to Athens in 335 after twelve years' absence attracted a great deal of attention. He came with ample means; with books and teaching materials of all kinds, maps, models etc., and a staff of assistants, the most important of whom was Theophrastus. All this is reliably recorded; in addition it is related that personally too he was splendidly equipped, luxuriously attired, with gold rings on every finger; that he dined like a prince and was waited on by an unusually large number of slaves.[1] Such accounts may of course be based on later gossip, of the kind directed against other school heads and philosophers. What is certain is that he did not return to Athens as a travelling Sophist, unsure of the future, but as a man

[1] Regarding Aristotle's luxury see Diog. L. v, 16; Düring, pp. 374 (Lyco the Pythagorean) and 381 (Theodoretus).

appointed to his task by Alexander, then the ruler of Greece, soon
to be master of the world. Consequently, everything he needed in
Athens was readily placed at his disposal.

In Athens a radical change of government had taken place. One
of the orators, Lycurgus, who, with Demosthenes, had previously
opposed Philip, had gone over to the Macedonian party and, as its
new leader, had become the dominant statesman. Since Aristotle
as a non-Athenian—a metic—was not permitted to own land, the
Athenian government under Lycurgus acquired for him the site
essential for his undertaking. He was assigned the grove consecrated
to Apollo Lyceus, which probably lay to the north-east of the centre
of Athens, between the mountain Lycabettus and the river Ilissus;
a spot which Socrates himself had liked. In it stood shrines to Apollo
and the Muses, and perhaps other smaller buildings or huts which
could be used immediately; very soon, we hear, Lycurgus spent
great sums on embellishing the shrines or temples and on having
further buildings erected in the grove. A covered colonnade led to
the temple of Apollo, or perhaps connected the temple with the
shrine of the Muses; whether it had existed before or was only
built now, is not known. This colonnade or walk (*peripatos*) gave
the school its name; it seems that it was here, at least at the beginning,
that the pupils assembled and the teachers gave their lectures. Here
they wandered to and fro; for this reason it was later said
that Aristotle himself lectured and taught while walking up and
down.[1]

Since everything required for the establishment of the school
had been carefully prepared in advance (the material Aristotle
brought with him would no doubt have benefited the Academy
if he had become its head), we may assume that the new undertaking flourished from the outset. At a later date we hear expressly
of the great number of pupils who gathered at the Lyceum. The
Stoic Zeno had to admit (in about 300 B.C.) that the Peripatetic
school attracted more pupils than his own,[2] and Diogenes Laertius
records that Theophrastus had two thousand students. Eudemus
of Rhodes no doubt joined the staff immediately after the founding
of the school. Among the pupils a son of the Macedonian viceroy

[1] On the meaning of the name see Düring, pp. 404 ff. and Brink in *Pauly
Wissowa*, Suppl. VII, s. v. 'Peripatos'.

[2] See H. von Arnim, *Stoicorum Veterum Fragmenta (SVF)*, Leipzig 1905,
I, p. 64, 20.

Antipater is named; the later governor of Athens, Demetrius of Phalerum (born about 345 B.C.) was also a student there. The famous playwright Menander no doubt studied under Theophrastus. But these were only a few of the most distinguished of those educated in the Peripatetic school. In Cicero (*De Fin.* v, III) we read that 'from the Peripatetic school, as from a factory producing specialists, there went forth orators, generals and statesmen, also mathematicians, poets, musicians and physicians'. And it is well known that in the following century, and even later, Peripatetic philosophers were to be found all over the world, at princely courts and in cities, where, as experts, they performed various tasks, each according to his ability and particular training: the success of the school was such that for a time the designation 'Peripateticus' (for an educated and highly qualified man) replaced the older names 'Sophist' and 'philosopher'.

So the new school fulfilled the hopes which Alexander had placed on it, as a centre of education for the youth of the whole Greek world, reflecting the spirit of the new epoch that began with the great conqueror. It competed with the Academy, which it was intended to equal or to surpass; and this was all the more necessary since, after the death of its founder in 338, Macedonia could no longer count on the Isocratic school. One asks how the Peripatetics managed to outshine the Academy. Not through a new philosophy (which in any case could not be ready when the school was founded and would develop only gradually). In fact the philosophical foundation of the Peripatetic school was—and remained—dependent on Plato's work. It taught Platonism, as did the Academy, albeit an 'improved' Platonism. What differentiated this from the original will be discussed in a later chapter. Hence, the superiority of the Peripatetic school had to show itself in another way, in the range and number of the studies and courses which the new school was able to offer, partly thanks to its abundant resources. Besides philosophical dialectic, all the sciences known at the time were studied, and not only these but also rhetoric in all its aspects. So the list of subjects taught and studied at the Peripatetic school encompassed not only those of the Academy but also those of the Isocratic school, and, indeed, exceeded both combined. Never before had there been an institution with studies on a comparable scale. Thus Cicero wrote (*De Fin.* v, III): 'From the Peripatetics' writings and teachings can be learned all liberal arts, history and style; indeed, so great

is the variety of subjects treated by them that no one ventures to
approach any significant matter without prior knowledge of their
works.' Rightly, therefore, one sees the Lyceum as the first university
almost in the full, modern sense of the word, while this cannot be
said of the two great schools which preceded the Peripatos, the
Pythagorean and Platonic schools. Similarly, the library which
Aristotle installed at the school was the first comprehensive collection
of books in history, and later served as a model for the famous
State libraries of Alexandria and Pergamum.

Although Platonism was fundamental to the Peripatetic school, a
characteristic attitude became evident, whether deliberately
adopted from the beginning or developing gradually: an inclination
towards empiricism allied to contemplation. The Sophists and
philosophers of the early fourth century had directed their thinking
towards the question of how one could raise or improve man and
human society; Plato himself had outlined the ideal State. In the
Peripatetic school, however, observation took the place of specula-
tion, description (e.g. of constitutions) that of Utopias. Intuition was
replaced by research, the reforming zeal by an industrious collecting
of data. In short, philosophy became apolitical; the thinking power
of youth was directed towards the examination of minute detail
and disinterested contemplation. History was taught, not least the
history of philosophy. Jaeger justly emphasizes that Aristotle was
the first to treat even the Sophists impartially.[1] Earlier philosophical
views were collated and expounded, Plato no longer being considered the outstanding master but only one of the famous sages of
former times (*Metaph.* A). So one may well say that the move
away from the State and towards private life usually ascribed to the
influence of the Stoa actually had its origins in the Peripatetic
school. Its effect even seemed to reach the Academy. Its members
too refrained from all open political activity, and it is said that
Xenocrates, apparently as an example to others, led a secluded,
almost 'monastic' life. Of course, the Peripatetics' never-ending
attention to detail aroused the scorn of contemporaries. In a
comedy their investigations of fish and their habits are described as
'a wonder for fools'. Thinking, it appeared, had ceased to be
exciting, through the move to empiricism, which was soon regarded
as the hallmark of the Peripatetic school; especially as here the
criticism of the Platonic theory of ideas, whether in its original form

[1] See Jaeger, p. 129.

or in the shape which Speusippus and then Xenocrates had given it, continued indefatigably.[1]

During the period of the founding of the school and of Alexander's rule, the economy of Athens flourished. The city, no longer resisting Macedonian domination, enjoyed the advantages of Alexander's conquests. The Piraeus had always been an important port of trans-shipment, but now it served not only the Greek cities and scattered colonies, but the whole, ever-growing Hellenized world. Athenian banking establishments found themselves represented in Egypt and Persia. Their growing wealth under Lycurgus as treasurer made the Athenians complacent and conservative; even the 'ancestral' religion, scorned a century before, was revived, at least superficially. But at the same time some important social changes affecting Athens took place. Wherever Alexander went, he founded cities, for which he needed settlers from Greece in almost unlimited numbers. So, from the over-populated mother-country and the islands, where they had mostly led a strenuous, poverty-stricken life, emigrants moved to the 'new world', where, on the coasts or on river banks, they began to build large cities on what had previously been unused land. The native population provided them with servants; the continuing war kept the slave-markets supplied. They became wealthy, and in particular the earliest settlers soon formed the upper class of the empire. Every support was given them; after all, it was through them that the conquered world was Hellenized. This social development also set the Athenian schools new tasks, and the Peripatetics in particular attempted to master them. The sons of the Hellenistic ruling class were educated at the Peripatetic school, at least until universities had arisen in the new cities; its 'graduates' went out into the empire. Furthermore, an extensive popular literature was created, which was to acquaint those living far away with the thought and culture of the mother-country. And the Peripatetic school adapted its political and social attitudes to suit the needs of the colonial upper class. It strove to establish a theoretical foundation—as it were, the ideological basis—for its rule. This is shown, among other things, by the fact that in the Peripatetics' writings, in contrast to those of all other contemporary schools of philosophy, particularly the Stoa, slavery is described as good and natural, and the (racial) superiority of the

---

[1] That the rejection of the theory of ideas also had political significance can be inferred from *Eth. Eud.* 1217^{b}24.

Greeks over the 'barbarians', i.e. all non-Greeks, is asserted (*Pol.* I).

For these views expressed in some of the esoteric works, parallels are found in the fragments of books published by Aristotle himself. It is true that the dates of the *ekdota* remain uncertain, but at least the writings addressed to Alexander must date from this period. In one of them Aristotle demanded that Alexander should treat his Greek subjects as comrades but the barbarians as slaves, like animals and plants; fortunately Alexander did not follow this advice, as Plutarch relates: on the contrary, the king regarded all men as equal.[1] In writings on monarchic rule, Aristotle, in contrast to Plato, played down the importance of philosophers (as already mentioned). The book on riches may also belong to this period. Without wealth, Aristotle is supposed to have declared, nobody could be happy, or even virtuous,[2] and in another passage he enlarges on this: the 'good' are also good at making money, he says, while the 'bad' are not even capable of earning a living.[3] In *The Statesman* Aristotle justifies rage, which he says is noble, just, useful and pleasant (sweet); without it, he continues, a general cannot wage war, nor a ruler destroy his internal enemies and so rule successfully.[4] It is recorded that Aristotle also published works on famous philosophers; but it may be that these date from his period of preparation in Macedonia. In one of these works, on the Pythagoreans, Aristotle dwelt particularly, it appears, on the mystical personality of Pythagoras as well as on the Pythagorean theory of numbers. Of two other works, on Archytas and Democritus, too little is preserved for any impression to be gained.[5]

So Aristotle had in an astonishingly short time achieved outstanding results. He had founded a new school, which was to satisfy the highest demands; he had designed its comprehensive

---

[1] Ross, *Fragm.* p. 63.

[2] See Düring, p. 38.

[3] Philod. *Pap. Herc.* 3, p. 41, col. 211; see W. D. Ross's translation of these fragments in *The Works of Aristotle*, vol. XII, p. 57. A new edition of a large number of the Herculanean papyri is being prepared in Naples by F. Sbordone under the title *Ricerche sui Papiri Ercolanesi*. The first volume of this work was published in 1969.

[4] Ross, *Fragm.* pp. 64 ff.

[5] A single surviving fragment of the latter makes it appear doubtful whether we are dealing with an extract from a published work or rather a passage from an esoteric text-book; since in it the Atomic theory of Democritus (or even one of his followers) is described methodically and carefully (Ross, *Fragm.* p. 143).

teaching and research programme, whose execution he directed
and organized. He had attracted pupils from the entire Greek world.
And not only had he established the school, he also gave it once
and for all its character and direction, based on Platonism, despite
the move to empiricism, and although he himself as well as his
colleagues and successors adapted to the spirit of the new era in
several respects, particularly in political and social spheres. In the
following period, as we shall see, the Peripatetic school was to prove a
more faithful guardian of the Platonic tradition than the Academy
itself. Furthermore, as head of the school, Aristotle had to
perform other important duties; he had to steer a middle course
between the wishes of the Athenians and Macedonian interests.
In fact, he did manage to keep up good relations with the Athenian
government, and probably also achieved a harmonious relationship
with the Academy. On the other hand he kept up a constant,
official, apparently business-like correspondence with Antipater
who, as Alexander's viceroy, governed Greece from Macedonia,
and he also remained in frequent contact with Alexander himself.
In addition to all this he wrote a large number of semi-popular books
which were intended to satisfy the thirst for knowledge and education
of the Greeks in the mother-country and the developing empire,
while for Alexander and his advisers he drew up numerous
memoranda. No doubt, therefore, in the twelve or thirteen years in
which he directed the Peripatetic school, Aristotle was engaged in
many varied and important activities; which, one might assume,
filled his time and absorbed his strength. And yet, all that he accomplished in this respect is supposed to have been a mere *parergon*,
an almost insignificant fraction of his true achievement. According
to a tradition which arose about two hundred and fifty years after
his death, which then became dominant and even today is hardly disputed, Aristotle in these same years also lectured—not once, but two
or three times, in almost every subject—on logic, physics, astronomy,
meteorology, zoology, metaphysics, theology, psychology, politics,
economics, ethics, rhetoric, poetics; and he wrote down these
lectures, expanding and amending them several times, until they
reached the stage in which we read them. However, still more
astounding is the fact that the majority of these subjects did not
exist as such before him, so that he would have been the first to
conceive of and establish them, as systematic disciplines.

*   *   *

In 323 Aristotle's work in Athens came to a sudden end. Alexander died and the empire he had constructed broke up. Athens thought itself free again. The old, long-restrained hatred of Macedonia erupted violently. Demosthenes, recalled from exile, addressed the assembly, which gave him enthusiastic support. War against Antipater was decided on. Anti-Macedonian disturbances broke out; anger was directed against all those who had aided Macedonia's cause. Aristotle more than anyone was in danger. He could not stay. In good time, it appears, he left Athens with his family, for we read that he was able to take many of his possessions with him on his flight.[1]

Proceedings on a charge of sacrilege (*asebeia*) had already been instituted against him (Diog. L. v, 6; 8). And not only he, but also several of his assistants left Athens; whether they too had to flee, or only considered it pointless to stay on longer in Athens, cannot be said. Eudemus set out for his native Rhodes, Dicaearchus for the Peloponnese (Cic. *Ad Att.* vi, 43), though both later returned to Athens. Whether the school as such was closed at this time is not known; but it is certain that neither the buildings nor the library nor the teaching material came to any harm, and least of all the grove itself, which as we know had already been popular in earlier times as a meeting-place for philosophers, Sophists and their admirers.[2] Among those who stayed, however, was Theophrastus. He came from Lesbos, which had long been allied with Athens, and it was he who, as Aristotle's successor, became the head of the Peripatetic school. But in which year his appointment or election took place or became effective, whether during the war that the Athenians waged against Antipater, or only after Athens had been defeated and subjugated again, remains uncertain. According to Diogenes Laertius (Diog. L. v, 36) Theophrastus took over in the 114th Olympiad, which embraces the years 324–320.

Aristotle found refuge in his mother's native town, Chalcis, on the island of Euboea, which was securely in Macedonian hands. Here he still owned the estate of his maternal grandparents, which included a larger and a smaller house, where he now established himself. Whether he was still active in Chalcis cannot be said. A report, according to which he attempted to measure the ebb and flow of tides in the straits of Euripus and drowned in the attempt,

[1] See Düring, pp. 374 and 381.
[2] See Düring, p. 357; Jaeger, pp. 319 ff.

is certainly invented.[1] In almost poetic tones, Jaeger portrays him in the period of his retirement as withdrawn into himself, a hermit, losing himself in the wonderland of myth.[2] He died, only about a year after his arrival in Chalcis (322 in October?) at the age of sixty-two or sixty-three, of a stomach complaint that had perhaps been aggravated by grief over his renewed expulsion from Athens and, as he must have assumed, the failure of his life's work. Even Delphi had revoked the honour it had once conferred on him.

* * *

His will, in all probability drawn up in Chalcis, is preserved (Diog. L. v, 11–16)—a remarkable document, informative in many ways.[3] His humanity is revealed in the terms concerning his slaves: he decreed that they were to be freed eventually, and he wanted to see them generously provided for. It shows his practical wisdom and it confirms his wealth. The most carefully thought out provisions are those relating to his family, especially to Pythias, his daughter by his first marriage to the niece of the tyrant Hermias, and to his nephew Nicanor. Nicanor's parents were Aristotle's guardian Proxenus and presumably his sister Arimneste. Aristotle wanted Nicanor to marry Pythias as soon as she was grown up: obviously so that her fortune should stay within the family.[4]

Pythias's fortune, if separate from that of Aristotle, doubtless came from the estate of Hermias, and was either in Macedonia or still in Assos, which now belonged to the Graeco-Macedonian empire; this was probably an additional reason for Aristotle to appoint the Regent Antipater as chief executor of his will. And Aristotle ruled that even if something were to befall Pythias ('may it never happen') or if she were to die childless, Nicanor was to be her heir. But if Nicanor should suffer an accident, Theophrastus should be requested to take Pythias into his house as his ward, and to take decisions regarding the disposition of her inheritance, if he so

[1] Procopius, Eustatius etc.; see Düring, p. 347.
[2] See Jaeger, pp. 320–2.
[3] For literature on Aristotle's will see Düring, p. 61.
[4] It is doubtful whether Nicanor did marry Pythias. From Theophrastus's will it emerges that Pythias was married (for the second time?) to one Metrodorus and that from him she had a son called Aristotle. Theophrastus warmly recommended this younger Aristotle to the care of his colleagues (Diog. L. v, 53).

desired (Diog. L. v, 13) and, as it says in another passage (Diog. L. v, 12), if he were in a position to do so.[1] The cautious manner in which Theophrastus is mentioned in the will reveals how keenly aware Aristotle was of the delicate position of Theophrastus in Athens, which he did not want to be exacerbated in any way. Finally, if Theophrastus too were unavailable, the remaining companions (or colleagues) were to take the decision regarding the inheritance, in consultation with Antipater. Whatever happened, the will was so designed that in no circumstances should the inheritance fall into the hands of an outsider.[2]

Having made these arrangements for Pythias, Aristotle turned to the provisions for his companion or second wife, Herpyllis. He recommended her most warmly to his other survivors; she was to choose her house herself, either the smaller of the two houses in Chalcis or the house in Stagira; whichever she occupied, it was to be furnished according to her own wishes, and she was to receive an adequate capital sum. In this way, one may assume, his son Nicomachus, by Herpyllis, was also provided for; moreover, Nicanor was enjoined to take care of Nicomachus. Aristotle himself, however, wished to be laid to rest beside his first wife Pythias; wherever he was buried, there her bones should also be laid.

So the will reveals a great deal about Aristotle's personality: his generosity and warmheartedness, his sagacity, and his piety, which he wished to express in public. He had statues erected not only to his mother, his brother and his sister, but also to his guardian Proxenus, and to Nicanor; and as a thanksgiving for the latter's anticipated safe return from a dangerous journey, he provided for statues to be dedicated to Zeus and Athena. Moreover, the document proves that Aristotle was in very close contact with the Macedonian court until the end, despite, or just because of, his exile from Athens, for he was able to entrust the execution of his last wishes to Antipater. Finally, it is striking that in his will, in contrast to the later school

[1] Theophrastus did actually become the heir to Aristotle's property in Stagira; see Diog. L. v, 52.

[2] This part of the will broadly conforms with an old Attic law which stipulates that the nearest relative of an heiress should have the option of marrying her. However, Aristotle goes beyond this legal rule by designating Theophrastus and his other colleagues as the next executors-heirs in the event of the relative's (Nicanor's) premature death. See Bruns, 'Testamente der griechischen Philosophen', in *Zeitschrift der Savigny-Stiftung*, Rom. Abteilung, 1880.

heads, there is no mention of the school, its library, maps etc. Whether he regarded the Peripatetic school as lost, or only wanted to avoid embarrassing the school and Theophrastus through the connection with his name (since of course he stood accused of sacrilege in Athens) cannot be determined. In any case, Theophrastus was without doubt closest to him after his family.[1]

That Aristotle was a great, dominating personality, an outstanding writer, a man of comprehensive knowledge; an eminent administrator and organizer, gifted, too, with an unusual diplomatic skill—all this is certain. Whether he was also the author of the treatises of the Corpus Aristotelicum, and thus a creative philosopher comparable to Plato, cannot be established either by a study of the *ekdota* or the evidence regarding his life; although the latter causes one to doubt whether a man who, far from leading a quiet, undisturbed life, was uprooted several times and restlessly driven from place to place, could have found the strength and the opportunity required for such a work. A stronger or even irrefutable argument against Aristotle's sole authorship of the Corpus will emerge from an analysis of the treatises themselves. However, before we come to this, we must examine what happened to the Peripatetic school and its library after the death of Aristotle. For a study of their history, too, will shed some light on the nature and hence on the origin of the treatises.

---

[1] The opinion expressed by certain scholars, according to which the paragraph concerning the school has been lost, and the will is therefore incomplete, is quite unfounded. Equally untenable is the view, based solely on the absence of any reference to the school in the will, that Theophrastus was the founder of the Peripatos, and that Aristotle taught in Athens merely in a make-shift way. Against this see Diog. L. v, 5; 10; 36 ('Theophrastus succeeded to the headship'; *diedexato tên scholên*). See also *Vita Hesychii* with a list of scholarchs. Besides, Aristotle probably held the Lyceum only on a temporary lease; see p. 50.

CHAPTER TWO

The Peripatos after Aristotle's Death

After the death of Aristotle, the Peripatos continued to prosper in Athens for about another century. So much can be said with certainty; what happened to it after that is doubtful and much disputed.[1] In any case, for an understanding of its teaching and character, the first century is decisive. This was an era of political changes. Alexander's death was followed by a long period of wars between the rulers of Macedonia, Egypt, and the provinces of the Asian empire, whose vicissitudes again and again affected the fortunes of the Peripatetic school. Generally speaking, the school flourished whenever Macedonia was strong, and it suffered setbacks each time Macedonia was defeated. For, as the school had been founded with Macedonian support, it remained dependent on Macedonian protection.

The first phase of the war, the Athenian struggle for freedom after Alexander's death—at the beginning of which (323) Aristotle had been banished from Athens—did not last long. In 322 Antipater defeated the allied Greek States at Crannon, and Athens had to surrender and accept harsh terms. The abolition of democracy was decreed, and an oligarchic constitution proclaimed; a permanent Macedonian garrison was stationed at Munichia (near Athens). Antipater dealt more severely with Athens than had Alexander and Philip before him but even he spared the Academy. We hear that after the defeat its head, Xenocrates, who had no doubt had connections with Macedonia for a long time (Diog. L. IV, 8), was sent to Antipater in Thebes with other Athenian representatives, and that it was he who brought about the release of the Athenian captives (Diog. L. IV, 9). The Academy, one may therefore presume, was treated with tolerance by the Macedonians; the Peripatetic school however, was given wholehearted support. Its new head, Theophrastus (according to a Greek source, albeit a late one, nominated by Aristotle himself), could now begin his work confidently. The situation was advantageous, the tasks enticing. In Athens the

[1] See Brink in *Pauly-Wissowa*, Suppl. VII, s. v. 'Peripatos'.

4

political and social attitudes of the Peripatos were in harmony with those of the newly-appointed oligarchs, while in the empire founded by Alexander, even if it was still torn by strife, the newly-erected cities and, in particular, Alexandria soon flourished, and as the Hellenization of Asia in general had begun, it fell to the Athenian schools to direct its progress.

Nevertheless, in Athens itself the Peripatos was still threatened by hidden dangers. Here, opposition to Macedonia was only superficially suppressed and by no means extinguished. The first flare-up occurred only three years after the re-opening of the school, with the death of Antipater in 319, and the remaining diadochs' proclamation of the freedom of all Greeks. At once hatred of Macedonia erupted in Athens and it was again directed against the Peripatetic school. As a few years earlier Aristotle, so now Theophrastus was accused of sacrilege. But Theophrastus, it seems, was not compelled to flee at this time. His enemies had to exercise restraint as long as the conflict remained undecided. The uncertainty lasted two years; then Cassander re-established Macedonian domination. He entered Athens victoriously; thereupon the charge against Theophrastus was dismissed and the accuser fined (317).

The following decade (317–307) was probably the most significant in the development of the school; a period of consolidation, expansion and the most fruitful work. The external circumstances were more favourable than ever. As governor of Athens, Cassander had appointed one of Theophrastus's students, Demetrius of Phalerum, who had made a name for himself as a Peripatetic writer. In order to further the school, Demetrius, by altering an ancient law, made it possible for Theophrastus, a non-Athenian, to buy land on Athenian soil, probably in the grove of Apollo Lyceus,[1] which had already been assigned to Aristotle for the founding of the school (though at that time presumably only on the basis of a temporary lease). Thus the continuance of the school was legally secured, and the scholarch became its owner, or rather, its trustee, since, as is revealed in the wills of the school heads, each of them left the school to his successor or colleagues. Moreover, now that the land and buildings were the property of the school, many improvements were made. In the temple of the Muses (the Museum) the library grew and a wealth of teaching material was

[1] See Jaeger, p. 315.

gathered. Here a statue of Aristotle was placed with other votive offerings. Lecture rooms were added, their walls decorated with relief maps of the known world. Houses were probably also built and the already existing dining-hall enlarged. The number of students under Theophrastus was two thousand (according to Diogenes Laertius); whether this number was reached at this early stage of his headship or only later, cannot be said. As under Aristotle, the students were offered comprehensive courses in all the known fields of study, and indeed new subjects were added. Theophrastus himself established the science of botany, besides that of zoology which went back to Aristotle, Aristoxenus that of music. Medicine, too, was later studied at the Peripatos. Historical researches were undertaken with particular zeal and data of various kinds assembled. The development of city constitutions, of poetry, of rhetoric, was recorded; physical and theological theories were noted. We hear that Eudemus wrote the history, not only of geometry and arithmetic, but also of astronomy.

As the work of the school branched out in so many directions it was inevitable that its teachers and scholars began to specialize, making one or several of the fields of study their own—logic, ontology, physics, astronomy etc.—according to individual inclination and training. As a result, differing views began to be held within the school. Even at an early stage there were on the one hand philosophers who took the logical-ontological aspect of Platonism as their point of departure, and others who, starting from the *Timaeus*, sought a scientific explanation of nature and Being—opposite approaches which were bound to lead not only to differing theses on particular questions but also, in spite of efforts to achieve a united Peripatetic doctrine, to contradictory basic conclusions.[1] At the same time, it seems that the boundary between esoteric and exoteric became blurred as the works meant for a wide public became more and more specialized. Many of the collections or compilations of doctrines such as data referring to the history of medicine (Meno), and of music etc., were published, as was Dicaearchus's history of Greek

---

[1] Zeno, the founder of the Stoa, is reported to have said: 'His [Theophrastus's] chorus is larger than mine but the voices of my chorus are in greater harmony with each other.' See Arnim, *SVF* i, 64, 19. Another Stoic, Cleanthes, is said to have remarked: 'The Peripatetics are like lyres; their sounds are sweet but they cannot hear one another' (*SVF* i, 135, 32). A further witness to Peripatetic contradictoriness is Cicero, *De Natura Deorum* i, 33; 35; see also p. 76 n.

culture (*Bios Hellados*) and, of course, Theophrastus's *Characters*, as well as a work on monarchy which the latter dedicated to Cassander, just as, before him, Aristotle had offered a comparable book to Alexander. It is not surprising, therefore, that the Stoics accused the members of the Peripatos of spending too much time on their publications, thereby neglecting their own philosophic researches. In fact, the great majority of those Peripatetics of whose writings only fragments are preserved[1] achieved prominence mainly or solely through their published work; the most important exceptions are Eudemus and Strato.

On two or three further occasions the work of the school under Theophrastus was interrupted. As the wars of Alexander's successors dragged on, one of the diadochs, Demetrius Poliorcetes, 'liberated' Athens, from which he expelled Demetrius of Phalerum, the governor installed by the Macedonians (307). Thereupon, the rule of the *dêmos* was re-established, and presently a law was passed, under which all foreign philosophers were banished from the city. Although this new law was drawn up in general terms, it was in fact aimed at the Peripatetics, as is revealed in a bitterly anti-Macedonian speech by Demochares, a nephew of Demosthenes, who later defended the passing of the law.[2] As a result, Theophrastus had to leave Athens with all his colleagues and the school itself was closed (306). But the interruption lasted only a year. Then Cassander regained the upper hand; the anti-Macedonian law was repealed and its originator, Sophocles, was punished. Theophrastus and his companions could return to Athens, to resume their work. After Cassander's death (294), Athens was once more besieged, and it is also known that in 288/7 serious anti-Macedonian disturbances occurred in Athens. On one of these occasions, or both, the school suffered considerable damage. Aristotle's statue was removed or broken up, with other statues. One of the lecture-halls was partly or totally destroyed, together with the relief maps covering its walls. An altar was damaged. All this is evident from Theophrastus's will (Diog. L. v, 51 ff.), from which one may also conclude that none of this damage was made good until some time after Theophrastus's death.

For thirty-five years Theophrastus was in charge of the Peripatetic

---

[1] See F. Wehrli (ed.), *Die Schule des Aristoteles. Texte und Kommentar*, Basel 1944 ff.

[2] Baiter-Suppe, *Orat. Att.* II, pp. 341 ff.; Jaeger, p. 314.

school (from 322 until 287/6), almost three times as long as Aristotle himself, during which period he successfully continued Aristotle's work, both within the school and through his exoteric writings. His headship brought renown to the Peripatos throughout the contemporary world. But whether he merely preserved a philosophy bequeathed to him or independently added to it as a creative philosopher in his own right, it is not yet possible to determine; we still lack the precise scholarly basis for an evaluation of his own achievements. Still less is it possible to say to what extent he was influenced by contemporary thought outside the Peripatos. For two events of far-reaching significance for philosophy as a whole occurred during the time of his headship. In 307 B.C. Epicurus opened his 'garden' in Athens. And only a few years later, Zeno of Citium founded the Stoa in Athens, probably in 304 B.C. That these two philosophical schools, particularly the Stoa, exercised an immense influence throughout antiquity need hardly be stressed. But it is not yet appreciated that the new doctrines, soon after they became known, may well have had a deep effect on the thinking of contemporary philosophers of other schools, and in particular the Peripatetic school. As a teaching institution, however, the Peripatetic school, at least to begin with, was not affected by the rise of the new schools. The number of students under Theophrastus remained far superior to that of the Stoa.[1]

The third head of the Peripatos was Strato of Lampsacus, 'the physicist', whom Theophrastus had appointed in his will as his heir, passing over Neleus (of whom more will be said later). Strato's election seems to indicate that at this time the scientific trend was dominant within philosophy. Strato, too, was a thinker whose originality it is not yet possible to evaluate.

Strato's period of office (from 287/6 to 268/7) passed without political disturbances, as far as we can judge from the evidence. Athens was securely in Macedonian hands and the school could therefore accumulate wealth. The furniture and upholstery of the dining-hall, as well as the drinking goblets, are specifically mentioned in Strato's will, no doubt as particularly valuable objects (Diog. L. v, 61 ff.). In Strato's time, too, the school continued to serve as a centre of education for the Hellenic world; the famous astronomer Aristarchus of Samos, who worked in Alexandria, was a pupil of

[1] See p. 51 n.

Strato.[1] From the outset the conservative, quasi-'imperialistic' Peripatetic school had had a very close relationship with Alexandria. Aristotle himself, it is said, had been asked to establish a library there, and Theophrastus, too, had been invited to Alexandria by Ptolemy I.

The fourth scholarch, and perhaps the last in Athens, was Lyco from the Troad (266/5 to 225). During his period of office, too, Athens remained under Macedonian rule, after a new war of liberation (266–263) had failed. The luxury of the school increased under him. The students were offered many opportunities to celebrate and enjoy splendid meals, if one is to believe Athenaeus, who, however, preserves a tradition hostile to Lyco and the Peripatos (Ath. XII, 547ᵈ). The fees are said to have been so high that only sons of rich men could now study there. Lyco himself was wealthy; he owned houses in Athens and Aegina, and many slaves. In contrast to his predecessors he was neither a scholar nor a philosopher. He was famous as an orator and writer; and he also distinguished himself in the field of sport. Above all, however, he was an outstanding administrator, even a diplomat, respected not only in Athens but in the whole Greek world. The beginning of his headship coincided approximately with the founding of the kingdom of Pergamum, whose princes patronized the arts and sciences and founded a famous library in competition with the Ptolemies. Lyco always had a very friendly relationship with the kings of Pergamum, Eumenes I and Attalus I (particularly since he was a native of the Troad, which became part of the Pergamene kingdom). Besides, yet another ruler, who also wished to found a library, Antiochus of Syria, solicited Lyco's support—apparently in vain.

So under Lyco, too, the school remained an important centre of education, even if its intellectual achievements were declining. At this time it began to be said that the Peripatos was stagnating (Cic. *De Fin.* V, 5; 13), especially in comparison with its rivals, the Epicurean and Stoic schools. Moreover, yet another great school emerged at this time, the 'Second Academy'. In about the same year as Lyco took over the Peripatos, a Sceptic, Arcesilaus, became the head of the Academy, and through him Scepticism became the philosophy of the Academy. The Sceptics tried to undermine all dogmatic philosophy and it appears that the Peripatetics, confronted with

[1] See K. Vorländer, *Erwin Metzke, Geschichte der Philosopie* I, Hamburg 1949, p. 194.

powerful assailants from three sides, had to defend their own basic teaching in constant argument with the philosophers of other schools.

In contrast to his predecessor Strato, Lyco nominated no successor. Rather he bequeathed the school in an uncertain fashion to all his colleagues, expressing the hope that the Peripatetic school would survive or even develop further. But in fact everything indicates that with the end of Lyco's period as scholarch (which lasted forty years) the disintegration of the school set in. For the death of Lyco (225) coincided almost exactly with the collapse of the Macedonian rule over Athens. Wilamowitz presumes that from now on, or from 200 B.C. onwards, the school led only an 'ideal existence'. In any case its fortunes are from then on lost in obscurity. It is true that two centuries later, when the school was re-activated in Rome, it was claimed that during all this time the Peripatos had continued to prosper under scholarchs following one another in uninterrupted succession, but this can hardly be believed. On the other hand there is clear evidence that the Peripatetic philosophy was never quite forgotten. Some of its tenets were mentioned and discussed even in the late Hellenistic period, in the second century B.C.[1] a fact which, as we shall see, is of considerable interest.[2] In Athens, however, the Peripatetic school no longer existed. When Cicero visited the city in 79 B.C., after Sulla had plundered it eight years before, he found no trace of either the Lyceum or the old Academy; the places at which Plato and Aristotle had taught were deserted (*De Fin.* V, 1 ff.).

[1] See E. Zeller, *Die Philosophie der Griechen* 11, 2, Leipzig 1879, pp. 148 ff.
[2] See p. 70, n. 2.

CHAPTER THREE

The Emergence of New Philosophical Schools during the Fourth and Third Centuries B.C.

As we have seen, during its century of existence in Athens (335 to c. 225 B.C.), the Peripatetic school was successful in many ways.[1] It had attracted a large number of students, introducing them to all the disciplines known at the time, and it had provided a sound methodical training. Its graduates were employed throughout the Hellenistic world and everywhere highly regarded. Its teachers made many important contributions to the development of philosophy and empirical knowledge. Collectively they delivered and re-delivered lectures on their entire range of subjects, revising them from time to time for new classes of students. Some of them published books on their own doctrines, others—the majority—produced an increasing number of popular works on various subjects, physics, astronomy, politics, rhetoric, poetry, the history of constitutions and institutions, works which, as it seems, gradually became more specialized as the public requirements became more demanding, so that the gap between learned and popular works narrowed.[2] Still, the school lacked success in one important aspect. Its main message and fundamental teaching did not arouse the enthusiasm of the young and it had little impact on the thought or 'intellectual climate' of the age. Other schools were dominant to such an extent that interest in Peripatetic[3] philosophy was slight and its knowledge confined to a narrow circle of experts. In any case, this was so after the closure of the school in Athens. Retrospectively, the school was mostly regarded

---

[1] See J. P. Lynch, *Aristotle's School: A Study of a Greek Educational Institution*, University of California Press 1972. I regret that this work, which contains several valuable suggestions, only reached me when the present book was already in the press.

[2] An example is the *Constitution of Athens*, an exoteric work, but in style and structure nearer to the treatises than to many fragments of the *ekdota*.

[3] See p. 70, n. 2.

as merely an offshoot of the old Academy (with some justification, as we shall see).[1]

How could this happen? Aristotle, himself a pupil of Plato's, had founded the school as an alternative to the Academy, meant to outdo its rival on its own ground. In that it succeeded. But what could not be foreseen at the time was the emergence of two new philosophical schools in quick succession—the Epicurean and the Stoic—providing a challenge which the Peripatos, continuing on the lines laid down by its founder, was ill-equipped to counter. Pythagoreans also exercised some influence and, fourthly, a current of Sceptical thought, the beginnings of which went back to the time of Aristotle himself, gained in strength during the third century, plaguing and bedevilling all constructive ('dogmatic') philosophizing. Moreover, whereas the Peripatos had grown out of Platonism the two new 'dogmatic' schools deliberately went back to the pre-Socratic teaching of Leucippus and Democritus (the Epicureans) and of Empedocles and Anaxagoras (the Stoics), thus forcing the Peripatetic philosophers not only to record the views of the early thinkers doxographically, as they had always done since the inception of the school, but to discuss them searchingly and critically, as valid, living thought.

In short, the Peripatetic philosophers had to adapt themselves continually to changing trends of thought, which, in practical terms, meant that they were compelled to revise their lectures almost from year to year, so as to make them acceptable to succeeding generations of students. That this was the case is stated in so many words by Theophrastus, in a letter addressed to a Peripatetic, Phanias, and preserved by Diogenes Laertius (Diog. L. v, 37). 'It is not easy,' Theophrastus wrote, 'to find a large audience, or even a small one such as one would like to have. Delivering one's lectures means amending them. To put off ⟨revision⟩ and ignore ⟨objections⟩ is a thing which students nowadays no longer tolerate.' This testimony, with its valuable information about the relation between teachers and students at the time of Theophrastus, receives a special significance from the fact that traces of repeated revision are in evidence everywhere throughout the Corpus Aristotelicum.

---

[1] Antiochus of Ascalon (1st century B.C.), one of Cicero's authorities, considered the Academy and the Peripatos as merely two branches of the school of Plato. See below, p. 76.

Let us see how the new schools were able to appeal so strongly to the Greek world. Epicurus, who after teaching in Mytilene and Lampsacus opened a school in Athens in his own garden (*képos*) in 307/6 B.C., taught a philosophy designed to free man from the fear of death and of wanton, cruel, gods. His views were frankly materialistic, his explanation of nature and of its origin and changes, mechanical. Reviving the Atomistic theories of Leucippus and Democritus, he held that only the void and atoms were real, the latter both infinite in number and of infinitely varied shape. As the atoms 'rained' down, propelled by their own weight and slightly deflected by some kind of spontaneous inclination, they conglomerated to form bodies which, under the impact of other atoms colliding with them, dissolved, separated, and changed into new entities. From this explanation of nature the notion of purpose was thus eliminated, and the cosmos which had a beginning, would come to an end. Like the body, the soul was composed of atoms dissolving at death. All knowledge, Epicurus maintained, was derived from perceptions, aided by concepts stored in memory (*prolêpseis*), but pure thought (*logos*) could add nothing to knowledge (he explained how the images (*eidôla*) of objects were absorbed, physically penetrating the senses). And he claimed that his philosophy was complete, his views final. So, sure in their conviction that nothing could be gained by further inquiry and that all relevant knowledge had been obtained, the master and his followers who formed a closely-knit society, could lead a serene, unworried life, guarding against passion and intent on avoiding pain.

While it is true that the number of Epicurus's followers was not very large, the impact of his teaching, so incisive and clear-cut, could not but extend beyond his own circle. It could not be ignored by the teachers of the other schools, especially as students were accustomed to attend lectures under different masters and not infrequently left one school to join another. Least of all could it be neglected by the Peripatetic philosophers whose views were opposed to those of Epicurus in almost all aspects. They held that the cosmos had neither beginning nor end; that nature was not merely matter but also contained an (active) form; that its movements and changes were not solely due to causes but directed by purpose (*telos*); that knowledge was based both on perception and conception. Nor did they offer a uniform finite philosophy; on the contrary, the relation of matter and form, of cause and purpose, perception and conception remained problematical, subject to ever-renewed inquiry. Obviously, their teaching was less striking, and in that sense less attractive, than that of their rivals. Hence, they had to defend or modify it. That the Peripatetics took notice of Epicurean views, often polemically, is well known. What needs pointing out is the remarkable fact that not only in the fragments of the later Peripatetics[1] but in the Corpus itself one finds passages refuting Epicurean theories— those of the existence of a void, of atoms, of spontaneous movement— or ridiculing Epicurean cosmogony,[2] in short, defending Peripatetic against Epicurean views. One also discovers instances of Epicurean influence on Peripatetic thinking or, at least, terminology.[3]

[1] It appears that Strato, a materialistic philosopher influenced by Epicurean views, developed his theory of 'qualities' (*poiotêteis*) to improve Epicurus's theory of atoms. See F. Wehrli, *Die Schule des Aristoteles,* Heft V (1969), Strato, frs. 42–9, p. 19.

[2] See also S. Sambursky, *The Physical World of the Greeks*, 2nd ed., London 1959, p. 112.

[3] The relation of the Peripatos to other schools is a vast field which has been little explored until now. J. Zürcher in his *Aristoteles' Werk und Geist,* Paderborn 1952, has collected a number of Epicurean terms occurring in the Corpus. Besides, there is the mocking simile of a wall coming into being accidentally, probably a caricature of Epicurus's rain of atoms (*Phys.* 199^{b}34 ff.). A refutation of the theory of atoms is found in *Phys.* 232^{a}24; 233^{b}17. The theory of the void is rejected e.g. in *Gen. Corr.* 324^{b}35 ff., that of spontaneous movement in *Metaph.* Λ VI, 1071^{b}3 ff.

On the relation between Aristotle and Epicurus see further: J. Mau, 'Zum Problem des Infinitesimalen bei Epikur', *Deutsche Akad. d. Wiss.*, Berlin 1954 (*Sitzungsberichte*); P. Merlan, *Epicurus and Aristotle,* 1960. Contrary to the general belief, D. J. Furley thinks that, in some aspects, Aristotle's and Epicurus's doctrines are very similar, perhaps identical; see D. J. Furley, *Two Studies in Greek Atomists*, Princeton 1967.

Of course, it may be that all references to Atomic theory in the Corpus are to Leucippus, who lived before Aristotle. But there are serious discrepancies between pre-Socratic views as known from other sources and as presented in the Corpus. Be it added that H. F. Cherniss in his well-known books (*Aristotle's Criticism of Pre-Socratic Philosophy*, Baltimore 1935; *Aristotle's Criticism of Plato and the Academy*, Baltimore 1944; *The Riddle of the Early Academy*, Berkeley 1945) tries to explain those discrepancies by suggesting that Aristotle deliberately distorted earlier views either to fit them into his scheme of argument and make it easier for himself to refute them or, less convincingly still, to create a foil against which his own views would stand out more impressively.

It was customary for the Greek philosophers to refer to ancient rather than to recent or contemporary thinkers, and to attribute doctrines emanating from a school to the founder of that school. The Corpus Hippocrateum provides the

The dominant philosophical school in antiquity was, of course, the Stoic, founded only a few years after Epicurus had started teaching in Athens. Affinities between Stoic and Epicurean views have often been noticed. The Stoics, too, subordinated logic and physics to ethics, which they regarded as the crowning part of philosophy. Like the Epicureans, they paid much attention to the material side of nature but, in contrast to them, they excluded neither mind nor purpose from their physical explanations. They, too, believed that they had discovered the basic truths but, less dogmatic than the Epicureans, they regarded their doctrines as capable of refinement, and hence worked on them, observing and researching with infinite industry. Their courses, though less comprehensive than those of the Peripatos, embraced the principal branches of philosophy (rhetoric and poetics however were not included). In each of these branches, their contributions were considerable. Stoic logic, long neglected, has recently been re-discovered, as a logic of propositions anticipating modern logical theory. Whereas in physics the Stoics' doctrines were developed from the views of Heraclitus, Empedocles and Anaxagoras, their epistemo-logy was their own, and it may well be regarded as the soundest theory of knowledge ever devised; for, while distinguishing our various faculties of cognition, the Stoics precisely describe the process of cognition, stating the criteria of knowledge as compared with (false) opinion. Above all, they were famous for their ethical teaching, which dominated the thought and actions of the most remarkable figures of the Graeco-Roman world, and which has never ceased to inspire even to the present day.

Although the Stoic school was small at first, its adherents were distinguished by a deep earnestness and by the intensity of their beliefs. The Peripatetics, who stood in almost total opposition to the Epicureans, found some areas of consensus between themselves and

---

clearest evidence for this. Democritus is nowhere mentioned by name by Plato. In *Gen. Corr.* II, 3, a view which is manifestly not Plato's own but probably belongs to the post-Platonic Academy is ascribed to Plato, namely the view that there are three elements, the middle being a mixture (330^{b}17). Theophrastus's *Metaphysics* seems to contain references to the atomic theory of Epicurus, which however, is there attributed to Democritus (11^{b}21–3). It also includes a possible allusion to the Stoic doctrine of theodicy, without any Stoic philosopher being mentioned (11^{b}5 ff.). When contemporaries are referred to it is done anonymously: their theories are ascribed to 'some' (*tines, enioi*).

the Stoics. They, too, saw nature as both matter and mind and as impelled by purpose as well as cause. But while the two schools agreed they also competed with each other, each elaborating its own theories in logic, physics and ethics. At the same time, they influenced each other while yet endeavouring to clarify their own distinctive views. Moreover, one discovers indications both of the adoption of Stoic theories and of polemic against them, sometimes also deliberate attempts at improving or outshining Stoic doctrines, in the Corpus.[1]

As one considers the relation of Stoa and Peripatos two aspects are particularly relevant. The Stoics were the first to construct a 'system', that is, an edifice of ideas, all-embracing and complete in itself. While the idea of 'system' necessarily had an impact on the Peripatetic philosophers, it stood in conflict with their own dialectical tradition derived from Plato, which led them to pose basic questions again and again, subjecting all solutions to ever-renewed inquiry. Hence, as they tried on the one hand to build a harmonious whole founded on a central notion (namely substance), this notion itself remained subject to doubt, and equally, many derivative concepts and doctrines were frequently re-examined. As a result, the Corpus creates the impression that whoever wrote it continually aimed at 'system' but always failed to achieve it.

Secondly, the problem of the relation of matter and mind was, in a sense, solved by the Stoic thinkers. To them the divine *logos* was the moving force, the spirit (*pneuma*) in matter.[2] But the Stoic *logos* with its theological implications was alien to Greek thought. The Peripatetics could not accept it and instead tried to define mind in accordance with Greek traditions as the generic, as form or essence, and as mind (*nous*). No solution was final: hence, substance could never be validly clarified, and the relation of matter and mind had to remain an open issue. On the whole, therefore, dialectical questioning, not dogmatic teaching as with the Stoa, proved to be the chief characteristic of the Peripatos.

---

[1] In this instance, too, the evidence, which might be plentiful, remains to be gathered; see p. 60, n. 3. In particular there are connections between Peripatetic and Stoic epistemology, as clearly emerges from an analysis of *De Anima* III, and especially III, 3. In this chapter the concept of *phantasia* is discussed in terms which show that the Peripatetic lecturer was aware of the great epistemological significance which the Stoics attached to *phantasia*.

[2] See Arnim, *SVF* II, 335, 25; 310, 24.

Further, but less importantly, the Pythagoreans played a part in moulding the philosophical climate of the age. They had exercised some influence on Plato in his later years and, to a still greater extent, on Speusippus.[1] One also discovers traces of a reaction to the Pythagorean theory of numbers in the Corpus.[2] In addition, the Hippocrateans made an impact not only on biological conceptions but on thinking in general.

As often happens, the appearance of several philosophical schools with their divergent views provoked an aggressive reply. The beginnings of what may be described as methodical Scepticism reach back to Plato's time. Pyrrho is named as the original Sceptic.[3] Later Scepticism achieved an important victory when Arcesilaus turned the Academy into a school of Sceptical thinking about 265 B.C. The Sceptics, following all constructive (or, as they said, dogmatic) philosophy with keen attention, attacked all published theories to show (1) that in each case the opposite view could also be held and (2) that it was impossible to prove the truth of any doctrine, since all proof must contain either a vicious circle or an infinite regress. What followed was, if not the denial of all possible knowledge, at least a demand that all judgment should be permanently suspended. Inevitably, such radical doubt affected the students even of the dogmatic schools. Catching the spirit of disbelief, they began to query the teaching offered to them and the validity of accepted doctrines and methods in an attempt to shake the confidence of their teachers or to force them to revise their views. The Academy, as we have seen, actually fell victim to the Sceptical onslaught. The Stoa on the other hand, although it became the main target of the Sceptics, maintained its strength, as did the 'garden'. The Peripatos, however, so closely related to the Academy, was in a vulnerable position. It stood nearer to Scepticism, both

---

[1] On the relation of the Pythagoreans and Plato see W. Burkert, *Weisheit und Wissenschaft*, Nürnberg 1962. Analysing the Pythagorean theories of numbers, Professor Burkert argues that they contain a 'primitive' element and that this must be pre-Platonic.

[2] The (old) Pythagoreans continued as a school till *c.* 250 B.C. See Professor K. von Fritz's lucid account of their history and doctrines in *Pauly-Wissowa*, Halbb. 47 (1963), pp. 209–68.

[3] It is generally assumed that Scepticism did not become a force until after Pyrrho (who lived from 360 to 270 B.C.), through Timo of Phlius and Philo of Athens. But it seems that this assumption may have to be revised.

in thought and in method, than the two essentially dogmatic schools, the Stoic and Epicurean. It was in fact part of the tradition of the Peripatos to state antithetic views, placing them side by side without deciding between them, according to Plato's own precedent in the *Parmenides*.[1] Like the Sceptics, the Peripatetics were used to gathering the opinions of others, adding their own critical comment, following Aristotle himself who had initiated 'doxography' even before he founded the school. It is true that, as they discussed theories critically, their aim was to eliminate what they thought was mistaken and to retain what seemed to them valid. Still, there remained only a narrow path between the absolute doubt of the Sceptics and the Peripatetic attitude of never-completed questioning. To us, the Peripatetic way of thinking may appear the most fruitful of all; it is perhaps more congenial to the modern scientific approach than that of other Greek schools. But in its own world the Peripatos found it difficult to maintain its identity, since it had to defend its own position not only against the dogmatic views of others but also against radical doubt. Later on, from the second century to the time of Cicero, the identity of the Peripatos was entirely lost. Being too close to the Sceptical Academy it was no longer considered a school in its own right. Again, we note that the struggle against the Sceptics is reflected in the Corpus. There are passages which show that sometimes the Peripatetic lecturers made concessions to Sceptical opinion. More often they attempted to prove to their students that some basic views could be maintained with certainty. Or, they made great efforts to strengthen, by further elaboration, a Peripatetic theory against which Sceptical objections had been raised.[2]

With so many influences working on the students and, as may be assumed, also on the lecturers of the Peripatos, it is not surprising

[1] Cicero comments on this: 'Aristotle set on foot the practice of arguing pro and contra upon every topic, not like Arcesilaus, always controverting every proposition, but setting out all the possible arguments on either side in every subject' (*De Fin.* v, 10, translated by H. Rackham, Loeb edition).

[2] A prime target of Sceptical doubt was 'definition'. The Sceptics claimed that it was impossible to define anything validly. Hence, we find that the Peripatetic lecturers made ever renewed attempts to improve their own theory of definition. The Sceptics also assailed 'perception', which they said was unreliable and, therefore, unsuitable as a basis for knowledge. This attack, too, troubled the Peripatetics, although it was mainly aimed at the Stoics and Epicureans.

that the overall teaching in the school began to show signs of disharmony and eclecticism. The individual lecturers adopted differing views, according to special interest or inclination, or even changed their views as the times changed. Some of them were inclined to listen to outside opinion; others remained antagonistic to it. Inevitably, too, lecturers began to conduct polemics against one another, each defending his own variant of the Peripatetic philosophy, though with restraint, as all were interested in upholding the basic unity of the school's teaching. Again we find traces both of internal polemic and of eclecticism in the Corpus.

As an educational establishment, the Peripatos catered to students from different backgrounds and at various stages of their studies—in modern terms, both for graduates and undergraduates. The latter included those intent on serious work and others who merely looked for some kind of higher education. Accordingly, some courses of lectures were of a specialized nature, others on a more elementary level. And since lectures were frequently revised for re-delivery, we find that the treatises often contain parts which only advanced students could appreciate beside passages which are basic, even simple. Moreover, as has been pointed out, a Peripatetic philosopher is often at pains to defend the school's doctrines against Sceptical objections. Indeed, it appears that he sometimes tried to forestall his Sceptical critics by himself asking the questions which his doubting students might put to him, considering them unanswerable. A somewhat neglected book of the *Metaphysics*, *Alpha Elatton*, can afford an insight into the working of the school, its spirit and organization, provided it is understood as what it manifestly is—partly if not *in toto*—a presidential or inaugural address given by the scholarch or his representative to the assembled student body at the beginning of term. Here it is:

⟨You all feel⟩ [the speaker seems to have addressed his student-audience,] ⟨that⟩ the search for truth is difficult. And indeed it is; yet it is easy. For while no single person can find a significant measure of the truth it is possible for everyone to contribute towards its discovery, so by the combined work of many something considerable will be achieved. Who can miss the door, as the proverb says? For it is easy to grasp a whole ⟨we all know what health, what illness is⟩, but it is difficult to understand the

5

particular ⟨the precise nature of any one disease⟩.[1] Besides, the difficulty may lie in ourselves; we must not shut our eyes, like bats in broad daylight, to that which is abundantly clear.

Having thus both encouraged and admonished the students the speaker refers to the debt every generation owes to its predecessors, illustrating the point he is making by mentioning not philosophers but two early poet-musicians. He goes on to circumscribe the main object of the Peripatetic philosophers' teaching. Stressing that they are aiming not at practical but at theoretical knowledge, he says that their search is for ultimate truth, that is, the first principles of things. And explaining what he means by this the speaker betrays his own inclination towards the physical sciences, for he states that the ultimate truth of a thing is its cause (see also below, p. 109).

Now follows a disproportionately lengthy section entirely devoted to the refutation of Sceptical arguments (*Metaph.* α 11). The speaker states emphatically that there must be first principles and first causes, and presupposing—as may be noted—that his (advanced) hearers are familiar with the Peripatetic doctrine of the four causes, he proves that neither the material nor the efficient nor the formal nor the final cause is subject to an infinite regress; on the contrary, he says, there *is* a first cause, an ultimate goal (*telos*)—the good. Evidently the speaker felt that the students would not stay in the Peripatetic lecture-rooms unless they could be convinced that some basic tenets were unshakeable.[2] In the last part of the chapter the speaker refutes two further Sceptical objections against Peripatetic

---

[1] Compare *Metaph.* A, 981ᵃ21 ff. with this passage. There are some similarities between *Alpha Meizon* and *Alpha Elatton*. *Alpha Meizon*, too, contains passages which may well have been part of an inaugural address (980ᵃ22; 982ᵇ12 etc.). It refers to the relative difficulties of different studies (981ᵃ21 ff.; 982ᵃ25 ff.). It is concerned with the concept of cause. Reflections on the difficulties of the search for knowledge and, in particular, on how one should progress in this search, namely from that which is plain to that which is obscure and hard to find, seem to have been a *topos koinos* in inaugural addresses or at the beginning of courses. See *Metaph.* Z IV, 1029ᵇ3 ff.; XVI, 1040ᵇ21 ff.; also *Metaph.* Δ, 1013ᵃ2, *Phys.* A 1 and *Eth. Nic.* 1095ᵇ2. However, the views expressed in these passages are not unitary: to a Platonizing philosopher the universal (982ᵃ25), to an empiricist the particular (981ᵃ21; 993ᵇ6), is the most difficult to grasp.

[2] That it was part of the Sceptical attack on the existence of cause to point to an infinite regress is shown by Sextus Empiricus, *Outlines of Pyrrhonism* III, 24: 'To prove the existence of cause it would be necessary to show a cause of a cause, *ad infinitum*. But this is impossible: hence, it cannot be proved that anything is caused by anything.'

views, namely that the definition of essence involves an infinite regress and that there is an infinite variety of kinds of causes. It is not unlikely that this part was added when the lecture was revised for re-delivery, for the students addressed now do not appear to be Sceptically inclined but rather anxious to acquire knowledge and hence to be protected from Sceptical arguments (994[b]21–3).

The speaker ends as he has begun, by addressing himself to the needs and expectations of his hearers. So far he has had mainly the advanced students in mind. Now he turns to beginners and near-beginners. To the first group he says that they must not be put off by technical language, the use of which, he says, is a necessity for them so that they can wean themselves of childish notions derived from myths. Such notions, he explains, have a strong hold on the mind, as is proved by the fact that our laws are still permeated by them, in spite of our better judgment. Next he talks to those who are new to the Peripatos but have had some previous training elsewhere, some at the Academy or under Pythagorean leaders, others at rhetorical schools. The first type of students, he says, will only consider what is expressed in mathematical terms; the second expect all statements to be followed by illustrations, or to be corroborated by sayings of the poets. In short, he continues, there are those who want everything set out in a strictly methodical (i.e. mathematical) way, others who reject methodical precision as tiresome and pedantic. Hence, there must be classes to train students in (general, philosophical) method, as a preparation for the study of any subject: 'For it is absurd to aim at knowledge and at the method of obtaining knowledge at the same time. It is difficult enough to acquire either of these.' And once again showing that he tends towards the natural sciences the speaker concludes by pointing out that each subject requires its own approach and that, in particular, the mathematical method is unsuitable for the study of nature, which contains matter.

I hope it has become evident from my paraphrase that *Alpha Elatton* is not a course of lectures on metaphysics, nor even the introductory part of such a course, but an address guiding students to the theoretical study-programme of the Peripatos.[1]

---

[1] It is true that the last sentence, of which the second part is omitted by Alexander, makes it appear that the book is an introduction to a course in physics, as Jaeger wrongly concludes. But the sentence is at variance with the whole tenor of the book and was obviously added (see commentary to Ross's edition of the *Metaphysics*, Oxford 1953, 2nd ed., ad loc.).

It is general in its approach and, except for the more intricate middle section, avoids difficult concepts. It uses the commonest term, *alêtheia* (truth), to describe the aim of the philosopher. It dwells on practical aspects of instruction. That its author is aware of student opinion is shown not only in the strong stand he takes against the Sceptics or in the emphasis he places on the physical study of nature, but also in his apparent awareness of the strength of Stoic views and their influence upon him. For instance the sentence at 994^{b}15 ff., ' . . . there would be no mind (*nous*) in the things that exist, for he who has *nous* acts for the sake of something, the end, the goal (*telos*)—the good', reflects views akin to Stoic doctrine.

Another point of significance is the philosopher's remark about the value, indeed the necessity, of team work in the acquisition of knowledge; a remark which we are surely entitled to apply to the Aristotelian treatises themselves and to the manner in which the great store of knowledge recorded in them was obtained.

Summing up, *Alpha Elatton* throws a light on the intellectual climate of an age or, at least, a decade. According to a scholion on Codex E, it was commonly regarded as the work of Pasicles of Rhodes, a nephew of Eudemus and pupil of Aristotle, who flourished during the headship of Theophrastus. There appears to be no good reason to disbelieve the tradition preserved in this scholion (although it has at times been rejected as false).[1] It is confirmed by the tone and contents of the book, which is surely post-Aristotelian. For Aristotle would not have been troubled by the Sceptics to the extent that its author is. Nor is it likely that Aristotle himself would have referred to several intricate Peripatetic tenets, i.e. the four causes or the doctrine of essence, summarily, and in a manner suggesting that he expected his hearers to be thoroughly familiar with them.

---

[1] See Ross, *Comm.* II, p. 213.

CHAPTER FOUR

The Library of the Peripatos and its History

We now turn to the important question of the school library: its composition and its history. Here, direct information is scarce; no ancient source tells us exactly how the library was formed or what happened to it in the course of time. So we depend on indirect evidence, biographical, historical and literary, of which, as we shall see, there is a good deal.

The books of the Peripatos were housed in the temple of the Muses. It is likely that some of them were copies of published books, partly by Peripatetic writers, partly by other authors, for the Peripatetics were students of history and compilers of *doxai*. It is certain that the library contained unpublished work, that is, records of lectures delivered at the school.[1] These must have been kept, for lectures were delivered more than once and revised for re-delivery, as we know from a letter of Theophrastus (Diog. L. v, 37). Legally, the rolls with all the other property of the school belonged to the scholarch, although in practice they were the common possession of the senior members of the school, who could use and amplify them as they wished, basing their own teaching on them.[2] So, as the need arose, copies of lecture records were made, which often contained variants of the original lectures. These, too, were retained and gradually rolls accumulated, constituting a large treasure of knowledge which was kept up-to-date.

On the other hand, the library was from time to time depleted. It is known that members left the school, for example Eudemus and Dicaearchus after the death of Aristotle, and it may be assumed that they took rolls with them. In one case, we have definite information about the loss of books from the school library. In his will Theophrastus decided to leave 'all the books' to Neleus, who took them to his native city, Scepsis, in the Troad (Diog. L. v, 52

---

[1] The treatises we read do not consist of lecture *notes*, as has long been assumed, but of lecture *records*.

[2] See Jaeger, *Entst.* and Brink in *Pauly-Wissowa*, Suppl. VII, p. 924.

and Strabo).[1] Strabo describes the bequest as 'the library of Theophrastus which included the library of Aristotle'. Still, what we are told does not enable us to decide whether Theophrastus left to Neleus his private library only, consisting mainly of published works, or also records of school lectures, of which copies may have been made. In any case, it is certain that an adequate stock of books remained at the school because its teaching went on uninterrupted, and because eighteen years later the next scholarch, Strato, was able to bequeath a library to his successor, Lyco.

Moreover, the rolls along with all the other property of the school, were continually at risk during the entire period of the school's existence in Athens, through bombardment and pilfering in time of war and through rioting in the city at other times, for the Athenians were consistently hostile to the Macedonian-supported Peripatos. At least once, the school suffered serious damage (see Chapter Two). Finally, when after the fall of Macedonia the school was closed, its stock of books somehow vanished; whether they were destroyed at this time or transferred elsewhere it is not possible to say. In any case, no trace of the library could later be discovered in Athens. Still, the knowledge of the Peripatetic teaching was never completely lost. There are references to it in the centuries of the school's abeyance, from which it follows that philosophers were always able to consult many of the esoteric treatises.[2] The question

---

[1] Strabo's account of the bequest and of the subsequent history of the library is, of course, our main source for the antecedents of Andronicus's edition of the Aristotelian treatises (Strabo XIII, 1, 54 ff.). Another source is Plutarch, *Sulla* 26.

[2] See E. Zeller, *Die Philosophie der Griechen* II, 2, pp. 148 ff. From one of the papyri from Herculaneum it emerges that an Epicurean acquired, or wished to acquire, the Aristotelian *Analytics* and *Physics* (no doubt, including at least parts of the *Metaphysics*), along with such works as Plato's *Apologia Socratis*; from which it must be inferred that *apographa* of the esoteric treatises, even if difficult to get hold of, were not unobtainable (*Pap. Herc.* 1005, fr. 21; see W. Croenert, *Kolotes und Menedemus*, Leipzig 1906, p. 174; E. Bignone, *L'Aristotele perduto*, Florence 1935, I, p. 41, n. 3 and II, p. 108; P. Moraux, *Les Listes anciennes des ouvrages d'Aristote*, Louvain 1951, p. 4). The last mentioned, while suspending judgment on the story of the disappearance of Aristotle's manuscripts, offers much evidence to show that the esoteric treatises were known before Andronicus. After referring to the Epicureans, Moraux particularly points out that the Stoics were profoundly influenced by the Aristotelian logic as well as physics, and concludes: 'Les échanges spirituels entre les deux écoles [Peripatetic and Stoic] paraissent avoir été abondants et suivis.'

Further, there are close similarities between *Gen. Corr.* and Ocellus Lucanus's

therefore arises: where could the Peripatetic lecture records be read? No doubt, even while the school still flourished the scholarchs were aware of its precarious position, so they may well have wished to see their records or copies deposited in a safe place.

Now, this was the epoch of the foundation of the great libraries of the ancient world: at Alexandria, Pergamum, Antioch and Rhodes. Both Aristotle himself and Theophrastus are said to have been asked to help organize the first and most famous of the libraries, that at Alexandria. Strato is said to have taught Ptolemy II. Lyco was in touch with Pergamum and was also invited to help create a library at Antioch (but he refused this request; Diog. L. V, 67). Eudemus may have contributed to the stock of rolls kept in Rhodes, his native island.

Of all the libraries the one at Pergamum grew fastest as it tried to compete with Alexandria, which had had a considerable start. Its patrons were the keenest, and it was with Pergamum, too, that several members of the Peripatetic school were closely connected. Aristotle himself had lived in Assos, later part of the kingdom of Pergamum, where he had collaborated with philosophers from the Troad. One of these was Coriscus, the father of Neleus, who after lecturing at the Lyceum returned to his native Troad with a large stock of books.[1] Lastly, Lyco, the third scholarch, was born in the Troad. Of him we learn expressly that he entertained the friendliest relations with the kings of Pergamum, obliging them to the exclusion of another ruler, the king of Syria.[2] At the time of Lyco, Pergamum was a rising power while Macedonia was already in decline, so it was only natural for Lyco to look to the kings of Pergamum for protection. Hence, if Peripatetic lecture records found their way into libraries (and we shall presently show proof that they did) it was in all probability in Pergamum that a great many of them were collected. This we may gather not only from the fact that Lyco was a loyal friend of the Pergamene king but also from Strabo's well-known story[3] which points to a link between Aristotle's books and the

---

On the Nature of the Universe, although the time of Ocellus Lucanus is contested; see Diels, *Dox. Graeci*, pp. 187 ff. and R. Harder, *Ocellus Lucanus*, Berlin 1926.

[1] See Strabo XIII, 1, 54ff. and Diog. L. V, 52. Coriscus is one of the addressees of Plato's *Sixth Epistle*.

[2] See Diog. L. V, 67.

[3] See p. 70, n. 1.

Pergamene library. There are two further reasons for this conclusion. We possess several lists of the works of Peripatetic philosophers (preserved by Diogenes Laertius in the lives of Aristotle, Theophrastus and Strato, as well as by Hesychius), and these must have been compiled at libraries. Secondly, the treatises of the Corpus are arranged in an order based on Stoic principles and although this arrangement may have been introduced later (see below) it is worth noting that the librarians at Pergamum included a highly regarded Stoic philosopher, Athenodorus, who was actually accused of interfering with the text of some of the books in his charge (Diog. L. VII, 34). In short, Peripatetic lecture records, all or some of those given to Neleus, were probably kept at Pergamum, and if the scholarchs were aware of this it is only natural to expect that they, and especially Lyco, offered to supplement the Peripatetic section of the library by periodically sending them further rolls, duplicates or specially ordered copies of original lectures.[1] In doing so they certainly obliged their patrons. For whereas it was always possible for the kings of Pergamum to acquire copies of published works, only the scholarchs themselves could supply them with copies of the esoteric writings. According to custom these rolls were inscribed in the name of the founder of the school, Aristotle, or in the names of the two most famous scholarchs, Aristotle and Theophrastus, and perhaps even some in the name of Strato. The rolls sent at any time would contain the latest version of a treatise on a subject. In many cases, libraries would acquire a large number of rolls under the same title; Alexandria possessed, *inter alia*, forty rolls of the *Analytics*.[2] But let it be emphasized that even if Lyco supplied Pergamum with rolls as late as 260 or 250, or even 240, the original treatises (apart from some slight revisions or additions) would go back to the early time of the Peripatos. Under Lyco, as we hear from Cicero among others (*De Fin.* v, 10 ff.), the thinking in the school had become barren, and nothing new was added to what had already been discovered. So considerable evidence points to

---

[1] Even if the books given to Neleus had not gone to Pergamum it was known that the kings of Pergamum were anxious to acquire Peripatetic treatises and the scholarchs were eager to oblige them.

[2] See Philoponus, *In Categorias*, in *Commentaria in Aristotelem Graeca* (*CIAG*), Berlin 1882–1909, vol. XIII, 1 (1898), pp. 7 and 26; compare Düring, p. 68.

Pergamum as the main recipient of Peripatetic lecture records but it is also certain that other great libraries, especially Alexandria, succeeded in obtaining copies of esoteric treatises (see Athenaeus I, 3).

The kingdom of Pergamum had a short history. Founded as an independent State about 283 B.C., it flourished notably under Eumenes I (263–241) and Attalus I (241–197) who patronized the library. But then Rome became an overwhelming power, and the last king of Pergamum, Attalus III, realizing that Pergamum could not hope to retain its independence, bequeathed his kingdom to Rome. So, on his death (133 B.C.), the senate and people of Rome became the rightful owners of all the possessions of Pergamum, and we hear of treasure-laden ships arriving at Ostia from Asia Minor and of auctions in Rome, at which the booty from Pergamum was disposed of in tremendous lots. Still, the transfer of power was accompanied by a severe upheaval. The population of Pergamum, or in any case the lower classes, were violently opposed to the dissolution of their State and finding a leader, Aristonicus, supposedly an illegitimate son of Attalus II, they rose in rebellion against their overlords. Inevitably, Rome won in the end; Aristonicus, the Pergamene Spartacus, was captured and executed. But during the two years in which the war was fought the insurgent forces occupied much of the territory of Pergamum, plundering the royal treasures wherever they could to finance their campaign and, in particular, to pay their mercenaries. It is true, they never succeeded in establishing themselves fully in the capital, but at some time or other they must have penetrated into the city, especially since the lower classes there were on their side.[1] The temple, with the library it housed, contained many treasures worth taking and indeed it appears that for a decade or two the market was swamped with goods that had never before been available for sale.[2] Speculators quickly grasped their opportunity. We hear of one of them, Apellico of Teos (c. 150/40 to 87/6 B.C.), described as a collector of books, who amassed a fortune in Athens, presumably by selling 'pirated' editions of works which had not been known to the public before. He filled his large house with books. He was convicted of stealing

---

[1] See Karl Bücher, *Die Aufstände der unfreien Arbeiter*, 143–129 a.Chr.n., Frankfurt 1874.

[2] 'From the time of C. Gracchus Asia had been the principal hunting ground of the Italian fortune-seekers, official and private' (M. Cary, *History of Rome*, 2nd ed., London 1957, p. 333).

public records from the Athenian archives and of him it is reported that he acquired rolls containing Peripatetic treatises, 'the books of Aristotle and Theophrastus', and that he soon had them cheaply and badly copied.[1] How had the rolls come into his possession? If it is right to assume that directly or indirectly they had been obtained from the booty of Pergamum, this had to be kept secret. Legally, the treasures of Pergamum[2] were Roman property and whoever bought them bought stolen goods. So a story had to be told to prove that the books had been lawfully acquired.

At this point, let us consider, in some detail, Strabo's account of what happened to Aristotle's books. Theophrastus, Strabo relates, bequeathed his library, which included that of Aristotle, to Neleus, son of Coriscus, who took them to his native city, Scepsis, in the Troad. There they were neglected after Neleus's death. Later, Strabo continues, at the time of the foundation of the Pergamene library, the kings of Pergamum had their entire kingdom searched for books (presumably offering good prices for them); whereupon— Strabo paradoxically says—the heirs of Neleus, who were *not* interested in philosophy, determined to keep the rolls to themselves, burying them in a hole in the earth where the kings of Pergamum could not find them. And there they lay hidden for nearly two hundred years, suffering a great deal of damage from moisture and from moths.

Now several aspects of this story conflict with what we know from other sources. Many tenets of the Aristotelian philosophy were frequently debated throughout the time when the rolls are said to have been buried.[3] Secondly, the text (of the Corpus), in contrast to what Strabo says, is a very good text and by no means bears out

---

[1] There are three Greek words for 'copy': *anagraphê*, *antigraphon* and *apographon*. It seems that *antigraphon* is used for what may be called a 'pirated copy' (Strabo XIII, 54 ff.); *anagraphê* means 'record', officially made. *Inter alia* this word is used for the copies librarians ordered to be made for the libraries (Athenaeus VIII, 336e). It is perhaps synonymous with *pinax*. *Apographon* is a general term, later used by Cicero (*Ad Att.* XII, 52, 3), and seems to mean copies ordered by private persons for their own use.

[2] The Pergamene library remained an important one under Roman rule, at least for another century. It emerges from Plutarch's life of Mark Anthony (chapter 58) that about 35-30 B.C. the library still contained a large number of books—whether or not the story is true that Anthony gave 200,000 books from Pergamum to Cleopatra. Of course, it must be assumed that the library was periodically replenished in the Roman era.

[3] See p. 70, n. 2.

the story of the moth-eaten manuscripts with their many gaps. It would follow that the rolls were always expertly cared for and also that it was always possible to consult them, two conditions which could only have been fulfilled in a library. It appears, therefore, that the main point made in Strabo's story is that the books had, of course, been expected at one time to go to the Pergamene library but, in fact, had remained in the hands of their rightful owners who had lawfully sold them in the open market.

We hear a good deal about Apellico from Athenaeus (Ath. v, 213ᵉ ff.), who amplifies what Strabo tells us about him (Strabo XIII, 1, 54–609; 644). He was not so much a public figure as a political adventurer who during the wars of Mithridates (who occupied Pergamum) joined the anti-Roman faction and associated with the notorious Athenio, an agent of Mithridates and usurper of power in Athens. By him he was sent on a plundering expedition to Delos but there his small army was surprised and beaten by a Roman general. He managed to escape from the slaughter and to return to Athens from the island, but it seems that he died soon afterwards during the ensuing siege of Athens. However disreputable, Apellico deserves notice as one of the key figures in the history of the transmission of the Aristotelian writings to posterity. For it is almost certain that the story of the burial and rediscovery of the books first gained currency in his time and, indeed, through him, and also, that the rolls in his possession had formerly been the property of libraries.

Both Strabo and Plutarch tell us what happened next to the Aristotelian books. Early in 86 B.C. Sulla entered Athens, which suffered severe damage and losses during and after a prolonged siege. Among other measures the victorious Sulla had the contents of Apellico's house, including his stock of books, confiscated, and by his orders the books were shipped to Rome. There they were put in the charge of a (public) librarian. It appears that for some time the Aristotelian rolls attracted little attention in Italy. But then the grammarian Tyrannio, a scholar and philosopher of some note and a client or friend of Cicero's, saw them.[1] 'Ingratiating himself with the librarian', as Strabo puts it, he was allowed to handle the books.[2]

It appears that Tyrannio, too, had bad copies of them made but

---

[1] Cicero refers to Tyrannio in: *Ad Att.* IV, 4*b*, 1; IV, 8*a*, 2; XII, 2, 2; XII, 6; *Ad Q. fratrem* II, 4, 2; III, 4–6. See Düring, p. 412.

[2] I read ἐνεχειρίσατο.

he also studied the treatises and began to arrange them. More important still, he spoke about them to Cicero, whose library he had been invited to arrange, and Cicero himself at least glanced at them. And now a remarkable phenomenon occurred: a complete reappraisal of Aristotle as a philosopher. During the entire Hellenistic period Aristotle had been known as a leading Platonist and author of fine popular works, but from the time when Cicero conferred with Tyrannio, Aristotle began to be admired as a great philosopher in his own right, as a critic of Plato and the creator of many profound (and conflicting) doctrines. This change in the image of Aristotle, which proved so significant, is reflected in Cicero's writings, his letters and his philosophical works. Both the earlier and the later estimates of Aristotle's achievements find expression in them. Following the Hellenistic tradition of his sources Cicero describes Aristotle as the rival of Isocrates and teacher of rhetoric (*De Oratore* III, 35, 141; *Tusc.* I, 4; *Orator* XIV, 46). He praises the 'golden flow' of Aristotle's style (*Acad.* II (*Lucullus*), 38, 119). He calls him a leading Platonist, mentioning him with Speusippus, Xenocrates and Polemo (*Tusc.* V, 10; 13; 31; *De Fin.* IV, 3). He speaks of the Academy and the Peripatos as 'one school with two different heads' (*Acad.* I, 4, 17 and 22). But then he comes to know the esoteric treatises (*De Fin.* V, 4; 12; *Ad Att.* IV, 16, 2). He now realizes that Aristotle's and Plato's views differ (*Acad.* I, 9, 33). He calls Aristotle by far the greatest mind after Plato (*Tusc.* I, 22; compare *Acad.* II (*Lucullus*), 43, 132). But as he becomes more closely acquainted with the esoteric treatises he begins to be troubled by their difficulty and seeming contradictions (*Fragm.* Klotz, p. 289; *De Fin.* V, 12). At one stage he seems uncertain if there are contradictions (*De Fin.* V, 12) but in an often debated passage he strongly accuses both Aristotle and Theophrastus of gross inconsistencies (*De Nat. Deorum* I, 33; 35).[1]

Still, however unsure Cicero's judgment of the treatises was,

---

[1] It is generally assumed that Cicero's criticism, in *De Natura Deorum*, of Aristotle's cosmology and theology was entirely based on a study of Aristotle's *ekdoton*, *On Philosophy*, but this assumption cannot be correct. For although Cicero in the quoted passage expressly mentions *On Philosophy*, the details of his criticism make it almost certain that he, or the Epicurean on whom he drew, also had knowledge of esoteric treatises—*Metaphysics* Λ and probably *Physics* Θ—and that he was referring not to an incipient but a fully developed theory of the unmoved mover; but see Jaeger, *Aristotle*, p. 138.

it is clear that a new estimate of Aristotle began to be formed in the second half of the first century B.C. And a further point of significance emerges: Aristotle was revalued not because the esoteric treatises were newly discovered—they had been known before, though not widely—but because they were only now attributed to Aristotle's sole authorship.

*   *   *

With the fame of Aristotle spreading, the ground was prepared not only for a close study of the treatises but for a revival of the Peripatetic school. Until about this time the Stoic school had enjoyed a unique position of influence but it had also aroused a great deal of jealousy and animosity, as we know from Plutarch's anti-Stoic writings. It appears that this was not solely the result of personal rivalry between teachers and philosophers but that there was a political side to it. The two most famous statesmen of the republican era, which had come to an end, Cato and Brutus, had been known to be Stoics. Hence, the emergence of a large body of writing, at least equal in depth to Stoic writing, must have appeared to be a most welcome aid in the struggle against the predominance of the Stoics. So, during one or two decades after the battle of Philippi— between 40 and 20 B.C.—another scholar-philosopher, Andronicus of Rhodes, himself trained by Stoics, set himself a double task: to make a new, scholarly edition of the treatises brought to Rome by Sulla, and to re-establish the Peripatetic school. He himself became its scholarch; the eleventh after Aristotle, as he claimed.[1]

Andronicus's edition was an epoch-making event. From the time of its appearance the fame of Aristotle became firmly established, and the study of the treatises under his name has gone on almost uninterruptedly to modern times. All our knowledge of the work of Aristotle and his school is based on this edition which, apart from a few minor additions which occurred later, is practically the Corpus as we read it. Andronicus published the treatises as the sole work of Aristotle himself. At the same time, to explain why it was only now possible to publish the works, three hundred years after the philosopher's death, it appears that he or his friends gave wide publicity to the story, which we know through Strabo, of the long

---

[1] Andronicus may have studied under Posidonius (born 135 B.C.) who taught in Rhodes and came to Rome in 51 B.C. where he died soon afterwards.

disappearance of Aristotle's own manuscripts which had only come to light in Apellico's time. It is likely that he himself believed the story and most unlikely that he invented it. Still, the story cannot be true, as we have seen: the text of the Corpus is too good to have come from moth-eaten originals and the knowledge of the Peripatetic teaching was never completely lost. The conclusion is that the rolls had been in libraries and if this was so there are many indications which show that the treatises published by Andronicus were not exclusively, or even predominantly, the work of Aristotle himself but the work of many members of his school over a lengthy period of time. While final proof for this assertion can only come from an analysis of the treatises themselves it is possible to present some evidence for it at this stage.

(1) It is confirmed by an examination of the lists of the works of Aristotle, Theophrastus and Strato, preserved for us by Diogenes Laertius and Hesychius.[1] These lists, based on library catalogues, include esoteric as well as exoteric works. In three instances works are described as lecture records (*hypomnêmata*)—Aristotle no. 33, Theophrastus nos. 170 and 198—and in two instances as courses of lectures (*acroasis*)—Aristotle no. 75 and Theophrastus no. 15. Some of the titles coincide with those known to us either from the fragments or from the Corpus; others seem to cover the matter treated in works of the Corpus. But there are also titles which it is difficult to relate to any of the works preserved.[2] As we look at Diogenes Laertius's list of Aristotelian titles[3] we find that the list begins with Aristotle's best known exoteric works (nos. 1–19). There follow Platonica and titles of esoteric works—logical, political, physical, mathematical and musical (nos. 20–116). Then we find works for 'seminars' (*aporêmata kai problêmata*, nos. 117–27), and after this collectanea and letters and poetry—146 titles in all.

(*a*) Some of the known works of the Corpus—*De Sensu, De Somno, De Insomniis, Meteorologica, De Caelo* and *De Generatione et*

---

[1] The middle section of Hesychius's list contains several titles of treatises not included by Diog. L., but it is generally agreed that that section of Hesychius's list is post-Andronicean (see Düring, p. 91).

[2] On titles in general compare Ernst Nachmanson, *Der griechische Buchtitel*, Göteborgs Högskolas Arsskrift XL, VII, 19, Göteborg 1941. Nachmanson points out that an ancient book was often referred to by its opening words, not its title.

[3] See Düring, pp. 68 ff.

Corruptione—are not included in Aristotle's list (see Diogenes Laertius) but they are found in the title lists of Theophrastus or Strato.[1]

(*b*) In one instance a work of Aristotle is described as similar to, or identical with, a work by Theophrastus (Aristotle no. 75); in three instances a work by Theophrastus is said to be similar to, or identical with, a work by Aristotle (Theophrastus nos. 49, 170, 179).[2]

(*c*) We find a great many identical titles in the lists of the three scholarchs (on politics, physics, poetics etc.).

(*d*) We find titles referring to special subjects within a discipline, especially physics and politics (*On Motion, On Causes, On the Just, On Kingship* etc.); and then again collective titles (*Physica, Politica*). Evidently, there were rolls devoted to special subjects and also other copies of the same or similar treatises bundled together into a book covering a whole discipline. The books of the *Metaphysics* were probably listed as *Physica*; also as *Principle* or *Principles* (*archê, archai*) and as *Causes* (*aitiai*).

It follows that several treatises on a subject reached the libraries at different times and that they bore different names, that of the founder or of the reigning scholarch. It may further be concluded that the various copies on a subject were not merely duplicates but in many instances revised up-to-date versions or even alternative treatments of the same theme.

It is remarkable that some of the subjects treated at length in the *Physics* appear in Strato's title list (*On the Void, On Time, On the Light and the Heavy*). It does not, of course, follow that the

---

[1] On this see Moraux, p. 96, n. 3; also Heitz, *Die verlorenen Schriften des Aristoteles*, Leipzig 1865, pp. 203 ff. Moraux explains the absence of many well-known titles from the list by suggesting that at the time the librarians compiled the list Aristotle was still at the beginning of his work so that only his early treatises had been collected; Moraux, loc. cit., pp. 317 ff. See also Düring, pp. 67 ff.

[2] It appears that Cicero had seen two versions of a Peripatetic work on cosmology and theology, one under the name of Aristotle and the other under the name of Theophrastus. This can be inferred from *De Natura Deorum* I, 33 and 35, where Cicero first criticizes Aristotle for his inconsistent views on these subjects and then criticizes Theophrastus for the same reason and in very similar terms. Nor is it likely that the criticism here expressed by Cicero in the name of an Epicurean was solely derived from the study of an *ekdoton*; see p. 76 n.

Corpus discussions are the work of Strato but merely that lecture records on these subjects probably reached the library in Strato's time, were inscribed in his name and, though basically composed much earlier, were brought up-to-date under Strato.[1]

Returning to Theophrastus: at one time, he and Aristotle were considered the joint *eponymoi* of the Peripatetic school (Cic. *Acad.* I, 33; *De Fin.* IV, 3 and V, 10 ff.). The *Politics* of the Corpus was regarded as the work of Theophrastus (Cicero, as above). Moreover, Cicero's criticism of Theophrastus's theology (*De Nat. Deorum* I, 35) may well refer to the *Metaphysics* (see above, p. 76). Further, the so-called *Metaphysics* of Theophrastus should be regarded, not as the work of Theophrastus, but as another of the esoteric school treatises on the subject, the record of which reached a library in Theophrastus's time. It should also be noted that Cicero believed the *Nicomachean Ethics* to be by Nicomachus (*De Fin.* V, 10), from which it may be inferred that this work, which is not included in the lists of any of the scholarchs,[2] was catalogued in the libraries as a book by Nicomachus.

(2) The Corpus itself, as every student of Aristotle knows, contains duplicates and even doublets. In *Metaph.* M (1078^b34–1079^b3; $^b12$–1080^a8), the argument of *Metaph.* A (990^b2–991^b8) is repeated. *Metaph.* K (1065^a26–1069^a14) contains a series of extracts from *Physics* II, III and V.[3] The Corpus includes not only

[1] There are affinities between the *Physics* and Strato's *Regarding the Void and Time;* see Wehrli, *Die Schule des Aristoteles,* Heft V, Strato, pp. 57–9 and 64. It has always been presupposed that Strato knew the *Physics* as we read it and that the author or authors of the *Physics* knew nothing about Strato's views. The question whether perhaps parts of the *Physics* were written or revised under the influence of Strato has never been asked.

Following a tradition established by Aristotle himself, many of the Peripatetic philosophers, in particular the scholarchs, wrote books for publication— *ekdota*. Their lists, therefore, included esoteric and exoteric writings. We may conclude that the *ekdota* of the lists are the scholarchs' own works, the treatises lecture records sent to the library under their names.

While essentially the treatises were composed during the early decades of the existence of the Peripatetic school, their text was probably established much later. An interesting parallel is afforded by the text and canon of Plato's works, which were probably established by the Academy at the beginning of its middle period (266–150 B.C.), from Arcesilaus to Carneades. See P. Merlan in *Ency. Brit.,* s.v. 'Academy'.

[2] Title no. 38 in Diog. L.'s list of Aristotle's works (*Ethikôn,* 5 books), apparently refers to an *ekdoton.*

[3] See Ross, *Comm.* I, pp. xxi and xxv.

three works on ethics but also—and this, too, should be generally recognized—several works on metaphysics, physics and politics. In the *Metaphysics* one finds several treatises on principles and causes, and on Being and substance, as well as a book on the One, and a book on pure, divine form. Indeed, as we shall see later, a single book of the *Metaphysics*, Z, incorporates several lectures on Being and substance or, more precisely, several new starts. In the *Physics*, at least book A and book Θ are altogether independent of each other. The *Politics*, too, contains several independent treatises. So, the Corpus confirms the conclusion obtained from an analysis of the titles: there existed a wealth of Peripatetic lecture records, many of them alternative treatments of the same subject.

(3) As we look for general characteristics of the Corpus treatises we note, first of all, that taken together they cover a wider range of subjects than any other ancient school of philosophy ever attempted to teach or study. But we also note that the preserved treatises are of unequal quality, some elementary, others specialized and methodically admirable, indeed unrivalled. We find that they were revised, often several times, incorporating polemical replies to objections, or taking account of new discoveries or trends of thought. As a result, they are full of excursions and sudden twists, while their main argument is interrupted, often to the extent that it is almost completely lost sight of. In fact as regards both their meaning and their structure, the treatises become intelligible only when it is realized that *they are part of a dialogue carried on between the lecturer and rival philosophers.* Many of the lectures were evidently meant for advanced students, since the main teaching in them is often merely briefly alluded to as though it were fully familiar to the hearers, while the bulk of the lecture consists of discussions of loosely connected problems, arising from objections to the main doctrine. In such discussions one often perceives echoes of philosophical views prevalent in the third century—Epicurean, Stoic and Sceptic-Academic. Moreover we find that many books of the Corpus consist of individual treatises, which were combined to form volumes. This was done in the libraries as the title lists show, rarely convincingly, more often artificially, for the unity brought about is often merely that of a concept indicating a theme, e.g. Being (*to on*), while the treatment of the theme is different in each of the treatises which make up the volume. We come upon varying and conflicting views, indicative of the

6

different inclinations, eidetic or materialistic, and interests, logical, mathematical and physical, surely not of one but of many philosophers.[1] We meet with manifest contradictions. We discover that in one treatise one view is dominant, in another treatise another; that views are propounded, discarded and revived probably in accordance with successive changes in contemporary opinion. Nevertheless, we also find a persisting tendency towards harmony or even system but, as would be only natural if the lecture records were made and collected over a period of time, the impression one gains is that of a unity often aimed at but never achieved, of a never-finalized order or system.

It appears, therefore, that Andronicus's edition of the Corpus reflects the teaching, not only of Aristotle, but of two or three generations of Peripatetic philosophers. Nevertheless, Andronicus published his edition as the sole work of Aristotle. Nor could he have done otherwise because, at least since Apellico's time, the treatises had been known as the work of Aristotle. And as Andronicus was intent on producing a pure and reliable edition, in contrast to his predecessors who were supposed to have tampered with the text by filling in gaps of the manuscripts arbitrarily (see Strabo), it is just possible that he expunged from the text anything that he regarded as indicating a non-Aristotelian origin, including names of post-Aristotelian philosophers, which he may have replaced by such pronouns as some or several (*tines, enioi*).

It is certain that Andronicus had before him a far richer material

---

[1] Diogenes Laertius mentions the following: Aristomenes, Timarchus, Hipparchus, Dioteles and Theophrastus, under Aristotle (v, 12); Hipparchus, Neleus, Strato, Callinus, Demotimus, Demaratus, Callisthenes, Melantes, Pancreon and Nicippus, under Theophrastus (v, 53); Olympicus, Aristides, Mnesigenes, Hippocrates, Epicrates, Gorgylus, Diocles, Lyco and Athanes, under Strato (v, 62); Bulo, Callinus, Aristo, Amphio, Lyco, Pytho, Aristomachus, Heracleus, Lycomedes and Lyco 11 (the scholarch's nephew), under Lyco (v, 70).

It is often assumed that those Peripatetics of whose works fragments have been preserved were the principal members of the school, but this may well be a wrong assumption. For men like Dicaearchus, Aristoxenus and the others whose fragments are found in Wehrli's edition all wrote for a wider public and for this reason became well known; whereas those who contributed to the evolution of the Peripatetic philosophy *within* the school, have largely remained obscure—with one or two exceptions, notably that of Strato. The rest are shadowy, and only their names, compiled by Diogenes Laertius, have come down to us.

than he used. His edition is severely selective. Not only did he omit many of the works of which the titles are preserved in Diogenes Laertius's list, for instance all the medical works (no. 110), but as every reader of Aristotle knows there are many references in the Corpus to which no corresponding work or passage can be found in the text we possess. So our knowledge of the Aristotelian work is defective and restricted. We only know what Andronicus included and thereby preserved; what he left out is lost. Another noteworthy feature of Andronicus's edition of the Corpus is its arrangement, which, as may be expected of a Stoically-trained philosopher, follows a Stoic pattern. In the Stoic view all philosophy culminated in ethics. Accordingly, their pupils had to study logic (dialectic) as a preliminary; then they had to study natural science to obtain the kind of knowledge that would enable them to understand the 'good'. Only at this stage were they ready to grasp the problems of ethics and finally, to lead the good life. Similarly, the Corpus is arranged as logic, physics and ethics, in this order.[1] Still, Andronicus faced two problems, arising from the comprehensive range of the Peripatetic teaching. The Stoic system had no room for a separate metaphysics, which to the Stoic philosopher was implicit in physics on the one hand and in ethics on the other, nor did the Stoics regard rhetoric and poetics as part of philosophy. Hence, without disturbing the basic order inherited from the Stoics, Andronicus decided to group together the treatises on basic questions and to insert them, not as a separate main section, but rather as an additum, immediately after the books on the natural sciences (*meta ta physica*).[2] This he probably felt all the more

[1] Although according to Pohlenz (*The Stoa*, Göttingen 1948, p. 33) this threefold division of philosophy goes back to Xenocrates, it was due to the Stoics that it became a generally accepted principle.

[2] Many attempts have been made to find a deeper meaning in the name 'metaphysics'. Recently Hans Reiner in *Die Entstehung und ursprüngliche Bedeutung des Namens Metaphysik*, published in *Metaphysik und Theologie des Aristoteles*, (ed.) F.-P. Hager, Darmstadt 1969, has suggested that the name arose because the study of metaphysics followed that of physics in the Peripatetic curriculum as the highest subject. But this explanation, like others before it (see Reiner's copious bibliography), remains unconvincing, and there is no reason to doubt the correctness of the traditional explanation of the name 'metaphysics', as the treatises placed after those on physics. We do not know when the name arose or by whom it was first used. It was certainly not used by Andronicus who, indeed, may not have given any special name to the treatises on 'principles' and 'substance' but regarded them as covered by the name *Physica*.

justified in doing since the problems discussed in these treatises were above all those basic to the study of nature. Consistently, he allowed the theological book *Metaph.* Λ to stand at the end of the collected treatises, as a work most suitable to lead on to the study of ethics.[1] To the books on ethics, *Eth. Nic.*, *Mag. Mor.*, *Eth. Eud.*, in this order, he joined 'politics' and 'economics'. Finally, he added the treatises on rhetoric and poetics to the completed Corpus, loosely attaching them, as a kind of *parergon*.

It emerges that the Peripatos as a whole is characterized by a spirit of inquiry extending to every field of study known at the time; that it was the one school which carried on the tradition of general Platonism after the Academy itself had abandoned it, first in favour of dogmatism, then of a radical Scepticism. Ever open to a reappraisal of their own doctrines, its philosophers produced treatises reflecting a wealth of new insights and discoveries, and of concepts capable of acquiring new and deeper meanings as the relation between them was determined and re-determined.

In its turn, the Peripatetic philosophy has stimulated great thinkers throughout the ages—Aquinas, Kant, Hegel. It has done so, not because it is a completed system; on the contrary, because it is unfinished. Precisely because its doctrines overlap and its arguments are intertwined it has challenged later philosophers, by re-interpreting its statements and concepts, to complete what had been begun and to erect that great edifice of which they admired the foundation. There is no single Aristotelian philosophy in the sense in which there is a Stoic philosophy, or a Kantian or Hegelian system.

At the same time, the founder of the school, Aristotle himself, stands out as an eminent Platonist, writer and administrator, who not only devised the most comprehensive study programme known in ancient times but was able to give the school he organized its permanent, philosophical direction. It should be understood that as we characterize Aristotle in this manner we are not expressing a new opinion but merely reviving a tradition older and much nearer to Aristotle himself than the one we are used to. Nevertheless whenever a view similar to this has been voiced in

---

[1] *Metaph.* M and N were later added to Andronicus's edition; see J. H. Randall Jr., *Aristotle*, New York 1960, p. 108.

recent times—by Cook Wilson, Shute and Zürcher—it has been rejected with disdain, or even fury.[1]

* * *

We now turn to the text. It is a mistake to assume that it has been often or materially interfered with by unphilosophical editors and that it is possible to emend it by alterations, deletions or transpositions (except in isolated instances where a copyist may be at fault). It is true that the writings were arranged by librarians and editors, who combined treatises or parts of them to make up volumes and in the process sometimes added an introductory or connecting phrase, but they did not interfere with the text. Equally, the early Peripatetic philosophers, who revised lectures as they re-delivered them, left the already recorded texts untouched. It follows that the contradictions found in the Aristotelian treatises should not be laboriously interpreted and re-interpreted until they appear to be resolved, but should be explained naturally, as expressing differing views.[2] In any case, the usual explanation of the discrepancies, namely that they are due to Aristotle's numerous 'false starts' and 'afterthoughts' resulting in as many corrections and insertions, has again and again been proved inadequate.

---

[1] A recent example is P. Moraux's criticism of Joseph Zürcher's *Aristoteles' Werk und Geist* with its angry invective, in *Aristoteles in der neueren Forschung*, (ed.) P. Moraux, Darmstadt 1968, pp. 69 ff. That Aristotle's authorship of the entire Corpus was not doubted in the Middle Ages, or even during the period from the Renaissance to the eighteenth century, may seem understandable. But it is surprising that it was hardly disputed at all by the great scholars of the nineteenth century. However, since this was so, for whatever reason, it is less astonishing that the question has scarcely been raised since then.

[2] The first to accept the contradictions instead of explaining them away was W. Jaeger (see above, Introduction, pp. 9 ff.). Jaeger understood them as reflections of Aristotle's developing thought in its various stages, and he visualized Aristotle's development as an almost unbroken, straightforward progress from an early idealistic, Platonic position, to his own mature, realistic, standpoint—from apprenticeship to mastery. But Jaeger's conception of Aristotle's development is not borne out by the testimony of the treatises. Some of the indubitably late books of the Corpus contain eidetic, earlier ones empiricist views (see p. 10 n). More important still, the contradictions in the Corpus are too frequent, too deep-rooted and too wide-ranging to be attributable to the philosophy of one man. In spite of the undisputed excellence of many of Jaeger's analyses, his basic conception cannot be maintained: it is romantic rather than critical.

Part Two

CHAPTER FIVE

The Structure of Metaphysics *Z*

(*a*) *The Parts of* Z

Z, a volume on the subject of substance, is arranged in seventeen chapters. We begin by outlining the main arguments of each of the parts of the book while, at the same time, drawing attention to points of structural importance. In section (*b*) we continue the analysis of the individual arguments and attempt to reach a conclusion about the structure of Z.

In Z I, after explaining that Being is principally substance, and substance essence, the philosopher emphatically states that the problem of substance is of the highest importance and that, as it has always been investigated by philosophers past and present, it is to be investigated again.

Z II begins with the statement that substance most manifestly belongs to 'bodies'. These are named: animals, plants and their parts; the elements, their parts and what is composed of them; the heavens and its parts, the stars, the moon, the sun. Then follow questions. Are those mentioned the only substances, or are there others besides them? Or are only some of those mentioned substances (the heavenly bodies), or these and some others besides them? Or are none of those named substances and only others (the incorporeal ones)? These questions are to be examined. But no such examination follows here. Instead there follows a broad or even comprehensive survey of the conceptions of substance formed by the early philosophers. The views of the Pythagoreans, of Plato, of Speusippus and of Xenocrates are sketched. Finally a promise is given that all the opinions described will be critically analysed until it is clear which of them are valid and which are not. The question of the possible existence of separate substance is also to be examined. However, once again, no such analysis or examination is offered here.

Z III opens with the statement that the word 'substance' is used in four principal senses, if not in more: 'The essence, the universal and the genus are regarded as the substance of the individual (*hekastou*), and fourthly the substratum.' We notice

89

that none of the basic physical meanings of substance given in Z II is now referred to.[1] We also find that the remaining part of Z III is almost entirely devoted to the discussion of one of the four interpretations of substance now mentioned, the substratum. Of the other interpretations essence is discussed in Z IV and V and the universal in Z XIII, while the genus is not discussed at all in the Corpus that we read. The substratum is first understood as the grammatical subject and this as signifying matter, form, and the compound of matter and form—the concrete whole. But then it is explained that if the substratum is understood as mere matter an impossible conclusion follows, namely that mere matter is substance, a view which is emphatically rejected. The chapter closes with a promise to discuss form, the most difficult aspect of the problem of substance. But no such discussion follows.

Z III and IV are linked by several transitional clauses (29ª34–29ᵇ12). Disregarding these at present, we find that Z IV begins by stating that essence is to be discussed, at first logically (29ᵇ13). Three doctrines are expounded in this chapter. (1) Essence is that which is said of a particular something *per se*.[2] (2) To state the essence of a something is to define it, i.e. definitions must always refer to essence. (3) It follows that only species can be defined. For a definition must have two terms both of which must refer to the primary nature of the something to be defined. This condition is fulfilled for species only. In all other cases, a description must include accidentals, or else one can refer to a particular only by naming it.

This is the clear teaching of Z IV to 30ª17. In the last section of the chapter, as well as in Z V, the doctrine of definition as expounded earlier is modified. Both definition and essence, the philosopher continues, may have different meanings. In one sense, essence signifies substance and the particular something (*tode ti*), in another the remainder of the categories, quantity, quality etc. Hence, he concedes that terms belonging to categories other than substance can also be defined, but only in a derivative sense (*hepomenôs*, 30ª22).

A similar conclusion is reached twice in Z V. It is true, the

---

[1] The four meanings of substance given in Z III are all of logical origin, pointing to the problem of definition. How is the substance of a given something to be determined? As its essence? As a universal concept covering it? As its genus? Or as its substratum?

[2] I read ἑκάστῳ with Bonitz (29ᵇ14).

philosopher says, that certain quantitative and qualitative terms can only be defined in conjunction with a substance (as odd with number, male with animal); and he concludes that such terms either have no essence or definition, or that they have essence and definition in a different sense from that referred to before.

Moreover there is a second difficulty (*aporia*), for it may be held that the definition of such terms (which are understandable only in conjunction with a substance) must either be tautological or involve an infinite regress. (Odd is a number which is odd; odd is an odd-number number; an odd-number number is a number that is an odd-number-number; etc.) The conclusion is once more that in such cases one can speak of definition only in a derivative sense. Here we discern the two stock objections of the Sceptics who denied the possibility of defining anything on the grounds of tautology and an infinite regress.

Let us note that, in this section, essence is said to belong to substance and to the particular something (*tode ti*), whereas, in Z IV, it was said to be implied in species only.

In Z VI the inquiry into the possibility of defining essence is not continued. Instead, the discussion turns to the problem of the reality of essence. Only one question is asked: whether essence and the individual (*hekaston*) are one and the same. The answer given in the first place is that individuals *per se* are the same as their essences but not individuals with their accidental predicates. Later in the chapter this answer is extended to cover unitary concepts, or 'individual ideas' such as the good and the beautiful (31^{b}11–14). These can have no accidental predicates and they are described as 'primaries' (*prôta*), a term which denotes individual substances;[1] and they, too, are said to be the same as their essences. The point now made is that what the Platonists call 'idea' is, in fact, essence. (On ideas as individuals see below on Z xv, pp. 106 ff. with note.)

Z VI is a polemical chapter in a twofold sense. (1) It refutes Sophistical objections raised against all theories of definition and consequently, of essence, on the grounds that essential and accidental predications cannot be separated from each other (31^{a}19–28). (2) It offers a critique of the theory of ideas which may well have been prompted by the question whether (Peripatetic) essences and (Platonic) ideas are at all distinguishable from one another (31^{a}28–^{b}18). In fact, Z VI is unusually close to Platonic thinking. The good and

---

[1] See *Cat.* v, 2^{a}11 ff. and *Metaph.* Z 1, 28^{a}30 ff.

the beautiful are given as instances, and it is left undecided whether the 'primaries' are forms (31^b14 ff.). All the same, the doctrine of immanent substance is strongly maintained throughout this chapter. It is clearly stated that essences, unlike ideas, are not separable, and that essences are either the same as individuals or inherent in them (31^b29; 32^a6).

It is conceivable that Z VI originally stood by itself. It is not linked to Z V by any connecting clause, but begins with a new question, the discussion of which, it says, will be useful for the study of substance and hence, essence. Its concluding statement refers to its own teaching only. Besides, the chapter contains repetitions: the twofold polemic against Sophists and Platonists, which occupies most of the earlier part of the chapter, is re-launched towards its end (31^b18–32^a11). On the other hand, Z IV–VI may be a unit, dealing with one subject, essence; progressively discussing this, first from a logical standpoint, and then in a basic (metaphysical) sense. There is also a reference to the epistemological aspect of essence: to know the individual is to know its essence (31^b20 ff.). Further we find several allusions in Z VI to points made in Z IV and V, and the same example as before, *white, white man* (compare 29^b21 ff. and 30^b12 ff. with 31^b27), is used here, to determine the scope of definition. Still, if Z IV–VI do in fact belong together, they do so in the sense that Z VI was added to Z IV–V by a philosopher re-delivering this course of lectures.

Whereas Z IV–VI deals with essence, Z VII–IX resumes the discussion of substance, but from a new angle: the genesis of individual substance is now to be investigated. Here essence is referred to only in passing, and we read that it is the same as form. The problem of definition is merely touched on, in connection with matter and form.

This section, which forms another unit,[1] contains a statement of the doctrine of immanent substance; perhaps its finest expression in the entire Corpus. Here, the emphasis is on form and it is the conception of form *in* matter which is expounded.

Z VII begins by distinguishing between natural, artificial and spontaneous creation but goes on to say that in *every* instance of becoming one can discern a 'from which' (matter), a 'by which' (form) and a 'what' (the compound product), in whichever category;

---

[1] Natorp thought that the section Z VII–IX was part of a separate treatise; compare Ross, *Comm.* II, p. 181.

still, the particular something is above all regarded as substance. On this basis the genesis of the individual is explained: in nature as in art the individual something is created through form entering matter. This is further clarified. For artistic creations, form is in the soul of the artist or craftsman; for natural genesis, it is in the parent or in the seed. Form is now described as the primary substance, essence; also, a little later, as substance without matter (*ousia aneu hulês*). Moreover, there is a reference to the logical aspect of the concept of immanent substance. Since matter is part of the product it must also be contained in the description (*logos*), one part of which must refer to matter, the other to form.

Z VIII begins by repeating the opening statement of Z VII (about matter, form and the compound product), then teaches that form is neither created nor exists separately but pre exists in nature, nor is matter created, only individual substances are. This doctrine is maintained against Plato's theory of ideas through the argument that from separately existing ideas or forms no individuals, only universals, could be generated. It is forms immanent in compound substance which, as they enter new matter, create new individuals by recreating themselves. The matter of different individuals— Callias, Socrates—differs, but their form, the human form, is one and the same as well as indivisible.

In this exposition of the doctrine of immanent substance, form is the predominant concept, to the exclusion of another well-known concept of the *Metaphysics*, cause. Indeed, it is expressly stated that it is useless to speak of the forms as causes—as if they were acting from outside—for there is no other cause of the creation of the individual except the union of form and matter. We also note that the substratum[1] is described as matter ($33^{a}10$; 28; 32);[2] further, that the notions of potentiality and actuality are not

---

[1] The question whether change should be described as an affection of the substratum which in itself is indeterminate and persists, or as a movement from opposite to opposite is debated in *Metaph.* Z VII ($33^{a}9$ ff.); there the second view is said to be the better of the two. But according to *Physics* A VII ($191^{a}15$), the second view is an early (and by implication, a mistaken) view, superseded by the first.

[2] D.M. MacKinnon in 'Aristotle's conception of substance', in R. Bambrough, *New Essays on Plato and Aristotle*, London 1965, points out that two views of the substratum are found in the Aristotelian writings: (*a*) the bare substratum, 'a clothes horse on which qualities are draped'; (*b*) 'the truly individual, the concrete thing, the table which is what *it* is'.

developed in Z VII and VIII,[1] although matter is vaguely described as potentially both something and nothing (32ᵃ20).

Z IX is like a collection of annotations to Z VII and VIII. It answers some questions arising from the doctrines already expounded, without varying those doctrines themselves. (1) How is it, the chapter starts, that some things are generated both artificially and spontaneously, e.g. health (by the physician and by nature) and others only artificially, e.g. a house? The reason is that in some cases, matter can initiate its own motion, e.g. heat in the body can induce health. This explanation implies the biological and medical theory of the natural movement of elements or their properties (*dynameis*)—the hot and the cold, the moist and the dry. (2) Both the products of art and of nature are created not only from existing products of the same kind but also from parts of those products. For example, the seed of an animal or a plant is productive of its own kind as it contains its form potentially within itself. (3) Form pre-exists not only in the case of substance but also in that of the other categories (this is a view implied but not explained in Z VII, 32ᵃ15). For example, only bronze is created, 'bronzen' is not. The form, i.e. the abstract quality 'bronzen', pre-exists; it creates bronze as it enters matter (metal) (see below, pp. 193 ff.).

The three points made all add subtler details to the theories of the preceding chapters. So Z IX is supplementary to Z VII and VIII. The examples it uses are the same as those used before: health and heat as in 32ᵇ7, the bronze circle as in 33ᵃ28 and 30, the mule as in 34ᵃ2. On the other hand, the notions of actuality and potentiality are now fully developed; indeed, they are introduced as familiar concepts. For what was merely called a something or a compound in Z VII and VIII, *ti, tode ti* (33ᵃ31); *hapan* (33ᵇ17 and 24, 34ᵃ6), *synhodos* or *synholos* (33ᵇ17), is described in Z IX as substance existing actually (*ousia entelecheiai ousa*). The forms in the other categories are described as only pre-existing potentially (*dynamei*, 34ᵇ18).

Looking at the entire section Z VII–IX, there can be little doubt that it is a self-sufficient unit, though not complete. It appears that both its opening paragraph and its final statement are lost. Most

---

[1] That the concepts of actuality and potentiality were formed at a late stage in the development of Aristotle's thinking is a view strongly held by P. Gohlke (but disputed by W. Theiler). See P. Gohlke, *Die Entstehung der aristotelischen Prinzipienlehre*, Tübingen 1954.

other sections of Z or even the *Metaphysics*, begin with a 'let us discuss' (*eipômen*), 'let us investigate' (*skepteon*), 'there is a difficulty' (*aporia estin, aporeitai*), or 'it is manifest' (*phaneron, dêlon*), followed by a clear indication of the argument to be developed, whereas Z vii–ix begins abruptly with the first premiss of the argument itself. Correspondingly, the section does not close with a summary restatement of its contents, at the end of Z viii or ix, as most sections do. Nor is it linked by a connecting clause either to the preceding Z vi or the following Z x. So it appears to stand by itself. Its approach is consistent: it discusses the problem of substance from a scientific, more precisely, biological starting-point and its concern is with becoming rather than with Being.

Z x and xi resume the discussion of the problems of definition begun in Z iv but interrupted by Z vii–ix. However whereas matter was not referred to in the earlier investigation it is now a prominent issue. In other words, whereas the argument in Z iv belongs to 'formal logic' and is conducted in terms of the categories, subject and predicate, substance and attributes, essence and accidents, the argument in Z x–xi belongs rather to 'philosophical logic'. It concerns the relation of thought to reality, of the definition to the thing to be defined. The philosopher looks to science; he wants to defend the validity of logical patterns in view of scientific theories— presumably widely held—in the fields of biology, psychology and epistemology. At the same time, he takes notice of Sceptical and idealistic objections and attempts to steer a middle course.

Z x deals with two problems: (1) How are the parts of a definition related to the parts of the thing to be defined? (2) Is the whole prior to the parts, or vice versa? (1) While the concepts of the whole and the part are old and already inherent in pre-Socratic philosophy, it was the Stoics who methodically set out the parts of the proposition.[1] The Sceptics, on the other hand, disputed both the possibility of defining anything and of distinguishing at all between a whole and its parts.[2] (2) As the parts were often identified with matter and the whole with form, the question of the priority of the whole or the parts implies an antithesis between an eidetic and a materialistic approach.

Z x is divided into four sections. The first contains a discussion of the first problem (definition and its parts), interrupted by an

---

[1] See Arnim, *SVF* ii, 31, 27; 44, 44; iii, 213, 25; 247, 24.
[2] See Sext. Emp. *Outlines* iii, 98 ff.

allusion to the second (the priority of the whole or the parts) (to
35^{b}2). The second section, beginning with the phrase 'we have now
stated the truth; nevertheless, let us resume the discussion and
express ourselves more clearly', deals with the second problem (to
35^{b}33). The third (to 36^{a}12) returns to the investigation of the
first question, adding further points (see below). The fourth seems
to concede that the investigation of the second problem has not been
conclusive and that no general answer to it can be found.

We now sketch the main arguments of z x.

Since a definition is a proposition and a proposition has parts, and
since a definition corresponds to the thing to be defined, and its
parts to the parts of the thing, the question arises whether the
definition of a whole should contain the parts of that whole. The
difficulty is that, *realiter*, in some cases it does, in others it does not.
For whereas the definition of the circle does not include the segments
of the circle, the definition of the syllable contains the letters of the
syllable. We may add here that the definition of man, whose essence
is life (*psychê*), includes such parts of man as are imbued with life,
especially the organs of perception (35^{b}17).

The philosopher solves the problem he has stated by explaining
that the material parts of a thing (the segments of the circle) are
not included in the definition while the formal parts (letters of the
syllable) are. He then interrupts his argument by referring to the
problem of the priority of the whole or the parts but says that this
should not (now?) be discussed. Resuming the former inquiry, he
offers a second solution to the problem of the parts. On the basis of
the threefold distinction of substance as matter, form, and the
compound of matter and form, he explains that even material parts
may be included in a proposition referring to substance *qua* the
compound (a bronzen circle) but not substance *qua* form (the
circle, mathematically) (to 35^{b}2).[1]

Then the problem of the priority of the whole or the parts is

[1] There follows another reference to the difference between 'snub', which is
partly material, and 'hollow', which is purely formal (35^{a}5); compare 30^{b}28 and
37^{a}32. 'Snub' includes flesh as its part, but 'hollow' does not. S. Mansion
in 'Tὸ σιμόν et la définition physique' (in *Naturphilosophie bei Aristoteles
und Theophrast*, Verhandlungen des 4, Symposium Aristotelicum veranstaltet
in Göteborg, August 1966, (ed.) I. Düring, Heidelberg 1969), after discussing
various passages in which the two terms occur attempts to prove, from the
viewpoint of modern logic, that the distinction between them is inadequate
for the purpose for which it was apparently designed.

discussed at some length and it is stated, in line with the solution to the problem of definition, that formal parts are prior, material parts posterior to their wholes.[1]

After this the discussion of the definition is continued (35ᵇ33) from where it was left off (35ᵇ2). It is stated that the parts of the definition or proposition (*logos*) correspond to those of the form only—the universal—not to those of the individual compound. Emphatically it is added that it is impossible to define the individual and that knowledge of it is gained by means of the understanding and perception. In speaking of the understanding the philosopher refers to intelligible mathematical matter, the lines forming a triangle (to 36ᵃ12).

In the final paragraph of Z x the lecturer returns to the question of the priority of the whole or the parts, not so much to modify what was stated before but to add that an absolute answer is impossible:

How the whole and the part, the prior and the posterior are related to one another has been stated. Still, when we are asked whether the whole of the right angle, or the circle, or the animal is prior to its parts there is no absolute answer. For even if it is held that, in each case, a thing and its essence are the same, that is, that an animal and its soul, or a circle, or a right angle, and their essences are the same, still, in one sense, the whole must be said to be posterior to its parts and, in another sense, the parts posterior to the whole. For (1) an individual whole is posterior to the parts of a proposition referring to it and also to its own parts (and this is true even of individual, material right angles, e.g. those made of bronze). Indeed, even the immaterial right angle is posterior to the parts of a proposition referring to it but (2) it is prior to the parts of individual right angles. In short, there is no absolute answer to the question: what is prior, the whole or the parts?

Although one may suspect that this entire argument was prompted by Sceptical objections the philosopher himself does not adopt a radical Sceptical view. He does not conclude that there are neither wholes or parts nor a prior or a posterior. His approach is impartially to state the reasons for concluding that in one way the

---

[1] On 'ultimate matter' (1035ᵇ32), see below, pp. 100, 134.

7

whole and in another the parts are prior.[1] One can hardly deny that this last paragraph exhibits a different spirit from that of the earlier sections of Z x. The lecturer now steers a middle course; he attempts to reconcile the opposing views of eidetic and material-istic thinkers. Besides, there is a slight change of terminology: whereas the word *meros* was used for part before, now *morion* is used, a term indicative of the growing influence of scientific thinking.

Z XI appears to be in the nature of an appendix to Z x. Its main objective is to defend the theory of formal and material parts against those who would discount matter altogether. But although matter is the point at issue, the stated subject of the chapter is still definition. There are references to the problems of definition both at the beginning and the end of Z XI. Moreover, this chapter is of interest both for its forward references to discussions still to come and for the extended summary at its close.

There are those, the lecturer says, who hold that all is form, not only the lines of a triangle or the circumference of a circle but also the flesh and bones of a man. The true nature of what is thought to be matter they believe is numbers; to them the dyad *is* the line. Rejecting this (Pythagorean) view the philosopher says that if there is one form for things, however different, all will be one. And he concludes that it is a mistake to ignore matter altogether. There is matter in all individual things. In parenthesis he rejects the analogy of man with a 'bronzen' circle. For while the essence of a circle is not in its material part (bronze), the essence of man, life, is also in the parts of man, in particular, in his organs of perception.

However, a little later the philosopher concedes that an inquiry into the deeper nature of matter may reveal a principle (presumably the Platonic principle of *mallon/hêtton*). What follows clearly marks Z XI as the final lecture of a course. The philosopher makes the interesting remark that a scientist studying perceptible sub-

---

[1] Cicero observes that 'Aristotle . . . set on foot the practice of arguing pro and contra upon every topic, not like Arcesilaus, always controverting every proposition, but setting out all the possible arguments on either side in every subject' (*De Fin.* v, 10, translated by H. Rackham, Loeb edition). But it is interesting to note that Diogenes Laertius ascribes this very practice of arguing pro and contra not to Aristotle but to Arcesilaus: 'Arcesilaus was the first to suspend his judgment owing to the contradictions of opposing arguments. He was also the first to argue on both sides of a question' (Diog. L. IV, 28, translated by R. D. Hicks, Loeb edition).

stances (the business of 'second philosophy', *deutera philosophia*) should not content himself with knowledge gained through experience but should also seek knowledge through reasoning (*kata ton logon*). The question to be asked, he says, that of the nature of matter, will be discussed later. Also, *the* problem of definition, namely how it is that the two terms of a definition mean one thing, is to be discussed later. So, by pointing to the related problems of the nature of matter and the possibility of definition, the lecturer outlines the programme of a new course of lectures, presumably to be held in the following academic term or year; while, at the same time, he clearly rounds off the teaching of a term just ended by a summary of the lectures on essence and definition, already delivered.

The reference to lectures on ideas and numbers is usually taken to point to *Metaphysics* M and N, the reference to a further course on definition, to H VI. But the latter is doubtful, since definition is also discussed in the immediately following chapter, Z XII. Indeed, the problem of definition (how its two terms can signify one thing) has been discussed and, as it seemed, solved three times before: (1) by the doctrine of the definability of species (Z IV); (2) by the doctrine of matter and form (Z VIII); (3) by the doctrine of the whole and the parts (Z X). It is, therefore, surprising to find the lecturer posing the problem of definition at this juncture, presumably because he felt the earlier solutions to be open to criticism or to be in need of further elaboration (the solution in Z X), or even because they were not yet known (the solution in Z IV). The next answer, similar to that in Z IV and based on the concept of the last differentia, is given in Z XII. The 'final' answer, arising from the theory of potentiality and actuality, is contained in H VI.

To the summary in Z XI, which refers to Z IV, X, XI and VI, in this order, we shall return later. Be it noted that in the summary *morion* is used for part although *meros* occurs throughout in the bulk of Z XI.

Comparing Z X–XI with earlier chapters we notice, if not a contradiction, at least a change of emphasis. Whereas form is stated to be indivisible (*atomon*) in Z VIII, and the same view is probably implicit in the doctrine of essence expounded in Z IV, form is now said to have parts. It is true that what is one *realiter* can have parts *logice*, but the emphasis in Z X is on the division of real form: the letters of the syllable are said to be the parts of the *form* of the syllable. So, there is a new approach to the concept of form, which as the rest of the chapter confirms, is due to the influence of scientific thinking, especially perhaps to a new interest in psychological studies; for the essence or form of man, the soul, was seen to consist of parts, the faculties of thinking and perception. Generally, neither form nor matter are taken as ultimates but are subjected to further analysis. And, although the standpoint remains eidetic, there is a growing awareness of the importance of matter. The notion of 'ultimate matter' (*eschatê hylê*), which is taken up in H VI, is found here. It signifies the individual in whom matter and form are practically indistinguishable as form is finally particularized; it is the material equivalent to the formal concept of *infima species*, as represented *realiter* by one of its individuals. To the scientist all things, the wholes as well as the parts, are matter formed; neither form nor matter exist by themselves (except potentially; compare p. 141). Hence, we grasp individual objects by the understanding and by perception; it is impossible to define them.

Further, comparing the present section with earlier ones, we find that the logical and the scientific analyses of substance are now more closely interrelated than before. Of course, in its earliest phase philosophy was undivided; the emergence of strictly separated disciplines marks a late stage and may well be associated with the Peripatetic school. Logic developed as a special discipline. But then, as scientific thinking became prominent again, it proved difficult to maintain a strict separation of disciplines. Hence, we find that the Peripatetic scientists discuss logical problems arising from their own theories (*Metaph.* H), while, on the other hand, philosophical logic takes shape as the logicians attempt to prove the validity of logic in the light of scientific concepts (especially the concept of cause; see *An. Post.*).

It is also apparent that the lecturer, conscious of the weaknesses of the theories of definition expounded so far, is here attempting to meet his critics. The theories of definition were, of course, a favourite target of the Sceptics. 'The dogmatists,' Sextus Empiricus says (*Outlines* II, 205), 'take great pride in their methodical treatment of definitions.' But, he goes on to say, one of two conclusions will emerge: either it is impossible to define anything, or definitions are utterly useless either for apprehension or instruction. Of the whole the Sceptics said that it was one and the same with its parts; so either only the whole or neither the wholes nor the parts existed (*Outlines* III, 98 ff.). We shall find an even closer correspondence between Sextus Empiricus and Z XII. So, it is probably in the context of Sceptical criticism that the Peripatetic philosopher here states the problem of definition with great precision, and forecasts yet another attempt at finding a satisfactory solution (37ᵃ18).

Of the remaining chapters, Z XII–XV are interconnected but they do not form a unitary section. Z XIV reverts to a point made in Z XII (*dihaeresis* and differentiae), Z XV takes up a point raised in Z XIII (the individual cannot be defined). All these chapters are concerned with the logical problem of the definition of substance: Z XIII–XV deal with this question critically. On the other hand, Z XVI does not deal with logic but is linked to Z II and I (the questions of bodily substances and their parts, heavenly bodies, and whether there are separate, non-corporeal substances). Finally, Z XVII offers a new, physical approach to the problem of substance. We now consider these chapters one by one.

Z XII seems originally to have stood near the beginning of a fresh course on definition, perhaps the course foreshadowed in Z XI. Once again, the problem of definition is stated: how can the definition with its two terms refer to a thing that is one? If man is defined as a two-footed animal, how can man be one thing, since two-footed and animal are two different representations? The first answer to this question, the lecturer says, is to be given on the basis of definition by *dihaeresis*. There follows an analysis of this method, from which it becomes clear that the dihaeretic definition refers to the primary genus and the last differentia only, and that the last differentia contains within itself all the marks of the intermediate differentiae or species (37ᵇ32). Hence, the thing is one and the definition is one because substance resides in the last differentia.

This is a mature statement of the doctrine of immanent substance, as applied to the logical problem of definition. Each species, of which the individual is a representative, is matter formed. In Z VII–IX (which deal with becoming) it is taught that form comes into existence by imposing itself on matter; here, form is shown to be already implanted in the individual, as its ultimate species. The lecturer emphasizes that there is no prior or posterior with regard to Being (38ᵃ32 ff.), only with regard to becoming.

Once again, it is probable that the discussion in Z XII was prompted by Sceptical queries. We find a close correspondence between this chapter and Sceptical discussions of the *aporiae* of definition as stated by Sextus Empiricus (*Outlines* II, 223; 225). According to the latter the genus is either the same as all its different species or it is none of them; in either case, genus does not exist. To this, there is an echo in Z XII (38ᵃ6). But the Peripatetic philosopher overcomes the objection by concluding that species exists and that it contains the genus within itself (while genus does not contain the various species).

The teaching in Z XII resembles that in Z IV, with the later chapter providing an elaborate proof of the thesis stated in the earlier chapter, that only species is definable. Nevertheless, Z XII contains no reference to Z IV. On the contrary, it expressly refers to a preparatory, purely logical course, in which the problem of definition was not solved but merely posed (*An. Post.* 92ᵃ29).

Z XII closes with the statement that, with the foregoing, a first attempt at analysing definition by *dihaeresis* has been concluded. No further attempt at such analysis is contained in the Corpus. Nor is 'the other method of definition' alluded to here, that based on the constituents of substance (*ex enhyparchontôn*), discussed in this chapter (it is mentioned in *Metaph.* B III). One may conjecture that a section containing such a discussion was included in the full material of rolls available to the editor of the works, but was omitted here because it was felt that this method of defining had been adequately treated in earlier chapters, in which it had been shown that the two terms of the definition correspond (1) to matter and form (Z VII–IX), (2) to the parts and the whole (Z X and XI), and (3) to genus and differentia (Z XII).

As we shall see, the line of thought begun in Z XII is continued in Z XIV, though even there not directly or without a break.

Z XIII clearly starts a new course.[1] This chapter not only begins with the phrase 'let us cover the ground again' but also with a summary reference to an earlier discussion, now to be continued, of the logical side of the problem of substance. It is a summary

---

[1] This chapter has been closely analysed by M. J. Woods, who rightly points out that its main part ends at 39ᵃ14. See 'Problems in *Metaphysics* Z', in Moravcsik (ed.), *Aristotle*, London 1968. Woods finds that the universal is treated differently in different treatises and that even Z XIII by itself does not arrive at a clear-cut conclusion. But then he attempts to remove the inconsistencies he has discovered by drawing a distinction between the universal and that which is universally predicated, and by arguing that Aristotle only denies that anything universally predicated can be substance, without necessarily denying that the universal itself may be substance.

which vaguely but not exactly conforms with statements made in Z III and IV; it accurately repeats three of the meanings of substance given in Z III but leaves out the fourth (genus) and adds a new meaning (the compound). We shall return to this summary later, along with others, for it is a general feature of summaries in the Corpus, or at least the *Metaphysics*, that they loosely but not precisely refer to previous analyses, a fact from which we shall be able to draw some conclusions (see below, p. 117).

Z XIII is one of the sections devoted to a critique of the theory of ideas. Its chief purpose is to show that the universal cannot be substance. So, it is important to realize that, throughout this chapter, the universal is understood, not as immanent—the primary genus—but as a transcendent idea, separately existing. The chapter is divided into three parts: the main argument, a paragraph to show that substance is actually, though not potentially, indivisible, and a corollary from the preceding, dealing with the difficulties of definition.

The main argument is fourfold.

It is shown that the universal cannot be substance, because as it applies to many instances it would be the substance either of all of them or of none (1*a*). It is always predicate whereas substance never is (2). If it were substance in the sense that it is present in an *A* as its essence, as genus is in species, it would indeed be definable though its definition would not cover all its instances (1*b*). Logically, this makes no difference but *realiter* it does. For as substance the universal would be present in individuals, and so, once again, it would be many things: e.g. 'animal' would be the substance of a man or of a horse. If substances were composite their elements would be particulars, not (universal) qualities, and qualities do not exist separately (3). If the universal were implicit in the individual as its separately existing genus it would be the same as the individual yet different from it (4). The general conclusion is that the universal never signifies 'this' but only 'of such a kind', and hence cannot be substance. It is clear that the whole argument is firmly based on the doctrine of immanent substance, stated expressly in 38^{b}10.

Next comes a paragraph, attached to the preceding by the connecting phrase, 'further, this is also clear in the following way' (39^{a}3), stating the doctrine that substances cannot be composed of substances actually and that, if they are so composed potentially this does not affect the doctrine because what exists only potentially does not exist at all. (This view is paralleled in Z XVI.) The examples given clearly link this argument, too, to Sceptical thinking. Either the double, the lecturer says, is not one or, if it is one, it does not actually contain any singles. Sextus Empiricus reasons in a similar manner, using the decad as his example (*Outlines* II, 215 ff.; see also II, 225 ff.).[1]

Yet another remarkable fact emerges. It follows from this section that philosophers had used the concepts of actuality and potentiality in the defence of separately existing universals. But these are two truly Peripatetic concepts, not known as such to Plato and his school; so it would follow that the polemic in this paragraph is directed not against Platonists but Platonizing philosophers, not improbably Peripatetics. Therefore, this passage, and others where arguments based on actuality and potentiality are refuted in the Corpus, would be instances of intra-school polemic.

In the last paragraph (39ª15 ff.) a dilemma (*aporia*) is expressed. If, in accordance with the preceding, all substances are monads it would be impossible to define anything. (In *Metaph.* B IV a similar *aporia* is expressed, from an epistemological viewpoint, 'the greatest of all *aporiae*' (99ª24 ff.): how can we know the infinite number of individuals, although all our knowledge depends on universals which do not exist except in individuals?) However, the chapter does not end on a Sceptical note, but with a phrase, similar to the one at the close of Z X (see p. 98 and n.), stating the answer from two viewpoints. 'In one sense,' the lecturer says, 'it is impossible to define things, in another it is possible.' And he adds that this (ambivalent) statement will become clearer at a later time. No such further clarification follows; it was probably omitted by an editor. The allusion cannot be to H VI because there the potential —matter—plays an important part in the argument whereas it is discounted as non-existent in Z XIII. The reason why the promised further clarification was omitted may well be that it would have formed a repetitive section at this point.[2] For in what sense definition is possible had been amply explained before in Z (see above, p. 102). Finally, it is possible that the entire Z XIII was inserted here for the

---

[1] The impression of Sceptical influence is further strengthened by the mentioning of Democritus whom Sextus Empiricus expressly associates with Scepticism ; see *Outlines* I, 213.

[2] Alternatively, this may be a retrospective reference.

sake of its last, aporetic paragraph on definition, which is the main theme of the bulk of Z.

Like Z XIII, Z XIV is devoted to the critique of the theory of ideas. The chapter begins with the phrase, 'from these same considerations there follows . . .'. One might be tempted to connect Z XIV with the main argument of Z XIII (to 39ᵃ2): a point made there is reinforced here (regarding the impossibility of the universal existing separately in the individual); and what was stated generally in Z XIII is applied specifically in Z XIV (to definition by *dihaeresis*). Nevertheless, a clear change of terminology leads to the conclusion that Z XIV and Z XIII do not belong together: the term 'universal' is not used in Z XIV nor is 'idea' used in Z XIII. Nor is it surprising that in two chapters criticizing Plato, similar or even identical arguments occur, while the opening phrase quoted above is too vague for any conclusion to be based on it.

On the contrary, Z XIV appears to be linked to Z XII, as a critical corollary to the teaching offered there. In Z XII, definition by *dihaeresis* was explained; it is added now that definition by *dihaeresis* is not thinkable on the basis of Plato's theory of ideas. The lecture recorded in Z XIV is full of spirited polemic; it consists of a great many arguments, some of which are rhetorically phrased as questions, while all are designed to show what absurd consequences would follow from the theory of separately existing ideas.

The reasoning falls under three heads. It is shown (1) that the theory of ideas splits every substance (genus and species, animal and man, would both exist in man as two separate substances; parts, animal and two-footed, would both be substances, separately existing); (2) that every substance would be composed of substances (a substance, man, would consist of innumerable substances, its parts; the genus would consist of all its different species—animal would be both two-footed and many-footed); (3, concluding) that the theory of ideas would mean the coexistence in separation of genera, species and essences in individuals. With regard to perceptibles, the lecturer adds, even greater absurdities would follow, for instance that a man and his bones would each exist separately.

Once again, the critique of Platonism, so vigorously conducted in this chapter, is based on the doctrine of immanent substance. Only one substance resides in any one entity. We could not represent a species or an individual as a unity unless we considered the genus in the species and the species and genus in the individual, not as transcendent ideas but as their immanent aspects. From the theory of ideas it follows that *as many substances exist as there are representations*.

Z xv re-affirms the thesis of Z x (also referred to in Z xiii, 39ª15 ff.), that individuals are undefinable, but carries it one step further, proving that even ideas themselves are not definable because, conceived as separately existing, they, too, are individuals. With this, the critique takes a new, sharp turn for, of course, the Platonists regarded ideas as above all definable, and hence as the basis of knowledge.

Starting from the Peripatetic distinction between the essence (here called *logos*) and the compound, the following points are made: (1) that the compound is not definable because, containing matter, it is subject to destruction and generation; hence, no knowledge of perceptibles is possible, only opinion (*doxa*); (2) that ideas are not definable either, since, as separately existing, they too are individuals; also their component parts are individuals; (3) that ideas, if thought to be composed of ideas, cannot form unitary wholes, since each of the component ideas refers to a multiplicity of diverse objects; (4) that such eternal and unique entities as the sun and the moon, if definable at all, are definable not as individuals but, like any other perceptibles, as species, even if the species contains one member only. The main critical point made in Z xv is this: it is self-contradictory to assert that ideas refer to many objects yet exist separately by themselves.

Although Z xv does not arrive at a Sceptical conclusion (that it is impossible to define anything) it is, nevertheless, true to say that its author has carefully considered Sceptical arguments. An indication of this is the frequent use of the phrase 'maybe not' (*ouk endechetai*), which here occurs four times (it is also found in Z xiii, 38ᵇ17), and which is described by Sextus Empiricus as 'a Sceptical expression' (*Outlines* 1, 187–208; 194). One also finds several points of affinity to Stoic thought and terminology in this chapter: a marked interest in epistemology in the emphasis given to the distinction between knowledge and opinion, and the unexpected use of the word *logos* instead of the customary term 'essence'. Moreover, while the interpretation of ideas as individuals is, no doubt, wrongly ascribed to Plato or his followers,[1] there is a

---

[1] P. Wilpert rightly points out that the view that ideas are individuals is not Plato's own but merely ascribed to Plato. See 'Zur Interpretation von Metaphysik Z 15', reprinted in F.-P. Hager, *Metaphysik und Theologie des Aristoteles*, p. 383.

parallel to this conception in Stoic literature where we learn that Chrysippus deliberated whether the idea should be described as an individual (*tode ti*).[1]

Z XVI does not belong to the same group of lectures as the preceding chapters or indeed the bulk of Z. Essence and definition are no longer discussed; the chapter reverts to the themes and problems of Z II and I and also, to some extent, of *Metaph*. E: corporeal substances and their parts, the elements; eternal substances; the possible existence of separate ideas; Being; causes and principles. Nevertheless, it differs in spirit from the earlier sections: questions merely raised there are answered here, statements made before are now corrected. Whereas in Z II bodies, the elements and their parts are said to be 'the generally accepted substances', they are rejected in Z XVI as merely ostensible substances. Being is described in Z I as almost synonymous with substance, but according to Z XVI neither Being, nor 'principle', nor element, nor 'cause' can be the substance of things.

Moreover, Z XVI is a composite chapter—as nearly all commentators agree—consisting of three sections (40^b5-16; 40^b16-24; 40^b24-41^a5) loosely joined together. Still, a polemical spirit is common to them all. It is directed (1) against the natural philosophers, (2) against Speusippus, Xenocrates and the Pythagoreans, and (3) against other Platonizing philosophers. First, it is stated that parts of organisms and the elements cannot be substances since, if they exist, they only exist potentially, as matter, and hence are mere aggregates, not unitary entities. Secondly, that the One and Being cannot be substances because they are predicated universally whereas substance only belongs to itself and to that in which it resides. Thirdly, the universal cannot be substance because it belongs to many things at the same time whereas a unitary entity can only be in one place at one time. Indeed, no universal exists in separation from its particulars. Hence, the philosopher continues, the Platonists rightly ascribe separate forms to eternal entities (in which form and individuality, the universal and the particular coincide), but they are wrong in assuming the parallel existence of separate (transcendent) forms and perishable entities. The eidetics, however, falsely argue that if there are perceptibles which are imperishable there may well be an imperishable substance belonging to man as well—'man himself'. But no such conclusion

[1] See Arnim, *SVF* II, 91, 25.

can be drawn from the existence of eternal substances. For the stars are there whether we perceive them or not; they are imperishable by necessity (while man is not).[1]

It appears, then, that Z xvi stood at the end of a course of lectures, for it contains what purports to be definitive statements on problems raised in earlier lectures, e.g. Z ii and Z i. As it reads now, it was probably arranged by an editor, who selected the three passages combined in it from a large body of material (for a great deal of what must have stood between the beginning and the end of the course by way of explanation or demonstration is here missing). Besides, these passages are (if at all) connected with each other by verbal association only: the elements and the One—the One and Being; substance and the One—the One and the universal; the universal and substance—substance and substances.

A special question is posed by the closing sentence of this chapter, which contains a summary, not of Z xvi, but of parts of Z xiii (especially 39^{a}3 ff.) and Z xiv and xv (especially 40^{a}23). This sentence obviously serves the purpose of binding Z xvi to Z xiii–xv. We will return to the question of this summary later (see below, p. 117).

The last chapter of Z, Z xvii, starts a new course on substance, as is expressly stated. Its approach, too, is unique for Z since it makes principle and cause the starting-points of the argument and arrives at the conclusion that nature is the ultimate substance. So Z xvii is concerned with basic reality, the roots of existence, not primarily with the critique of earlier views or with logic. It is therefore closest to Z vii–ix although its subject is Being rather than becoming and although it also diverges from Z vii–ix in a point of doctrine. It is related, too, to *An. Post.*, to *Metaph.* Δ and to *Physics* B i–ii. Its argument is unitary: the question asked at the beginning is answered in the conclusion. Still, it is convenient to outline it under three heads.

(1) Logically we describe a thing such as it is in most cases by using the formula '*A* belongs to *B*'. So when we inquire why a thing is such as it is we ask: 'Why does *A* belong to *B*?' Rejecting

---

[1] In Z xv the eternal substances are mentioned as constituting a problem in the theory of definition (40^{a}28), and in this context, too, the argument is aimed at the Platonists. It appears therefore that the question of the eternal substances was an unsettled issue leading to recurring controversy between Peripatetics and Platonizing thinkers.

such summary and facile answers as 'because a thing is itself' or 'is inseparable from itself', the lecturer states that the existence of a particular thing is in each case due to a cause, a final cause (bricks and stones are made into a house), or an efficient cause (the clouds produce the thunder). Reverting once more to logic, he adds in passing that the cause of a thing is, in logical terms, its essence.

(2) Searching deeper into the cause of Being, the lecturer continues as follows. The question *why* is most difficult to answer when we describe a something merely by one term, e.g. man, asking 'What is man?'. This is an impossible question unless we articulate it, realizing that there is matter in everything that exists and that matter is turned into a definite thing, a substance, by a cause; further that this cause is form. Hence, he goes on to say, the usual kind of analysis, by the formula '*A* belongs to *B*', is manifestly not applicable to absolute entities (*hapla*), like 'man'. A different kind is required, one that searches for matter and cause.[1]

(3) Finally, repudiating the views of those who ascribe to matter, especially the four elements, the power of originating movement and thus creating entities, the philosopher states his two conclusions. No unitary entity is equal merely to the sum total of its components; rather, it is something other over and above its parts and this 'other' —its substance—is the cause of its being. Now since all substances are what they are by nature (artefacts are ignored at this point), not the elements but nature itself is the principle and ultimate substance; nature which contains within itself both matter and all causes (forms).

It appears that Z XVII, which offers its own version of the doctrine of immanent substance, was originally a course of its own consisting perhaps of two or three lectures. The chapter is highly condensed, especially towards the end and it is not improbable that it was designed as an additional or supplementary course for students who were well acquainted with the logical aspects of the theory of substance but who had to acquire some understanding of its physical side. The opening sentence of the chapter confirms this impression. Substance had been dealt with;

---

[1] The term *ta hapla*—'absolute entities'—has been taken to mean 'pure forms' (41^b9; see Ross, *Comm.* p. 225). But as the same term in its adverbial form *haplôs* occurs once before in this paragraph (41^b2), referring to entities described by one term only ('man'), it is apparent that *ta hapla*, too, means such entities. In *Phys.* B I, 192^b10, *ta hapla* signifies the elements (*stoicheia*).

now 'a new start, as it were'[1] was to be made in the discussion of substance, in the course of which, the lecturer adds, perhaps some light will be thrown on separate substance, too. To logical problems, essence and definition, he refers only as an aside, as though his audience was fully familiar with them. He stresses the concept of cause; and it is on this point that Z XVII diverges most noticeably from Z VIII and also from H VI. For form as cause is stated to be a useless concept for (an understanding of) generation and existence in Z VIII ($33^{b}27$ ff.), and in H VI we read that it is in vain to search for any cause of generation because becoming is adequately explained as the transformation of the potential into the actual ($45^{a}30$); but in Z XVII both essence and form are said to be aspects of cause. So views diverged and indeed—as other passages confirm[2]—the significance or otherwise of cause was a major debating-point within the Peripatetic school.

The dominant concept of Z XVII is nature, as we have seen. This concept is, of course, old. Anaximenes used it (Diels, I, 91, 14). Democritus made nature the cause of all generation (Diels, II, 101, 21). According to Empedocles, on the other hand, nature is but a name given by man to the processes of mixing and separating (*Metaph.* Δ, $1015^{a}2$). Then the Stoics revived the concept, as is well known. Still, the doctrine of nature found in Z XVII is manifestly Peripatetic, for nature as the principle of Being is here conceived as that which contains within itself both matter and all the causes, which are the forms.[3] Two parallel discussions of nature occur in *Metaph.* Δ IV and *Physics* B I and II, both more copious than that

---

[1] Professor Allan has rightly pointed out (in a private communication) that an expression closely similar to the one used here (viz. 'let us make a fresh start—as it were'), occurs in *Eth. Nic.* $1145^{a}15$. Still, whereas in *Eth. Nic.* the expression introduces a discussion of subjects not dealt with before though 'integral to the *Ethics*', in Z XVII it leads on to yet another analysis of problems already examined.

[2] 'Cause' is the highest principle, e.g. in *Phys.* $184^{a}10$ and in *An. Post.* $71^{b}9$; $94^{a}20$. In the theory of the 'four causes' form is merely one of the aspects of 'cause' (*Phys.* B III, $194^{b}16$ ff.). On the other hand, 'form' is essence and primary substance according to *Metaph.* Z, $32^{b}1$; it is (at least in artificial production) the efficient cause and originator of movement ($32^{b}23$). 'Essence' is the cause of generation and existence, logically speaking (*Metaph.* Z XVII, $41^{a}28$).

[3] It should be noted, however, that the concepts of 'nature' and 'cause' are often found closely linked in Stoic writings, too. See Arnim, *SVF* II, 112, 15; 118, 11; 264, 7 and 22. Of the pre-Socratics, Democritus taught that nothing happens without a cause; Diels, II, 101, 9 ff.

in Z. In *Metaph.* Δ, which can be described as a general inventory of Peripatetic concepts and doctrines, nature in the sense of 'matter and form' is mentioned as only one interpretation of the concept beside others.[1] Clearly *Metaph.* Δ draws not merely from Z XVII as its source but from several other treatises as well. And it is interesting to see that even the point made in Z XVII is elaborated more fully in *Metaph.* Δ than in Z (indeed the explanation given in Z would be almost incomprehensible if we did not have Δ), so it appears that both these books draw from the same passages but Z condenses them more severely than does Δ.

Moreover, we notice an overtone of polemic in the last part of Z XVII. The philosopher stresses repeatedly that it is not the elements[2] but nature itself which is the cause of the existence of all things. Now the elements are the essential concepts of 'the theory of the natural place'—another Peripatetic theory, expressed chiefly in *De Caelo*, according to which all changes in nature are due to the natural propensities of air, fire, water, earth, of which the first two move upwards, the last two downwards. If, as seems likely, this theory is repudiated here (as also in parts of the *Physics*), Z XVII provides us with another instance of intra-school polemic.[3]

(b) The Composition of Z

I.

The first conclusion from an analysis of Z is that this book contains three different approaches to the problem of substance. (1) Earlier and contemporary conceptions of substance are outlined and a critical analysis of all of them is promised in Z II (compare also

---

[1] In Γ III nature is said to be only a genus of Being, and the study of nature, instead of the study of Being, is said to belong to an early, pre-Socratic phase of philosophizing.

[2] The term *stoicheion* occurs here in two meanings, a narrower—the elements of nature—and a wider—components of existing things. But the two meanings are united in the argument of this chapter in which *all* components, not only the elements of nature, are understood as mere matter.

[3] Another discrepancy or unresolved question: according to Z X 'form' has 'parts', and the example of the syllable is used to make this clear; the letters as the components of the syllable are said to be parts of its form (34^b26 and 35^a11). In Z XVII, on the other hand, form is not composed of parts, and the letters of the syllable are described as matter (41^b13 and 32).

Z XVI). (2) The logical side of the problem of substance is investigated, in Z III–VI and Z X–XV. (3) The relation of substance to becoming and Being is discussed in Z VII–IX and Z XVII. In other words, since the Corpus consists of lecture records, three courses on substance are combined in Z: *a doxographic-critical, a logical,* and an ontological or, rather, *basic-physical* course. It has often been observed that Z occupies a unique place within the Corpus in that it embraces nearly all the main tenets of Peripatetic metaphysics and indeed, as is evident from the *Metaphysics* as a whole,[1] the three courses preserved in it, which are complementary to each other, formed what may be described as the principal syllabus in metaphysics or 'first philosophy' in use at the Peripatos.

But although Z contains a comprehensive course on substance it cannot be maintained that what is preserved in Z is the one original statement of Peripatetic teaching on substance, perhaps going back to Aristotle himself. On the contrary, there is evidence to show that Z represents only one version of this course and that other versions must have existed beside it. A lucky chance has preserved for us the summary of such a course, in *Metaph.* H I. It is true that it is generally believed that this summary refers to Z as we read it, or nearly as we read it, but a close scrutiny of H I shows that this is by no means so.

H I: $1042^a 3$–25. Promising his hearers that he will offer them a definitive solution to the problem of substance the philosopher summarizes the teaching given before:

(1) He mentions an opening lecture on principles, causes and elements (missing in Z; see below, pp. 113 and 114 ff.).[2]

(2) He recalls that reference was made to the generally accepted substances, the bodily ones, enumerating most of them; also, that incorporeal entities were referred to and even held to be substances by some (this part of the summary closely corresponds to Z II; see also Z III, $29^a 34$).

(3) He recalls that the notions of substance derived from logical procedure were discussed. (He mentions all the four meanings of

---

[1] Doxographic-critical courses are preserved in *Metaph.* A, M, N; a logical course in *Metaph.* Γ; a basic-physical course in the bulk of H and the first half of Λ, as well as in *Phys.*, especially B; another combined course possibly in *Metaph.* K.

[2] An opening lecture to fit this description is found hardly anywhere in the *Metaphysics*, not even in E I. But *Metaph.* A III and IV, E I and Z XVII refer to principles, causes etc.

substance given in Z III but places them in a different order from Z III. Further, he adds idea as a fifth substance derived from logic.) Reference is also made to:

(4) An analysis of essence and definition (as in Z IV, V or VI).

(5) An analysis of the parts of speech and, correspondingly, of substance and the definition (as in Z X and XI).

(6) A refutation of the universal as substance (as in Z XIII) and of genus as substance (missing in Z).

(7) A future discussion of ideas and numbers (perhaps as in Z XI).

At this point the summary breaks off and the philosopher begins his own exposition of substance as related to Being and becoming, making the perceptible substances his starting-point.

No doubt, the course as summarized in H I is similar to the course recorded in Z. Above all, the underlying pattern is almost the same. In both H and Z, the course includes sets of doxographic-critical, logical and basic-physical lectures (the last if we take the whole of H into account). But there are also significant differences, omissions and additions, as well as a changed order within the pattern.[1]

(1) Omitted in Z but referred to in H:

    (*a*) An opening chapter on principles etc. Instead Z has an introductory chapter on the near-identity of Being and substance.

    (*b*) A discussion of genus as a possible substance.

(2) Contained in Z but not mentioned in H:

    (*a*) Z I (see above).

    (*b*) The refutation of the substrate as substance in Z III.

    (*c*) Z VII–IX, on substance as matter and form.

    (*d*) Z XII, on *dihaeresis*.

    (*e*) Z XIV, on ideas.

    (*f*) Z XV, on the definition of individuals.

    (*g*) Z XVI, on perceptible substances, the One and Being, forms and the universal.

    (*h*) Z XVII, on substance as cause and nature.

Most notably, the summary of H omits the entire basic-physical course contained in Z, which H replaces by its own course, and it

---

[1] H II, 42^{b}10 also shows that H does not refer to Z as we read it, but to a course of lectures based on the general acceptance of the substratum, or matter, as substance; whereas in Z III the substratum is not allowed to be substance.

8

also seems to omit almost the whole of the second half of Z, with the possible exception of Z XIII. The introductory chapter, too, is different in H and Z. So, manifestly, the course referred to in H was considerably shorter than the one preserved in Z. It was also more straightforward, consistent, and it is a fair assumption that Z contains a much-revised version of the course and that H is earlier than Z as we read it. This we shall now attempt to prove in some detail.

2.

There are clear indications in Z of the work of an editor endeavouring to compile a representative volume on substance by joining together suitable sets of lectures on the basis of a well-established pattern.

(1) For such a volume an opening chapter had to be found to suit, not a doxographic-critical course but a full course on substance. Now the introductory lecture sketched in H I was manifestly designed for a doxographic-critical course. It dealt with the elements, posing the question whether these contained the principles of motion within themselves (compare *Phys.* B, 192^{b}10; 21; also *Metaph.* A and Δ, 14^{b}33; 15^{a}14). Z I, on the other hand, begins with the concept of Being, which, in the sense of truth, is, of course, the ultimate object of all inquiry; and it concludes by stating that the problem of Being is, in fact, the problem of substance. To this extent, Z I is well suited to introduce the whole of book Z; nevertheless, there are signs to show that the chapter was not composed for this purpose but merely selected for it from available material. For an analysis of Z I reveals that the lecturer as he speaks of Being has the copula 'to be' in mind and that he conducts his argument on logical-grammatical lines, in a manner comparable to that of *Categories* IV ff. Moreover, a large part of Z I is occupied by the refutation of two objections, one referring to the use of verbal forms as predicates, the other to various meanings of the word 'primary' in relation to substance. It is clear, then, that only the main point made in Z I qualifies this chapter as an introduction to a full course on substance, but not its details. That it was not written for book Z is further confirmed by the fact that it is not linked with Z II, which starts afresh.

(2) Similarly, the last chapter of Z, Z XVII, suitably concludes a course on substance in the sense that it offers a final explanation of what substance is (nature containing matter and causes within

itself). But again it is clear that the chapter was not composed for Z but added to it, probably editorially, from ready material. It is a treatise by itself, unconnected with the chapters preceding it; also the notion of nature, which it introduces, is new to Z.

(3) The order in which the three courses follow one another has been changed from an earlier order. As we read Z, the lectures on the generation of substance not only split the logical course (IV–VI; X–XII) but are themselves divided (VII–IX; XVII). It appears that there were two possible arrangements: doxographic-physical-logical, and doxographic-logical-physical, and it can be shown, by an analysis of Z III/IV (28ᵇ33–29ᵃ14), that, in the course of a revision of Z, the first arrangement has been altered into the second.

However, before Z III/IV can be analysed, a textual problem has to be examined. Near the beginning of Z IV stands a 'famous digression' on the gradual acquisition of knowledge (29ᵇ3 ff.). 'One must advance,' the philosopher says, 'from the less knowable to the better knowable. Everyone must try to progress from what he knows himself though imperfectly ⟨the compounds of matter and form⟩ to that which is at all knowable ⟨form itself; empirical particulars⟩.'[1] In its original position this digression is preceded by the statement that essence has to be discussed and it is followed by a discussion of essence in logical terms. Now on the grounds that where is stands the digression interrupts the context, and that the most difficult knowledge to attain is logical knowledge, Bonitz has transposed the digression so that it precedes the statement about the necessity of discussing essence, and follows the reference to perceptible substances. All the editors of the *Metaphysics* since have followed him. Moreover, in nearly all modern editions the last sentence of Z III is printed as if it were the first of Z IV.[2]

However, Bonitz was wrong in assuming that, at this point, logical studies are regarded as the most difficult. On the contrary it

---

[1] There are parallels to this discussion in *Metaph.* A 11, 982ᵃ25 ff.; α 1, 993ᵃ30 ff.; Δ 1, 1013ᵃ2; Z XVI, 1040ᵇ20; *Phys.* A 1, 184ᵃ16 ff.; *Eth. Nic.* 1, 4, 1095ᵇ2. In spite of some variations the general meaning of these statements on how to acquire knowledge is: we naturally start in each instance with an immediate but vague conception of something, i.e. one that is easily grasped but contains little comprehension of the object in question, and from this, our own first but imperfect insight, we proceed to a clearer more detailed knowledge of the object itself. See above on *Metaph.* α, p. 66 and n.

[2] In W. D. Ross's edition, on the other hand, the digression is printed as part of Z III, which then extends from 28ᵇ32 to 29ᵇ12, with the exception of 29ᵇ1–2.

is stated expressly in 29ª34 that the hardest inquiry is that into the forms of things.[1] Nor is Bonitz's transposition satisfactory in a textual sense. If it is adopted the same expression 'about it',[2] namely essence, is used twice in successive clauses (29ᵇ2 and 14). Finally the transposition does not cure the lack of clear direction which has given offence in Z III/IV, but merely obscures it. One should therefore leave the digression where the codices have it and read the text as it stands. We then find that three different investigations are announced in succession (of which one—on essence—is actually carried out). 'As the compound of matter and form as well as matter are manifest we must investigate *form* which is obscure' (29ª30–3). 'Since the perceptibles are generally agreed to be substances we must first inquire into *the perceptibles*' (29ª33–4). 'Since, as we have said before, one meaning of substance is essence let us consider *essence*' (29ᵇ1–2).

What is more natural than to conclude that Z III/IV contains three different starts of discussion (of which one is followed up), and that this section of the book was severely cut and contracted? Manifestly, an inquiry into form, which is hidden in the perceptibles, followed the statement of 29ª30–3 at one time, probably one similar to the discussions of Z VII–IX, which start from the perceptibles. This discussion was taken out and replaced by the inquiry into essence which we actually read in Z IV–VI. It follows that Z III was originally meant for a course of the pattern doxographic-physical-logical but was revised to suit the pattern doxographic-logical-physical. A further conclusion is that at one stage, the basic-physical investigations grew out of a discussion of the perceptibles, which is inherent in the doxographic course; this is proved by H I, 42ª25 ff. At that stage, logical inquiries, as in Z X–XI, and as clearly shown in 37ª13–18, came last in a graded syllabus. But then the basic-physical course assumed greater

---

[1] It is, in fact, debatable whether the digression is intended to introduce an easier or a more difficult subject, and the former is more likely; see *Metaph.* A, α and Z XVI. For the digression essentially says that knowledge is graded and this observation could stand at any juncture of a course except its very end. Assuming that it was normally used to introduce an early part of a course, it may well have been added here when, during the revision of Z, the logical course was put in the place of the physical course, to justify the slow progress to be expected. Before the final teaching was offered logical problems had to be mastered.

[2] περὶ αὐτοῦ.

depth and significance, so it emancipated itself from the doxo-graphic course and became the crowning part of the entire meta-physical programme. A trace of the old connection between the doxographic and physical inquiries is found in the sentence, 'since the perceptibles are generally agreed to be substances we must first inquire into these' (29ᵃ33–4), which belongs to Z III and not to Z IV. This sentence might have followed Z II, but as we read Z now, Z III begins abruptly and its only link with Z II is a weak connecting phrase.

There is much evidence to show that the material of which Z consists was selected from different sources, that is, from several versions of the course originating at different times.

(4) In the composition of Z one detects a preference for lectures initiating and those concluding a course. The middle sections are less favoured. Apart from Z I, II and III, the beginning of new courses is expressly announced in Z XIII and XVII; Z XII seems to have stood near the beginning of a course. Beyond this several chapters start abruptly: Z II, VII, X and XVI. On the other hand, where two chapters appear to be joined together as at Z III and II, it is easy to see that the link between them is artificial.[1] Also, there are several concluding lectures, usually marked by summaries such as in Z XI, XVI and XVII.

(5) It is a characteristic of the summaries that they loosely but not precisely fit the discussions that have gone before; also that they refer only to a part of the previous analyses. The summary in Z XI merely recalls Z IV, X and XI, then adds a reference to Z VI (37ᵇ3). The summary in Z XIII refers back to Z III but not accurately (see above, p. 102). The closing sentence of Z XVI epitomizes parts

---

[1] The words 'first outlining what substance is' and 'if not in more senses, at least mainly in four' (28ᵇ32–4), appear to be an editorial addition (the first of the two phrases suggested by 'we have now stated in outline', 29ᵃ8). For the whole of Z II is devoted to a survey of the possible (physical) meanings of substance; it is therefore awkward for the chapter to close with the words 'let us first briefly outline what substance is'. This phrase is even less fitting when taken in relation to Z I. There substance was emphatically stated to be first of all essence: here, the question is wide open again. In Z III substance is said to be chiefly the following: essence, the universal, genus and the substratum. Similarly, the words 'if not in more, at least in four principal senses' only provide an artificial link between Z II and III. They are meant to refer to the many meanings of substance mentioned in Z II, but these meanings were not treated in Z II as secondary. In fact, Z III makes a fresh start by discussing substance in logical terms.

of Z XII, XIV and XV but hardly refers to itself (see above, p. 108). The lengthy summary in H I resembles the contents of Z but does not accurately reflect them (see above, pp. 112 ff.). Similarly, the forward reference at the beginning of Z III only partly corresponds to the rest of Z. Surely, the conclusion is that a number of parallel treatises on substance existed and that the editor drew on several of them at his discretion, ignoring the incongruities inevitably creeping into his volume?

(6) Z contains several doctrinal discrepancies. The concept of the formal cause is described as useless for ontology in Z VIII (33^b27), the concept of cause in general is said to be of little consequence in H VI (45^b5–24), but is given great prominence in Z XVII. Form is stated to be indivisible in Z VIII (from a scientific standpoint) but is said to have parts in Z X and XI (in a logical sense). Being is stated to be primarily substance in Z I but is rejected as substance in Z XVI. Z II poses the question as to whether there are separable substances, whereas according to Z III separable forms are above all accepted as substances (29^a27). (It appears that at one stage the eidetic outlook was predominant at the Peripatos.) The substrate is rejected as substance in Z III but it seems to have been generally considered as substance according to Z VI (31^b18). Equally, matter is repudiated as substance in Z III (29^a28) but according to Z XI (36^b22 ff.) it is idle to discount matter altogether,[1] and matter is treated as important throughout *Metaph.* H. (It was, in fact, on the problem of matter that the Peripatos was most clearly divided, as we shall see.) The individual is said to be substance (Z I), its essence definable as its species (Z IV) and 'to know the individual is to know its essence' (Z VI, 31^b20), yet the individual is expressly stated to be undefinable in Z X, XIII and XV (36^a5; 39^a15 ff.; 39^b28–40^a2). Z also contains several repetitions. Most notably, the problem of definition apparently solved in Z IV and by implication also in Z VII–VIII and Z X, is posed again in Z XI (37^a18), solved once more in Z XII, stated to have been for long intractable in H VI (45^a21) and, as is claimed, finally solved in H VI (45^b2–24) through the doctrine of the potential and actual.

---

[1] According to *Metaph.* Z X, 1036^a8–9 matter is in itself unknowable, but according to *Metaph.* Z III, 1029^a32 ff. it is in a sense manifest and less difficult to grasp than form. See J. Owens's interesting paper, 'The Aristotelian argument for the material principle of bodies', on the philosophical difficulties inherent in the Aristotelian—and the author's own—concept of matter (in Düring, *Naturphilosophie* etc.).

(7) Considerable parts of treatises joined together in Z are missing in that book but preserved elsewhere in the *Metaphysics* and even the *Physics*. Such omissions are manifest in passages where the expression 'is to be considered' (*skepteon*) occurs without being followed by an inquiry such as announced. A clear example of this is found in Z 11 which starts a doxographic-critical course and where the expression is used twice (28^b16 and 31) without its natural sequel, leaving an obvious gap. For the discussions initiated in Z 11 are merely indicated there and cut short at the very beginning. On the other hand, full critical discussions of the kind foreshadowed in Z 11 are contained in *Metaph.* M and N, also in *Metaph.* A and in *Physics* A and B.[1] It appears, therefore, that when the volume comprising the three courses was compiled, the doxographic-critical course was shortened, indeed mutilated, and its main part *transferred to separate volumes*. A second example of this procedure is found in Z III where a treatise on form is foreshadowed but not included (29^a33; compare above, pp. 116 ff.). These, then, are clear cases of editorial interference, a conclusion confirmed by the fact that in two other passages, Z III, 29^a1 and Z X, 34^b34, the same expression 'is to be discussed', is, in fact, immediately followed by a discussion such as announced.

Nevertheless, it does not follow that the shortening of the treatises in Z took place as late as the first century B.C. and that Andronicus, the editor of the Corpus, was responsible for it. For Andronicus had predecessors: the librarians of the State libraries and of the Peripatos itself. These, too, as the title lists show (see above, pp. 78 ff.), had combined several treatises to make up volumes[2] and it is not improbable that, ultimately, the pattern of the volumes was based on actual teaching practice (see below, pp. 124 ff.). Now, if a comprehensive course was held, the individual courses had to be shortened to be included, but it appears that the early cuts were far less severe than the cuts in Z as we read it. Once again, the summary

[1] O. Gigon, in 'Die Archai der Vorsokratiker bei Theophrast und Aristoteles' (in Düring, *Naturphilosophie* etc.), offers—I believe, convincing—evidence to show that *Metaph.* A as we read it presupposes Theophrastus's *Physikon Doxai*. This, however, does not exclude the likelihood that Aristotle *and* Theophrastus began to collect such *doxai* at an early date, for instance during their stay in Macedonia prior to Aristotle's return to Athens in 335 B.C.

[2] There is evidence for this in the title lists which sometimes include both full and abridged versions of a course: e.g. Theophr. no. 171, 'Physical Opinions, 16 books'; Theophr. no. 172, 'Epitome of Physical Opinions, 1 book'.

in H I serves as evidence. It refers at some length to both doxographic and critical inquiries, indicating a more copious treatment of these than found in Z II. Only one sentence of the summary deals with the large section Z X–XI, but two sentences are devoted to the short chapter Z II.

However, a clear distinction has to be made between the expressions 'is to be considered' (*skepteon*), and 'is to be considered later' (*skepteon hysteron*). The second of these need not refer to the current course: on the contrary, it is likely to point to a different, more specialized course to be held later. The phrase occurs twice in Z XI ($37^{a}11$ and 20) and, in the first instance, seems to allude to *Metaph.* I.

(8) But although the editor of the Corpus and his predecessors, the librarians, must be credited with arranging and re-arranging the order of treatises, with grouping units together and even— however sparingly—adding connecting phrases where this seemed to be required, there is no evidence whatever to indicate that they ever interfered with the text itself. On the contrary, the lectures given by the philosophers were regarded as authoritative and treated with the greatest respect. Thus, if nevertheless we find that some chapters are much-laboured and that some lectures are revised we have to conclude that it was the old philosophers themselves who revised the lectures and that the edition of the works as we read them was based on the latest, much-revised versions of the treatises. For the philosophers of the school not merely re-used earlier lectures but adapted them for re-delivery both by shortening and augmenting them. Hence, in this sense, and in this sense only, one can speak of 'revised' or 're-adapted' lectures, for a strict principle of revision was in force: additions and omissions were allowed but no alterations of the recorded lectures. It is, therefore, a mistake to attempt to emend the text of the Corpus on the hypothesis that a word here or a sentence there was changed or transposed by an ancient philosopher or editor (although modern commentators have often been inclined to make such attempts).

As a result of the repeated re-use of lectures, many of the treatises are not uniform but are composed of two or three strata, which it is possible to distinguish, and the contemplation of which is of great interest as the strata go back to different times of origin and thus afford an insight into changing outlooks and attitudes. Moreover, they are indicative of outside influences as they often contain polemical reactions to the views of other philosophers, sometimes even philosophers within the school.

(*a*) Added layers are recognizable by almost stereotyped phrases introducing them.

Z III: 'It has now been stated in outline what substance is . . . But we must not merely proceed in this way, for it is not adequate' (29^{a}8 ff.).

Z X: 'The truth has now indeed been stated; still, let us explain the matter more clearly, covering the ground once more' (35^{b}3).

In both these passages the words *men oun* (indeed) are used at the beginning of the introductory phrase, and they occur also in the following chapters to introduce additions: Z I, 28^{a}30; Z X, 35^{b}34 and 36^{a}13; Z XI, 36^{b}21. In Z XIII a new layer starts with the words, 'again it is clear in this way, too' (39^{a}3). In Z XI an outline of inquiries to come is placed before a summary of discussions already completed (37^{a}11–20).

(*b*) Added passages are also indicated by doublets.

In Z II the question whether there are substances beyond the perceptible ones is asked twice, in both instances followed by 'is to be investigated' (*skepteon*, 28^{b}13 ff. and 31 ff.). The first version of the lecture probably ends with the first 'is to be investigated'. Another lecturer re-delivering the lecture then added a sketch of opinions on substance and, in conclusion, repeated the questions already asked in a more copious but less precise manner than was done before. In Z III the definition of the substratum is stated twice (28^{b}37 and 29^{a}9); so is the view that matter might be substance (29^{a}11, 19 and 27), that the substratum is form, matter and the compound (29^{a}2–8 and 29^{a}29–32), and that the abstraction of all attributes leaves nothing to the substratum (29^{a}13 and 17).

These many repetitions confirm what we have noticed before: that Z III is a much-laboured chapter. Let us look at Z III once again. At its beginning four principal interpretations of substance are given. After this one naturally expects an inquiry into the relative merits of these interpretations, but no such inquiry follows. Instead we find that the rest of the chapter is almost entirely devoted to a discussion of substance in one sense, that of the substratum, presumably owing to a newly-emerging interest in this concept which, of course, played an important part in the controversy between materialistic and eidetic thinkers. At first the substratum, as the grammatical subject, and as long as it means form and matter along with form, is accepted as substance. But then the flow of the argument is interrupted. The definition of the substratum is repeated and we read: 'This definition is not sufficient, it is not adequate for it may lead to the view that mere matter is substance.' After this, the argument in favour of this view is copiously and repetitively stated and sharply rejected. And now the discussion returns to a point made in an earlier part of the lecture. What had been said before about form, matter and the compound is repeated and an inquiry into form announced. It is difficult to avoid the conclusion that the section 29^{a}8–33 is a new section by which an earlier lecture was augmented.

It appears that different strata are mainly found in Z I–XI and Z XIII (all the passages quoted belong to these chapters) and that the remaining chapters of Z contain hardly any additions. It would follow that Z XII and Z XIV–XVII are in their entirety of comparatively late origin, a conclusion supported by other indications, as has been pointed out (see above).

(*c*) It has also been explained that the added sections often serve the purpose of modifying what had been stated before and that they are characterized by an awareness of opinions differing from the basic Peripatetic teaching: Sceptical views, strictly materialistic views (those of Leucippus, Democritus and perhaps Epicurus) and various dualistic views (those of Heraclitus, Empedocles and perhaps the Stoics).

We find a significantly large number of probably added sections discussing objections especially to theories of definition: Z V (p. 91); Z XI (p. 98 ff.); Z XII (p. 101); Z XV (p. 106). Moreover, one notices the frequent use of such Sceptical expressions as 'maybe not' (*ouk endechetai*) in these sections; also of 'there is a difficulty' (*aporia*, *aporeitai*)—which although they are not expressions coined by the Sceptics were favoured by them. We also notice that Sceptical queries about the relative priority of the whole or the parts are taken into account in Z X (p. 97).[1]

Other probably added sections are marked by a growing influence of scientific thinking—Z X and XI (pp. 98 ff.). Still, the scientific

---

[1] The subtlety with which the relation of the whole and the parts is discussed in Z X and XI is paralleled by the Stoic teaching that 'the whole and the parts are neither different from each other nor are they the same' (Arnim, *SVF* I, 111 and II, 167, 15). The Stoics also taught that the body has no distinguishable parts (*SVF* II, 158, 32; 159, 5; 16; 22; III, 43, 24).

influence is seen more clearly in H than in Z where it is not improbable that the thought in some sections (especially in H II) was
stimulated by the Epicurean philosophy, as we shall explain in
Chapter Six.

There are signs of Stoic influence in Z. In Z XVII the concept of
nature is dominant and it is connected with the concept of cause,
as in Stoic philosophy.[1] In Z XV a central concept of Stoic philosophy,
logos, replaces the Peripatetic term, 'essence'; epistemological
problems are referred to, and the idea is described as an individual
(see above, p. 106). The later sections of Z III, too, appear to be
post-Stoic. The Stoics widely used the term 'substratum' both in
the context of grammar, where it means the subject, and in the
context of physics, in the sense of mere matter. It is true that the
earliest philosophers already spoke of matter as without any
quality[2] but it was the Stoics who described both the substratum
and substance as 'matter without any quality' (*hylê apoios*),[3]
and this is the conception of the substratum which is so vehemently
rejected in Z III. Also there occurs in Z III the Stoic term 'the
first substratum', although its use here seems to differ from the
Stoic use of the term.

The impression of Stoic influence in this chapter is further
confirmed by a difficult clause in Z III in which a subtle point
relating to indeterminate matter is made. Having said that 'the
ultimate substrate *per se* is neither any thing nor any particular
quantity nor anything else at all', the philosopher adds: 'nor is it
the negations of these, for the negations, too, would only apply by inference, predicatively' (*kata to symbebêkos*, 29ª26).[4] Ross in his *Commentary* (p. 165) draws attention to the obscurity of this clause and he
finds it difficult to explain within the context of the Aristotelian

---

[1] See p. 110, n. 3.

[2] So did Anaximander (Diels, I, 83, 10) and Anaximenes (Diels, I, 91, 14;
109, 10; 145, 14). Later, Anaxagoras regarded matter as indistinct and chaotic
(Diels, II, 5, 5; 8, 4; 16, 1; 19, 3; 20, 6) and Democritus called the perceptibles
and the elements bare of all qualities (Diels, II, 99, 17; 112, 28). However, the
term 'substratum' cannot be proved for the pre-Socratics; where it is used with
reference to their views it may well be the commentators' term (Diels, II,
120, 11; 135, 40; I, 91, 14; 109, 10; 145, 14).

[3] Arnim, *SVF* II, 125, 33; for *ousia apoios*, *SVF* I, 110, 27.

[4] See Bonitz's Index, s.v. *symbainein* (3b) and *symbebêkos*, and compare p. 209
with n. *Symbama* is a Stoic term for predicate; see Arnim, *SVF* II, 59, 15 and
31; 60, 12.

philosophy. However, the clause becomes meaningful when it is seen in relation to a Stoic method of distinction, that between absolutely opposite terms and terms opposed to each other by negation (*ta enantia, ta apophatikôs antikeimena*).[1] For example, virtue is opposed in the second sense to non-virtue but absolutely opposed to vice; and as non-virtue means anything between virtue and vice, non-virtue would be the same as non-vice—an equation described as absurd. It follows, generally, that a subject is not determined by a negatived term as the predicate and, in particular, that whether it is denied that the substratum is, or is not, a particular something or quality etc., both types of this negative proposition have the same meaning.[2] That is, the proposition leaves the substratum absolutely indeterminate in either case—which is the point the philosopher wishes to make as he attempts to repudiate the view that the substratum as mere, indeterminate matter can be substance.

Finally, one detects signs of intra-school polemic in Z, in Z XIII (see p. 104), and in Z XVII (see p. 111). In connection with doctrinal divergences one often finds that the opposition to a disputed view is expressed in sharp, almost contemptuous terms; in the defence of the significance of 'matter' (Z XI, 36^{b}22; see p. 98) and in the rejection of the relevance of 'cause' (Z VIII, 33^{b}27 and H VI, 45^{b}5–24; see p. 118).

*　　*　　*

The following picture of the origin and growth of Z emerges. The philosopher-librarians of the Peripatos, after collecting lecture records for some time, began to combine related records in volumes, e.g. on the subject 'substance', possibly basing the arrangement of the volumes on the structure of courses actually held. Soon the

---

[1] See Arnim, *SVF* II, 50, 28 ff. Compare also Kant's distinction between negative and infinite judgments.

[2] Only if the negation is prefixed to the entire proposition is the absolute opposite expressed: i.e. if we said 'it is not the case that the substratum is nothing, without any quality etc'. See Arnim, *SVF* II, 66, 26; 70, 16 ff. and compare Benson Mates, *Stoic Logic*, University of California Press 1961, pp. 31, 65, 95. A distinction between negative and infinite judgments is made in *De Interpretatione* (23^{a}40 ff.; ^{b}15 ff.), though less clearly stated than in the Stoic writings. But the genuineness of *De Interpretatione* was already doubted in antiquity (see Ross, *Aristotle*, p. 10). Moreover, *De Interpretatione* contains Stoic terms, e.g. *apophansis*.

librarians of the great royal libraries received copies of lecture records either separately or in volumes and it is probable that they, too, made up volumes of individual treatises. When at last Andronicus produced his edition he was able to draw on a number of volumes as well as single treatises on a subject, for the publication of his own volumes, on substance (Z, H, Λ), and on principles (A, M, N). In arranging the books he edited, he followed the patterns set by the earlier compilers, and as the material available to him often consisted of late, augmented versions of the various treatises, it is on these that his edition, the Corpus, to all intents and purposes is based.

It is not so much on account of the doctrinal discrepancies or the apparent influence of post-Aristotelian thought on some sections of Z that Aristotle's own authorship of the book is unlikely or even inconceivable. It is rather because it is impossible to read Z as a single philosophical treatise developing its argument, or as a continuous set of lectures discussing its subject progressively, whereas the book is intelligible throughout when read as an edited volume consisting of parts of treatises representing phases in the evolution of Peripatetic thought.

CHAPTER SIX

Peripatetic Ontology according to
Metaphysics *H*

The ontological philosophy of the Peripatos is mainly preserved in *Metaphysics* Z, H and Λ. We have seen that Z includes two onto-logical sections, two versions of a 'basic-physical course'. We now turn to the H-version of this course.

H announces itself as the final part of a comprehensive course on first philosophy (*prôtê philosophia*) such as is preserved in Z. It starts with the statement that it is 'necessary to compute the results of what has been said before, to gather up and unify what has emerged so as to arrive at a final, overall conclusion'. We shall see that H fulfils its promise of providing a definitive answer to problems raised, to many of which it refers explicitly and in detail; but that it does so in a spirit altogether different from that of the main parts of Z.

The opening statement of H is followed by a summary of the preceding course which we have discussed and which, as we have seen, omits the basic-physical sections of Z. It is these that H sets out to supply before offering its comprehensive solution.

H I (42ª25)—*résumé*
The philosopher starts with the generally accepted perceptible substances, which had been touched on in the summary in connec-tion with the doxographic section of Z, and says that they all contain matter. He then defines the substratum as substance (in contrast to Z III) in a threefold sense, as matter, as *logos* and shape, and as the compound. This, of course, is a well-known Peripatetic formula.[1] There follows the emphatic statement that matter, too, is substance (again in contrast to Z III), and this is proved by a brief outline of scientific, biological theory (all changes

---

[1] Of *logos* and shape the philosopher adds that, conceptually, they are entities by themselves, i.e. logically separable; of compounds that they alone are capable of coming-to-be and passing-away, and so are absolutely separable. He further adds that even of conceived substances some, those without matter, are absolutely separable, whereas others, shapes realized in matter, are not.

—local, quantitative etc.—occur to an underlying body, matter). For details the philosopher refers to lectures on the natural sciences (probably *Phys.* 201ᵃ12; 225ᵃ20 ff.; *Gen. Corr.* 317ᵃ17 ff.).

So by stressing the importance of matter, the H-philosopher reveals at the very beginning that his background is the natural sciences, especially biology, and that the ontological doctrines he is going to expound, with their application to logic, will be based on insights gained from the study of nature. Throughout Z, with the exception of Z VIII and XI, matter is treated as of small or no significance (see above, p. 118). A comparison of H I and Z III throws the divergence of views on matter within the *Metaphysics* into clear relief. There is a polemical tone in both these passages. Z III vigorously refutes the theory (said to be held by some) that matter can be substance (29ᵃ10 and 27): H I defends this view with an equal vigour.[1] The substratum, too, the theory of which is closely connected with that of matter, is rejected as substance in Z III but unquestioningly accepted in H I. More important still, the definition of matter in Z III differs from that in H I. In Z matter is defined as absolutely indeterminate, in H as that which is potentially but not actually a particular something. In Z III it is doubted if matter by itself exists while form dominates Being; according to Z X (36ᵃ8) matter by itself is unknowable. In H, however, matter is not merely indeterminate, it is also partially determinate (fire, earth etc.) and fully determinate. In other words, in Z matter and form are absolutely opposed to each other, as non-Being is to Being, whereas in H matter is as relevant as form. Here form and matter permeate each other; they are, in fact, merely two sides of the same thing—of substance or the perceptible body.

We shall later see that the conceptions of potentiality and actuality in H on the one hand and most of the remaining books of the *Metaphysics* on the other, differ from one another in an analogous manner.

---

[1] The question under discussion was whether matter by itself exists or does not exist, that is, is or is not substance. In the eyes of eidetic Peripatetics matter by itself does not exist. Although logically, i.e. in universal terms, one can refer to that which is not formed and in this sense know it, still, matter by itself is unknowable (Z X, 36ᵃ8). But to other Peripatetics matter, too, was substance; this is stated in *Metaph.* H, 42ᵃ32, where the point would not have been emphasized if no one had denied that matter can be substance. The view rejected in Z III, 29ᵃ19, namely that (prime) matter *alone* is substance, appears to be a Stoic, not Peripatetic view. See Arnim, *SVF* I, 24, 28; 25, 1; II, 114, 17; 115, 41; 116, 10; 126, 40; 140, 7; 172, 24.

The divergence of views on matter in H as compared with Z is reflected in a change of terminology. In Z III (29ª17–24) the terms 'prime matter' and 'ultimate matter' (*prôton, eschaton hypokeimenon*) are used for the original, indeterminate matter, in H they stand for the fully determinate, proximate matter (*eggytatê hylê*), i.e. the matter nearest to the particular something. Ultimate matter in this second sense also occurs in Z x (35ᵇ32). It may well be that the Z III lecturer had no knowledge of the notion of proximate matter; while H has its own term for original matter: 'the underlying body' (42ᵇ13).[1]

H II—*résumé*

In H I the substance—substratum—of perceptible things has been discussed as matter and as potential: in H II it is to be discussed as actuality. On the underlying matter as substance, the philosopher says, there is general agreement (in contrast to Z III); one may conclude that what follows is not generally accepted, i.e. the explanation that actuality lies in the several ways in which matter diversifies and combines. According to Democritus, the philosopher states, there are three diversifying factors, figure, inclination and contact or, in 'modern terms', shape, position and arrangement. But, he continues, there are, in fact, many more ways in which matter is determined than those stated. What follows is, in effect, a broad survey, partly of technical rules (e.g. a book is put together by glue), mainly of scientific theories on the various ways in which materials are combined or matter affected (by hardness, softness, density, rarity, dryness, humidity etc.), ending with a reference to a Hippocratean principle—all that happens is due to either excess or defect.

Here the lecturer interrupts the argument to point out the relevance of what has been said to logic. The copula 'is', he says, has as many meanings as there are ways of determining matter.[2] A threshold is defined by its position, ice as water condensed,

---

[1] For a recent discussion of Aristotle's acceptance or otherwise of 'prime matter' see W. Charlton, *Aristotle's Physics*, Oxford 1970, pp. 129–45; H. Happ, *Hyle. Studien zum aristotelischen Materie-Begriff*, Berlin–New York 1971, pp, 298–309.

[2] G. E. L. Owen in 'Aristotle on the snares of ontology' (in Bambrough, *New Essays* etc.), discusses this passage and points out that from what is said by Aristotle it is clear that 'the verb "to be" (even) in its existential role or roles can have many senses'—of some of which Aristotle himself is not aware. Professor Owen discusses the following three senses: (1) to be = to be something

a hand or foot by a whole range of processes, mixture, blending, binding, condensing etc. He adds that the classes of determination are, then, the principles of Being, a statement followed by a new summary of scientific theories partly corresponding to the earlier summary, partly introducing different conceptions, e.g. the Pythagorean principle of the straight and the curved.[1]

Now at last (43ª2) the philosopher seems to return to his initial explanation of how matter diversifies. For following up what he has said before, he concludes that, manifestly, the cause of the existence of individual things lies in those diversifying factors, or ways of combining materials, which he has outlined. They are not substances, even when combined but there is something similar (analogous) to substance in them. They are in fact the actuality in matter, the actuality which appears as the predicate in definitions, e.g. in definitions of the threshold or of ice (the same examples are used as before). There follows the important conclusion that both actuality and definitions vary with varying matter, i.e. that there are kinds of actuality and that these depend on kinds of matter. At this point, the philosopher turns his full attention to logic. One may define a thing as potential (a house as bricks and stone) or in its actuality (as a receptacle of goods and men) or as a concrete compound (as bricks and stones designed as a receptacle). And after quoting Archytas[2] for examples of the last type he concludes by saying that it has now been explained what perceptible substance is, and how it is, namely in one sense as matter, in another as shape, that is actuality, and thirdly as the

---

or other; (2) to be = *il y a*; (3) to be, as used in such statements as '"time"—"space"—"the void"=exists; does not exist'. R. Bambrough in 'Aristotle on justice' (in Bambrough, *New Essays* etc.), draws attention to the fact that Aristotle was conscious of the 'analogical' nature of words (concepts), including the verb 'to be'; and he stresses the significance of *An. Post.* I, 24: 'A word may have one meaning without necessarily referring to one thing' (Bambrough, p. 174). See also Charles H. Kahn, 'The verb "be" in ancient Greek', *Foundations of Language Suppl. Series* 16.

[1] See Diels, 1, 452, 43 (986ª25).

[2] It is remarkable that in both examples from Archytas actuality is not, as one might expect, a moving force but the absence of such a force—not the storm disturbing the air or the sea but the calm of the air or the sea. It appears that Archytas chose his examples to show how negatives are used in definitions whereas the H-philosopher takes them up to illustrate what he means by actuality, namely a condition of matter.

compound. The formula covering substance in its threefold sense is well known; what is new here is the interpretation of shape as actuality.[1]

Comment and conclusions. There is clear progress of thought in the main argument of H II. Actuality is stated to be closely related to its matter, as its position, density etc. Hence it is said to be the cause of the existence of the individual thing. An application is then made to logic: one defines a thing by predicating the actuality of its matter.

At the same time, there are clear signs of revision, that is, augmentation in H II. We find two sets of parallel passages: two summaries of biological theories partly overlapping in content (42^b16-25 and 42^b32-43^a2) and two logical discussions (42^b26-32 and 43^a6-43^a28), with partly the same examples used. Nor is it easy to deny that the paragraph starting 43^a2 follows naturally on the paragraph ending 42^b25: the various kinds of combination have been discussed; so manifestly, one must look for the cause of the individual's existence among these. The pronoun 'of these' (*toutôn* at 42^b24) is repeated by *en toutois* (43^a2); it must have the same reference.[2]

H II contains a detail of particular interest: the explanation in 'modern', current terms of the Democritean terms—figure, inclination and contact (42^b14-15). Their equivalents are said to be shape, position and arrangement. Still, the three sets of terms do not seem to coincide precisely,[3] and more important still, the new terms (*schêma, thesis, taxis*) are Epicurean terms, as the *Letter to Herodotus* reveals (Diog. L. x, 42; 44; 48). It could follow that *Metaph.* H belongs to a date after 307 B.C. (the opening of Epicurus's school in Athens) and that its philosophy, with its marked shift towards materialistic conceptions, grew out of a philosophical climate created by Epicurus at that time (compare *Metaph.* A, 985^b15 where the old and the new terms are also juxtaposed).

H VI follows naturally on H II.

[1] Alexander followed by Bonitz read καὶ, the codices have ὅτι—ὅ τι? (43^a28). Whatever the true reading, *energeia* explains *morphê.* καὶ can mean 'that is'.

[2] On the other hand, τούτων before ἕκαστον (43^a4) appears to be redundant. It does not refer to 'kinds of combination', as does ἐν τούτοις. It most probably refers to 'hand or foot' (42^b31) and is likely to have slipped in when the lecture was revised for re-delivery.

[3] The old terms are *rhythmos, tropê* and *diathigê.* The first may mean form or arrangement; the second, change of place; the third, touch or collision (see Ross, *Comm.* I, p. 140).

H VI

The philosopher has shown that actuality is that which determines matter. He has then applied this insight to logic and pointed out that, in definitions, actuality is the predicate. With this he has laid the foundation for answering that fundamental question concerning definition: how its two terms can signify one thing— the question asked in Z XI and Z XII (37ᵃ18 and 37ᵇ11; see pp. 99 and 101). And as he answers this question he also resolves several other dilemmas stated in Z, thus fulfilling his promise to offer definitive solutions of all problems posed.

The opening question: 'What is the cause of the unity in definitions?' takes in many points raised before. 'Number' is associated here with 'definition', as in Z XIII, 39ᵃ12, and also in H III, 43ᵇ22 ff. It is repeated that a thing has parts, as in Z XI, yet is not a mere aggregate or heap (see Z XVI, 40ᵇ9; XVII, 41ᵇ12; also H IV, 44ᵃ4 and VI, 45ᵃ9); and that the whole is something beyond the parts (see Z XVII; also H III). Some biological causes of unity are mentioned, as in H II. Finally, the philosopher recalls the counter-example of the *Iliad*, which is not a unity but one thing merely by connection (see Z IV, 30ᵃ10 and ᵇ9). However, the question is not answered now but repeated concisely, as in Z XII, 37ᵇ13: 'Why is man not two things; (*a*) animal, (*b*) two-footed?' The Platonists, the philosopher continues, using their conception of participation cannot solve the problem. But—this is the answer—the dilemma vanishes when it is realized that perceptible substance is, at the same time, matter and form, potential and actual, and that potential substance contains all that actual substance contains. In other words, the elements or parts that combine to make man are, in fact, man. So when in a definition a part (two-footed) is separated from the whole (animal) this does not make the parts and the whole two. They are one: what the parts are potentially, the whole is actually. Another example is given. If *X* is round and bronze, why is it one? Because bronze and round are one as matter and form; so whereas *X* as a potentiality is round *and* bronze, as an actuality it is *round bronze*. Hence it is vain to search for a cause of unity, except for an efficient cause. A potential sphere is all that an actual sphere is; the essence of a thing is in the potential as much as in the actual (45ᵃ34).

It appears that what is ruled out for natural substances is the final cause, though not for artefacts (see H II, 43ᵃ10); also possibly the ultimate cause or prime mover. Form pre-exists in the potential so only an efficient cause is needed to turn the potential into the actual. Water contains all that is necessary to change it into ice, including the solidifying factor; only the cold is required to bring about the actual transformation. It is clear that by this interpretation of matter as the potential, in the sense he gives to this concept, the H-philosopher *stresses the importance of the study of the particular in material nature.*

Next the philosopher discusses unity as such or 'the One'—a discussion easily suggested by the problem of the unity of perceptible substance. There is intelligible[1] and sensible matter, he says, but there are also concepts which have no matter, the highest genera, the One and Being, and the categories of Being, this, quality and quantity. These are unities by themselves. But they have no separate existence (see Z XVI). Rather they are inherent in all essences without any cause for them so to inhere; hence, they are never stated in definitions (although they are always implicit in them). The One and Being are also discussed in Z XVI but, as in all other cases, while Z is hesitant, H is positive and dogmatic.

The final paragraph of H (45ᵃ8 ff.) contains a second statement of the doctrine of potentiality and actuality. The philosopher reverts to the *aporia* stated at the beginning of H VI: what is the cause of the unity of a thing defined? The Platonists say that it is participation but then they look for a cause of participation and even wonder what participation is. Others—Sophists—speak of combination, connection and communion, words that appear to differ yet mean the same and hence can each be applied to everything. They try to explain how a potential and an actual thing can be two yet one. But the truth is that they *are* one. Ultimate matter is fully determined matter and thus is the same as form (in matter). What the first is potentially, the second is actually. There is no cause for this unity; unity itself is the cause for the existence of individual things, except that one may search for an efficient cause needed to turn the potential into the actual. And concisely stating what has been explained more elaborately earlier in the chapter, H ends with the words: 'That which has no matter is absolutely one.'

---

[1] Intelligible matter '. . . as in mathematics'; compare *Metaphysics* Z X, 36ᵃ9. For instance, the lines forming a triangle are the parts, or intelligible matter, of the triangle. The term does not mean logical genera or 'the generic element in species'; but see Ross, *Comm.* ad loc.

As this résumé shows, the earlier argument is repeated in this paragraph almost point by point, expressed here, if anything, more strikingly, so that one might conclude that it is this paragraph which contains the original inspiration and the earlier passage which is secondary. This assumption is reinforced by the observation that the opening phrase 'because of this *aporia*' connects this paragraph directly with the beginning of the chapter.

The doctrine of the unity of the potential and the actual is nowhere stated more incisively than in H. The question of which is prior, the potential or the actual—answered in favour of the actual in Θ VIII —is not raised here. It would appear that they are regarded as simultaneous or, if the efficient cause is taken into account, that the potential is considered prior. The nearest to H in outlook seems to be *Physics* Δ, 213^{a}1–11 (compare also *Phys.* Θ IV, especially 255^{b}6 ff.).

That ultimate matter is the same as form, the philosopher says, has been explained before. This, no doubt, is an allusion to a lost treatise, knowledge of which is also presupposed in Z X, 35^{b}32; a forward reference to it seems to be contained in *Physics* Δ, 213^{a}4. According to this treatise, substance belonged to the individual, and individuality was based on matter. For it emerges from Z that generic and specific concepts (of men and horses) have no substance, nor has generic matter, and that substance belongs to individual, ultimate matter, which, in fact, is the individual thing. So whether in logical *dihaeresis* one descends from the highest genus to the lowest species or scientifically one ascends from original matter to ultimate matter, substance resides in the individual representative of species. Hence, a man's character is not determined by species, but by the particular matter of which he—mainly, it is to be assumed, his heart or brain—is made.

These views seem to be implied in the concept 'ultimate matter' which, as emerges from H VI, is closely related to the twin-notions of potentiality and actuality. Let us now look at H III–V.

H III

H III has four parts: 43^{a}29–^{b}5; 43^{b}5–14; 43^{b}14–32; 43^{b}32–44^{a}14.

(1) A linguistic difficulty is stated. A word may signify both the form or actuality of a thing and the concrete thing itself—'house' or 'soul'. The latter case is said to be particularly puzzling because it is not certain whether the soul is *in* the animal, as its actuality, or the animal itself. Still, while this problem may be important for

other investigations such as psychological studies, linguistic ambiguity does not impede our inquiry into perceptible substance. For the essence of a thing is in its form or actuality. So whether we speak of the form or the thing the same definition applies.

(2) The point is made that neither the parts of a compound nor their combination suffice to explain the coming-about of the compound; nor does composition derive from the component parts. Hence, there is something beyond the parts (= matter), namely substance, which is the cause of composition, unity and existence. Yet there are philosophers who consider matter only, passing over substance.

In this, as well as in the preceding paragraph, the speaker is a natural philosopher with an eidetic outlook. The doctrine stated is the same as in Z XVII ($41^{b}11$ ff.); even the example of the syllable is repeated. But in contrast to Z XVII, the tone in H III is polemical; and the polemics are directed against those who give prominence to matter and who hold that matter and potentiality are the same as actuality (as in H VI and *Phys.* Δ). In short, it is directed against the main philosophy of H itself. The terms 'composition' (*synthesis*) and 'mixture' occur in H II as well as here. But whereas these denote two primary kinds of actuality in H II ($43^{a}14$), both are derivative according to H III.

(3) This paragraph, too, is related in outlook to Z XVII and Z VII–IX. Some possible sequels of the theory of immanent substance are rather hesitantly stated: (*a*) that perhaps only natural things, not artefacts, should be regarded as substances; (*b*) with Antisthenes, that only compounds can be defined, not such natural entities as silver—of such it can be shown only what they are like.

This limitation of the scope of definition seems a concession to Sceptical thinking. It is in contrast to H III (1). More important still, this paragraph contains no hint either of the definitive solution to the problem of definition, which is promised at the beginning of H and clearly stated at the end of the book, or of the concepts of potentiality and actuality on which that solution is based. According to H VI, everything is definable as potential-actual, with the exception of the One and Being. Silver would presumably be defined as water or vapour solidified by pressure (see *Mete.* $378^{a}28$ ff.; $384^{b}33$ ff.).

(4) Certain points of similarity between 'numbers' and definitions are stated: (*a*) both are divisible into indivisible parts; (*b*) neither

admit of addition or subtraction without being changed in essence; (*c*) for both numbers and objects of definition there is something beyond their parts that makes them unities, i.e. the actual nature of each; (*d*) neither admits of degrees unless (in contrast to *Cat.* 3^b33) perhaps the compound does.

The theory of numbers referred to is not Platonic but belongs either to the post-Platonic Academy or the Pythagoreans.[1] It is probable that this paragraph was added at a time when the philosophy of numbers attracted the attention of many. It is a variant of the theory of ideas. The lecturer's standpoint is eidetic.

The summary at the end of H III is surprising: it refers first to a passage not included in H and then to the last paragraph of H III only.

H III—*conclusions*. It seems certain that this chapter was added to the H-course of lectures. It differs in spirit from H I, II and VI. It nowhere refers to potentiality: in its middle section neither potentiality nor actuality is mentioned. In contrast to the main part of H, its standpoint is eidetic, sometimes near-Sceptical. It seems to belong to a time when naturalistic views had—temporarily —lost their appeal.

From the summary it appears that of H III, as we read it, only the last paragraph was added by a lecturer re-delivering the course, whereas the rest of the chapter was attached later. For paragraphs 1–3 consist of various observations joined together by verbal association. 'Shape, actuality, the compound of these' are found at the end of H II and at the beginning of H III; the composition of the compound 'house' occurs in H III (1) and is taken up in H III (2); 'substance' occurs at the end of H III (2) and is taken up by 'this', i.e. substance, at the beginning of H III (3). At which stage was H III (1–3) added? It would seem that these sections were inserted here by an editor and that they were taken from lectures not directly connected with H. An additional proof of this is the opening phrase, 'one must not fail to notice that', which can be cut out without any loss of meaning or damage to the construction. The original lecture probably began with 'sometimes' (*eniote*). We shall find a close parallel to this opening in H IV.

H IV

Whereas H III deals with the compound and stresses form, H IV discusses matter, which is the main concern of H as a whole. Its

---

[1] See Ross, *Comm.* ad loc.

explanations are biologically based but general and elementary; potentiality is not mentioned. H IV is unitary but for the purpose of explanation may be divided into two parts, the second part beginning at 44ª32. The chapter first makes the point that proximate, not original matter must be the basis both for scientific knowledge and for definitions. Secondly, it gives instructions about the correct way in which to state the material cause.

Résumé. It is pointed out that biologically one kind of matter arises from another so that a concrete something contains several kinds of matter, the last involving earlier kinds; conversely, that one kind of matter may be turned into different objects, but within limits. Not every type of matter can be used for every type of thing. This is an elementary reflection, of which the deeper philosophical meaning is expressed in H II (43ª12): actuality, which differs with different matter, depends on matter.

It is then explained how to state the material cause (along with the other causes), namely with reference to proximate matter. It is added that the procedure is different in the case of eternal substances which have no matter in the ordinary sense, and of natural phenomena which have no substance at all. Therefore a phenomenon has to be defined as occurring to an underlying substance, e.g. an eclipse happens to the moon, with the intervention of the earth as the efficient cause. Another example is sleep, which is immobility—but which substratum is affected? The animal? Or the heart of the animal? And which is the efficient cause? While sleep is here discussed in a thoroughly aporetic manner, it is treated dogmatically in *De Somno,* 456ª5 and in *Part. An.* 653ª10. According to the former the heart, according to the latter the brain, is principally affected in sleep.

One gains the impression that H IV is an elementary or indeed ancillary lecture on matter, given to beginners. If nothing else, the instruction on the double meaning of the phrase 'one thing comes from another' (*tode ek toude*) points to it. Students are told to realize that that often-used formula may mean, either that a higher entity *A* develops from a lower *B* or that a lower entity *A* is found when a higher *B* is analysed into its parts (44ª24). The lecturer himself may well be a junior philosopher. He expresses himself with caution, as though leaving it to others to give definitive explanations. He uses the word 'perhaps' (*isôs*) four times (44ᵇ1, 7, 12 and 44ª20), three times in his most essential explanations. His standpoint, however, though cautiously stated, is clearly materialistic rather than eidetic. Of the four causes he seems to recognize mainly two, the material and the efficient, like the philosopher of H VI. Of the final cause he says at one point that it *perhaps* coincides with the formal, and at another, regarding the eclipse of the moon, that *perhaps* there is no final cause—and, by implication, no formal cause—for it.

Like H III, the chapter is introduced by an editorial phrase, of which this time even the grammar is dubious:[1] 'As regards material substance one must not ignore the fact that....' The original text probably began: 'Even if from the same...' (*ei kai ek tou autou...*).

H V

This is a composite chapter, the first part of which is a continuation of H IV. Potentiality is not mentioned. The second part (starting 44^{b}29) deals with—probably Sceptical—objections against the theory of potentiality, which are answered in terms apparently borrowed from the Stoics.

(1) In H IV substances which have no matter in the ordinary sense have been discussed; the inquiry now turns to entities which have no matter at all. These are points—if they do exist, the lecturer adds with caution—and forms, which do not change as compounds do, but are or are not.

(2a) There is an *aporia* about the matter of an individual thing. How can it contain two contraries within itself? How can the body of an animal be potentially both healthy and sick? Or how can water be potentially both wine and vinegar? Could it be that in its positive state and (positive) form a body is healthy—and water is wine—while through privation and destruction a body is sick—and water vinegar? The antithesis between 'according to positive state' (*kath' hexin*) and 'according to privation' (*kata sterêsin*) or 'against nature' (*para physin*) is found in Stoic writings.[2]

(2b) But then there is also this *aporia*. A thing would be both

----

[1] λανθάνειν ὅτι is not classical Greek, least of all, in the sense 'to forget', 'to ignore the fact'. In its active form this verb is intransitive. It means 'to be hidden' and is construed with a participle, or with an interrogative clause, as in *Metaph.* E 1, 25^{b}29 or in *Phys.* Γ, 200^{b}13. In the middle voice it means 'to forget' and is construed with a genitive.

[2] Arnim, *SVF* II, 52, 1 and 17; III, 34, 37.

itself and its opposite—wine would be vinegar, a living man a corpse. But they are not. Individuals do not change into their opposites. It is their matter that changes while individuals perish as a result of the change of the matter (*kata symbebêkos*). Wine must become water, a living man his matter before turning into their negative opposites, and before new things arise. In short, any individual changing into another must first go through matter.

That the Sceptics tried to discredit the theory of potentiality is clear from Sextus Empiricus, *Outlines* II, 225. Their chief objection was that it implied that X would be A and not-A at the same time. This objection is dealt with in H v, and it is possible that the examples used are those of the Sceptics. Both the lecturer's preoccupation with difficulties raised in Sceptical thinking and his hesitant adoption of Stoic terms make it likely that the second part of H v is relatively late. Its connection with the first part is slender; the word 'the contraries' (*tanantia*) seems to be the main link. Nor is there any connection between the arguments of H v and H VI. The *aporia* stated at the beginning of H VI is not the *aporia* of H v but that of Z XI and Z XII.

Book H—conclusions

It has emerged that the set of lectures designed to complete a course such as contained in Z comprises H I and parts of H II and H VI, with the rest of the book added at a later time. It need cause no surprise to find that this original course was somewhat short, at least by modern standards. There are many more examples of short courses in the Corpus. Moreover, as the lectures were recorded (all the treatises are lecture records), only the essential teaching was reproduced, in as few words as possible, and it is fair to assume that in oral delivery the lecturer was more explicatory and generally far less sparing of words.

By its consistency, originality and clarity the H-course is one of the most remarkable of the Corpus. It stands out because of its purpose to offer a definitive solution to all problems raised, and it does so by expounding a theory designed to answer ontological and logical questions at the same time. It is as though the philosopher said: all the dilemmas that have continually troubled the logicians can be resolved by someone with a sound scientific training, which alone enables a philosopher to understand nature and to discover the universal—and hence logically usable—principle to which all changes in nature can be reduced. This principle is *the oneness of potentiality and actuality*, through which the emphasis is shifted from *form to matter*.

The (pre-Socratic) view that order and determination were contained in matter was regarded as primitive after Plato. As the H-philosopher revives this view he gives it a subtler and deeper meaning. He teaches that, although matter does not determine either itself or nature, it is identical with the capacity to be determined, i.e. it contains within itself all that is required for its determination; hence, in essence, the determinable is the same as the determinate. So substance belongs to matter, i.e. potentiality, as much as to actuality. Both are in fact the same, both pre-existent in nature. For form is only another name for actuality, which, as potentiality, is contained in matter. The philosophy of H is the nearest approach to a monistic, materialistic philosophy within the Corpus, and it is remarkable, too, in that—unusual for the Corpus— it is expressed with that dogmatic self-assurance often so characteristic of materialistic thinkers.

The rivalry which existed between scientists and logicians within the Peripatos has left many traces. In Z XI we read that however important the study of perceptible substances and matter may be it is part of 'second philosophy', and knowledge of substance according to the *logos* is more important (37ª15). This was, of course, a Platonic tradition. Observation of nature, which could never lead to certain results, was deprecated.[1] On the other hand, one finds slighting references to logicians, to those who 'deal in words'. 'There is a great difference between those who investigate first causes scientifically and those who discuss them logically' (*Gen. Corr.* I, 2, 316ª12). 'Only those who dwell in intimate association with nature and its phenomena see the great universal principles, while those who are devoted to abstract discussions have only a narrow understanding' (*Gen. Corr.* 316ª6 ff.; translated on the basis of Joachim's translation, Oxford edition). In *Gen. Corr.* 335ᵇ24, after a critique of the theory of ideas, those who study matter are described as the better experts on nature. In *Metaph.* Θ VIII those 'who deal in words' are derided as people who arrive at absurd results (50ᵇ35). In *Metaph.* H VI Platonists and Sophists are classed together as those who make pointless distinctions and ask futile questions (45ᵇ8 ff.).

As the problem of matter became a point of debate within the

[1] See Sambursky, p. 176.

Peripatos so did the concepts of potentiality and actuality. It seems that the terms had quite a wide currency and were sometimes used in a half-popular way. Philosophically, we find two antithetic interpretations of them. According to one view, that which is potential is merely an indeterminate heap (Z XVI); it depends on the actual which is prior to it in every respect (Θ VIII; also Z IX); substance, form and the end are in the actual (Θ VIII, 50^{b}2 and 50^{a}22); matter only appears to be something (Λ III, 70^{a}10);[1] matter underlies actuality (Z XIII, 38^{b}6).

The contrary view is stated in *Gen. Corr.* I, 3 (317^{b}18 ff.): 'potentiality is prior to actuality', although—the text continues— a wondrously difficult problem results from this doctrine.[2] It is stated at least as a possible view in *Physics* Δ (213^{a}6): 'Matter and actuality are one and the same.' Finally it is nowhere more strikingly expressed than in *Metaph.* H (45^{b}21): 'Somehow (*pôs*) the potential thing is the same as the actual thing'.

So, whereas according to eidetic doctrine matter comes to be through an immaterial agent, form, it was held by the empiricists that matter determines itself through its own potencies (*dynameis*); indeed is predetermined by them and hence, exists by itself, as a potentiality.

---

[1] In Jaeger's edition of the *Metaphysics* this clause, ἡ μὲν ὕλη τόδε τι οὖσα τῷ φαίνεσθαι (1070^{a}10), is marked as corrupt, but Ross—I believe rightly— upholds the text, quoting Alexander in support of his interpretation: 'The matter which is a "this" merely in appearance.' See also Z XVI, δοκοῦσαι οὐσίαι (40^{b}5).

[2] The dilemma as recorded in *Gen. Corr.* I, 3 is this. If the potential were determined its qualities would exist separately, i.e. ideas would be existing entities: if, on the other hand, it were completely undetermined, it would not exist at all. This passage is of interest because it shows that the conception of the potential as outlined in H was hotly debated. The two opposite views on which is prior, the potential or the actual, are referred to in *Metaph.* Λ, 1072^{a}4.

CHAPTER SEVEN

Peripatetic Ontology according to Metaphysics Λ

According to *Metaphysics* E and K (1026ᵃ19 and 1064ᵇ3) theoretical philosophy is divided into mathematics, physics and theology.[1] Λ is the only book of the Corpus to contain a combined physical-theological course. For this reason alone Λ occupies a unique place; beyond this—as has often been noted—it offers its own complete system of ontology, meant to be conclusive or definitive. Hence, it may well have been composed as a deliberate antithesis to views expressed in other books of the *Metaphysics*, notably Z and H, and as an attempt to direct the thinking on substance within the Peripatos into new, or disused, channels. The emphasis in Λ is on immaterial substance, although matter is not lost sight of, and its teaching is that nature with all its phenomena lastly depends on pure actuality, which is God.

Λ, or at any rate its first part, is the work of a philosopher fully trained in physics and astronomy, not quite so well informed on biology and only slightly interested in logic. Consequently, it searches not for the many causes which produce the changes in particular substances, as does H, but for the ultimate cause of all changes; not for the forms inherent in individuals and definable as their essences but for the highest form on which all forms depend. In other words, Λ takes its stand both against a materialistic philosophy, which allows matter to be a source of changes, and against a logical idealism (eideticism), which explains substance in terms of the universal, or of essence and accident.

In spite of its special character, Λ is closely related to other works, within and outside the Corpus, both in its physical and theological aspects—the first to *Physics*, *De Caelo* and *Gen. Corr.*; the second to other books of the *Metaphysics*, notably E, Z, H, K, M and N, as well as to *De Philosophia*, *De Anima* and *Eth. Nic.* Even the

---

[1] In K the order is: physical, mathematical, theological; compare also the six theoretical sciences of the Stoics, culminating in theology (Arnim, *SVF* I, 108, 12).

manner in which these two aspects are connected is derived from an earlier work, Plato's *Laws* (x); whereas the *Epinomis* seems to have served as a model for Λ VIII. The theology of Λ especially, appears to have a Platonic origin; nevertheless, as one more version of the doctrine of substance, Λ is characteristically Peripatetic: its theology is stated in the terms of Peripatetic ontology—substance, form and actuality.[1]

The book, which consists of ten chapters, may be divided into the following sections: I–II; III–V; VI; VII; VIII–X. The physical course comprises I–VI; the theological course begins with VII. That is to say, the incision occurs after VI, not after V, where it is usually placed (see below). The essential teaching of Λ is found in I–II, VI and VII.

The terseness of Λ in argument and language, especially in its first half, has often been noted. Here the whole of Λ's physical theory is sketched in bold, simple strokes, producing an outline of its essential tenets adequate for students who had attended full courses on physics and biology, and sufficient to show where the philosopher stood.

Λ I–II

Five main points are made in Λ I–II.

Λ I. (1) Λ begins by stating that its subject is substance; it adds at once that it will inquire into the principles and causes of all substances, that is, into the sources of becoming. There follow arguments to show (as in Z 1) that substance is primary, in a physical sense (if the universe is regarded as a whole) and in a logical sense (if all is explained in terms of the categories). Again as in Z 1, the authority of the early philosophers is invoked for the importance of the inquiry to be undertaken; then reference is made to contemporary thinkers—logicians—who regard universals as substances, principles or causes. The early philosophers discovered the four elements, fire, air etc., but did not think of the 'common body'— mere matter.

---

[1] The interconnection between Aristotelian theology and ontology is discussed by D. M. MacKinnon who, after pointing out the problematic nature of the distinction between essence and existence in its relation to the concept of God, emphasizes that 'engagement with the problems of Aristotelian ontology brings one at once up against absolutely central issues in philosophy'. See 'Aristotle's conception of substance', in Bambrough, *New Essays* etc.

(2) It is stated that there are three kinds of substances; two perceptible, of which one is eternal the other perishable (on which there is agreement, the philosopher adds, as in Z II); thirdly, the immutable (*akinêtos*) substance. The term 'immutable' substance for immaterial substance is peculiar to Λ; it points forward to the doctrine of the prime mover in which physical and ontological concepts are united. Nevertheless there now follows a reference to eidetic and mathematical views of immaterial substance. Plato himself regarded ideas and numbers, Xenocrates ideas-numbers, Speusippus numbers only, as separately existing substances (see Z II). Then it is said that the perceptible substances are the subject of the natural sciences, while immovable substance belongs to another science (logical, mathematical); unless there is a common source for all substances, in which case there would be one overriding science—theology.[1]

(3) Λ's theory of change is stated, which is closely based on *Physics* A. When perceptible substance changes: (*a*) the change is from opposite to opposite or from intermediate to intermediate, or from opposite to intermediate or vice versa; (*b*) the change is between contraries, i.e. cognates only (colour changes into colour, not into sound); (*c*) that which undergoes change persists. (The logical-grammatical term 'substratum-subject', *hypokeimenon*, is avoided.)

Λ II. After a brief recapitulation, indicating the beginning of a new lecture, the persisting body is described as matter.

(4) The doctrine of the four types of change is briefly referred to; it is treated at length in *Gen. Corr.* I, 4 and 5 (see also *Phys.* 201ª12 ff.). The four types, in accordance with the categories, are: generation and destruction (substance); growth and diminution (quantity); change of affection (quality); change of place (locality).

(5) The doctrine of change is stated in terms of the theory of potentiality and actuality. All change is from what exists potentially to that which exists actually; from the potentially white to the actually white. Hence, all things originate from something that exists potentially though not actually (water in air); and this unity (of what is potentially, and is not yet actually) is the One of Anaxagoras

---

[1] On the question of the possibility of a universal science and the contradictory answers to it found in the Corpus, see G. E. L. Owen, 'Logic and metaphysics in some earlier works of Aristotle', in *Studia Graeca et Latina Gothoburgensia* XI. See also Owen, 'On the snares of ontology', in Bambrough, *New Essays* etc.

10

(see below). Other philosophers wrongly make matter a uniform mass, instead of correlating a potential A to an actual A, for matter is different for different things. Even the matter of eternal substances is changeable, but only in respect of place.

There follows a paragraph to confirm and explain further what has just been said. The philosopher begins by referring to the three meanings of not-Being[1] and making the third meaning, namely unrealized potentiality, the sole basis of his argument, states that not every potentiality can turn into every actuality; on the contrary, different things come from different origins. He adds that if matter were a uniform mass there would not be this infinite variety of things in the world, but as the ordering principle, mind, is one, all things would be the same.

Returning to the beginning of Λ 1 the philosopher sums up: there are three causes, three principles of perceptible substances, form, privation, matter. In other words, the Λ-philosopher's theory of change or becoming has been outlined as far as the material and formal causes are concerned; what remains to be explained is the doctrine of the moving cause or causes.

Λ I–II—*comments and conclusions*. While Λ I is based on physical theory Λ II draws on biological knowledge. In *Physics* A IV–VII a copious discussion of the theory of the three principles and causes, as outlined in Λ I, is preserved. It is summed up in *Physics* A VII (191ᵃ4 and 20) in a manner comparable to Λ II.[2] But whereas the question whether there are two or three or more principles is debated in *Physics*, only the conclusion at which *Physics* arrives is tersely stated in Λ, namely that there are three principles; and on the assumption that a shorter, dogmatic version is later than a fuller, inquiring one, Λ presupposes such teaching as is recorded in *Physics* A.

Similarly, the theory of the four types of change, which is briefly referred to in Λ II is discussed at length in *Gen. Corr.* I, 2–5; II, 1. In this way[3] Λ combines physical and biological knowledge as

---

[1] The three meanings of not-Being alluded to here are stated in *Metaph.* N, 89ᵃ26 ff.; compare *Metaph.* Θ, 51ᵃ34 and *Phys.* A VII, 187ᵃ1 ff.

[2] See also *Gen. Corr.* II, 1, 329ᵃ32.

[3] G. R. Morrow in 'Qualitative change in Aristotle's *Physics*' (in Düring, *Naturphilosophie* etc.) rightly points out the contradictions between the Aristotelian theories of the four elements (*stoicheia*), and of the powers (*dynameis*). He then severely criticizes the conceptions of change (*alloiôsis*) and potentiality, as 'pseudo-explanations, detrimental to the clarity of Aristotle's insight on certain crucial issues'.

established in other departments to create a basis for its theory of the unmoved mover. While this may be regarded as certain, it is a question of considerable interest whether Λ also presupposes *Metaph.* H. In H the theory of the oneness of the potential and the actual is expounded, as we have seen,[1] and it appears that this theory is stated and accepted in Λ II: 'the potentially white changes into the actually white'; 'everything originates from that which potentially but not yet actually is' (i.e. such a thing). Then Λ describes this unity, which it considers as the right concept of unity, as the One of Anaxagoras, and it is not impossible that it is also the One of H VI. The One of Anaxagoras has puzzled commentators[2] but the reading is accepted as correct by Ross and Jaeger. What is this One? It is not the Mind, but matter in which the contraries are contained and from which they emerge by segregation (*Phys.* A IV, 187ª19). It is both One and many (187ª22). And One and many are the same: many is potentially, then actually One (*Phys.* A II, 186ª1).[3] This is a theory akin to both H and Λ II.[4] So it appears that Λ invokes Anaxagoras in support of its own teaching, re-interpreting Anaxagoras's concept of the One in terms of the potential and the actual. With this Anaxagoras seems to confirm that, as regards the particular, things arise from matter.

In contrast to Anaxagoras, three other philosophers are mentioned who also understood the importance of matter but failed to see that matter is diverse in kind or, as H II puts it, that a different actuality or form belongs to different matter (43ª12) and, hence, merely spoke of the togetherness of all or of mixture. The teaching of the last-named of these philosophers, Democritus, is also restated in the terms of potentiality and actuality: 'All things were together potentially though not actually.' But, the Λ-philosopher implies, this is not good enough, because different things have different

---

[1] This theory is mentioned as one which it is difficult to maintain in *Gen. Corr.* I, 3, 317ᵇ17 ff.; compare p. 141, n. 2.

[2] See Ross, *Comm.* p. 351.

[3] There are Stoic parallels to this view: 'everything originates from One', 'the One is many' (see Arnim, *SVF* I, III, 27 and II, 160, 12). Besides, the revival of interest in pre-Socratic philosophers, especially Democritus and Anaxagoras, is a feature of the last decade of the fourth century. In *Phys.* Γ IV, 203ª22 ff., certain views of these two thinkers are stated as though they were nearly identical.

[4] On the other hand in Λ x, where eidetic views predominate, 'one' is opposed to 'many' as form is to matter.

matter; hence, not everything can arise from everything: only what is potentially A can become actually A. The conclusion is that Λ at this point readily incorporates the teaching of *Metaph.* H in its own doctrine, although, as we shall see, this acceptance of H later met with opposition (see below, on Λ v).

There is a reference to 'contemporary philosophers' in Λ I (69ª26), who regard universals as substances. It is unlikely that the allusion is to Plato and his two immediate successors as these are referred to in the same chapter in another connection, namely with the theory of ideas in its varying forms. Alexander, too, denied that the Platonists were here meant.[1] It seems natural to conclude that the reference is to those Peripatetic logicians whose views are mentioned at the beginning of *Metaph.* Z III and expressly refuted in Z XIII; for there is no other school to which these views can be attributed. Within the Peripatetic school, on the other hand, they must have enjoyed a vogue at some time. The Λ-philosopher is out of sympathy with them, and it is interesting to note that the use of logical terms is avoided in Λ I–II and VI–VII: instead, physical terms are used. In place of 'substratum' one reads 'common body' (compare *Metaph.* H, 42ᵇ13, 'underlying body'; also *Phys.* 187ª12 and 203ª34);[2] for 'negation' (*antiphasis*), 'privation' (*sterêsis*), see *An. Post.* 73ᵇ21 and *Topics*, 143ᵇ34). Neither 'essence' (*to ti ên einai*) nor 'immaterial form or substance' (*eidos* or *ousia aneu hylês*) occur; instead the physical term 'immutable, immovable' (*akinêtos*) is used. Besides, we find the threefold division into matter, form and privation in Λ I–II as in the *Physics*, not the twofold division into form and matter, as in *Metaph.* Z.

The last paragraph of Λ II is likely to have been added on the occasion of a re-delivery of the course. It is introduced by 'one might be in doubt...' and it emphatically repeats points made before. Moreover, it anticipates knowledge on the part of the students of the concluding chapters of Λ. It refers to mind (*nous*), without giving any explanation of the concept.[3]

---

[1] See Ross, *Comm.* p. 350.

[2] According to *Gen. Corr.* 320ᵇ23, a 'common body' does not exist (see Ross, *Comm.* II, p. 350). But *Gen. Corr.* uses the term in a different sense from H and Λ, and denotes not mere matter as such (as in H and Λ), but a material element more basic than fire, air etc., and it is the existence of such an element that is denied.

[3] Only the One (*hen*), not the Mind (*nous*) of Anaxagoras is mentioned in this chapter.

Λ III

This chapter differs from Λ I–II both thematically and in its approach. It is not concerned with nature as a never-ending process of becoming through change but with problems connected with the structure of substance. It consists of four observations which, though related to one another, do not form a continuous argument: (1) on matter and form in general; (2) on accidental and spontaneous generation; (3) on the three meanings of substance and the possible existence of immaterial form; (4) on the efficient cause as prior to, and the formal cause as simultaneous with, composite substance. The chapter ends with an attack on the theory of ideas.

In approach Λ III is in line with those sections of the *Metaphysics* which, centred on the doctrine of immanent substance, explore the logical and general implications of that doctrine: Z VII–IX; Z XVII; H III—sections which, related to one another, seem to form an identifiable body of writing, characteristic either of a phase in the evolution of Peripatetic thinking, or of a school within the school.

(1) The first observation seems to answer a question such as this: how far back should one go in explaining the generation of things, with a view to defining them? The ruling is that although only primary matter and form are not generated (and, hence, stand at the end of all inquiries into generation), in practice, one has to treat such materials as bronze and such forms as the circle as primary in explaining—and defining—a bronze circle. (This same ruling is given in H III, 43^{b}24–33, an added chapter as we have seen.) In defining a composite substance, it is impossible to go back to original matter and form and one has to take its material side as though it were primary matter and its formal side as though it were primary form. For one cannot define such materials as silver, merely point out what they are like: e.g. silver is like tin (43^{b}26).

(2) Here the question seems to be: if both in art and in nature things of a kind evolve from things of the same kind, that is, the same form which is their cause, how do accidental and spontaneous generation fit into this scheme? The answer is that accidental and spontaneous generation are privations, i.e. the contraries to generation based on form as its cause. With this compare Z VII, 32^{a}24 and Z IX, 34^{a}22 (see also *Phys.* B IV).

(3) The question is: does immaterial form exist? After a restatement of the doctrine of the three meanings of substance which is in line with Z VII, 32ᵃ16 and Z VIII, 33ᵇ20 but here expressed in difficult terms, the answer is as follows. One must distinguish between art and nature. In art form does not exist except in the product (or the artist's mind). In nature, however, form may exist by itself, if Plato is right.[1] A parallel to this passage occurs in H III, 43ᵇ18.

(4) The question is: if the cause of a product precedes that product, must not ideas exist? The answer is that one must distinguish between the moving and the formal cause. The former precedes the product, the latter is simultaneous with it. (Whether form remains after the dissolution of the compound, e.g. the soul, or rather its rational part, after the dissolution of the body, let this be considered: it is not impossible.) In any case, one need not assume the existence of ideas. For the formal cause, and as far as these coincide, the moving cause, too, is immanent; man begets man, medical science reflects, and produces, pure health. In this paragraph the doctrine of immanent substance is upheld, followed by a rejection of the theory of ideas, as in Z VIII.

So Λ III consists of restatements with slight variations of points made mainly in Z, in contrast to Λ I–II where an argument is built up by means of precise extracts taken from fuller discussions, mainly in physical works. The conclusion that Λ III is inserted is strengthened by its use of the elliptical phrase 'further that . . .' which occurs twice, and which one might supplement to read after H III and H IV: 'Further one must not ignore the fact that . . .' (*meta tauta dei mê agnoein* . . .). Moreover, the moving cause, reserved by the philosopher in Λ I–II for the second part of his course, is anticipated twice in Λ III (70ᵃ1 and 21), nor are logical terms avoided, as in the earlier section (e.g. substratum, 70ᵃ11). There are also some repetitions within the chapter. The doctrine of threefold substance is referred to in 69ᵇ35 and 70ᵃ10. The words 'man begets man' occur in both 70ᵃ8 and 28.

Λ IV–V

These chapters form one section. They discuss the same questions,

---

[1] There is no need for a transposition of 70ᵃ20 and 21. I read 70ᵃ19 with Jaeger, ἀλλ'οὐ τούτων: forms may exist in the nature of wholes but *not* of fire, flesh, head etc. (i.e. parts), for these are all matter.

the relation between the universal, or the general, and the particular, and the part played by the moving cause. They both stress the importance of the particular against the universal, and to that extent they reinforce the doctrines of Λ I–II and of *Metaph.* H. They differ, however, especially from H, in that they also strongly emphasize the significance of the moving cause (which is subordinate in H), in anticipation of the teaching of Λ VI ff. All the main points are made in Λ IV. They are reaffirmed in Λ V in the light of the theory of potentiality and actuality. The theme of the section is indicated in the opening sentence of Λ IV: 'In one sense, causes and principles differ for different things, in another sense, speaking universally and broadly logically, they are the same for everything.' It is again referred to in the concluding sentence of Λ V. With the exception of the last paragraph of Λ IV and the first paragraph of Λ V, which appear to be added, the section is of one piece, although it is possible that it contains another insertion near the beginning of Λ IV.

Λ IV. (1) The statement of the question to be discussed is immediately followed by a lively polemic probably aimed at philosophers who regard numbers as the elements (*stoicheia*) of everything and consequently obliterate the difference between substance and the other categories.[1] But, the philosopher says, there is no common basis for the categories, no higher universal than these. Nor could any of the categories be an element in any other category. And further, no simple element can be the same as a compound of such elements, so if the categories were compounds they could not be basic; but they necessarily are, hence no elements basic for everything exist. A reference to the One and Being is included; they are indeed common to everything but may be discounted (see H VI and p. 133).

(2) After an elliptical, almost unintelligible repetition of the opening sentence (which may indicate that the preceding polemical paragraph is an addition), it is stated that such forming agents as the hot and the cold, the matter that can turn hot or cold as well as the products of such form and such matter as flesh or bone, are indeed substances, but even these principles (i.e. this form, this matter) only apply generally, not universally. Only in a broad logical sense (*kat' analogian*) are the principles the same. Only the abstract

---

[1] The polemic is probably directed against Speusippus; see H. J. Krämer, *Die Geistmetaphysik*, Amsterdam 1964, p. 153.

concepts 'form, privation and matter' apply universally. But different things have different principles. In other words, empirically speaking, genus differs from genus, species from species, the individual from the individual.

(3) After this the importance of the (proximate) moving cause is stressed and it is stated that this cause, too, is different in different cases. With this, it appears, the climax is reached. For deliberately amending the doctrine of the three causes and principles as stated in Λ II (1069^{b}33), the philosopher now teaches that four, not three, principles are involved in all changes: form, privation, matter and the moving cause. At the same time, the terminology is altered. A distinction is made between 'elements' and 'principles'. By themselves, the three causes, as listed in Λ II, are called 'elements'; in combination with the fourth cause or principle they are all called 'principles'. So the two terms are in one sense antithetic, in another their meaning is identical. Both uses of the terms are confirmed in *Metaph.* Δ. Here an 'element' is that which primarily inheres in a thing (1014^{b}14), while a 'principle' is a generating cause from without (1013^{a}7). On the other hand, principles are both inherent and external, and 'elements' are (one kind of) principle (1013^{a}20 ff.).

The amended teaching is illustrated by examples taken from art, not nature—from medicine and architecture. The first of these examples also occurs in Λ III but is there used differently; in Λ III medical skill is an example of the formal cause, in Λ IV of the moving cause. Further down in Λ IV it is once again an example of the formal cause.

(4) In the last paragraph of Λ IV the 'amendment' just introduced is amended once more. Repeating that in a certain manner three causes can be distinguished but in 'this manner' four, the lecturer now unifies the formal with the proximate moving cause and, anticipating the final teaching of Λ, describes the prime mover as the fourth cause. That this paragraph is an addition to the section IV–V is evident not only because it is at variance with its immediate context but also because it is preceded by a clause which occurs in an earlier paragraph, too: 'and the concept of principle is divided into these, namely inherent and external principles' (70^{b}29 and 24). This clause has been deleted here, wrongly; for it indicates that the explanation of the four causes given in the last paragraph is meant as an alternative to that given just before. Moreover, first

(*prôton*) here signifies 'ultimate' whereas before it meant 'proximate'.[1]

Λ v

This chapter begins (1) by restating the doctrine of the supreme importance of substance as compared with the other categories, as do Z 1 and Λ 1. (It appears that a constant fight was conducted against those who tried to obliterate the differences between the categories; see discussion of Λ IV (1).) And then, the philosopher unexpectedly continues, using the living creature as his only example, soul and body, or reason, appetite and body would presumably be the (principal, formal and material) substances. A parallel to this passage is found in Z XI (37ª5), but there the example is used to explain the compound, the living creature, both as a generic concept and as an individual; whereas at this point the example seems to occur without reference to any relevant thesis.

(2) The discussion of the main problem of Λ IV–V, the relation of the universal, general and particular, is resumed. In yet another manner, in a broad logical sense, the philosopher says, actuality and potentiality are principles which are the same for everything. Nevertheless, he adds, these too differ for different things and apply to them differently. And, it is further explained, they coincide with the causes mentioned before. The actual coincides with (separate) form, with the compound and with privation, the potential with matter. Now an approach from another angle is interwoven with the doctrine just expressed, that actuality and potentiality as principles are the same though they apply differently to different things. In one sense actuality and potentiality are the same as each other, in another sense they fall apart.[2] For of some things one may say that at one time they exist potentially, at another actually, for

---

[1] There is one other point of textual interest to be considered. The last sentence should be read as the codices have it—ὡς τό—and not as in Jaeger's edition, following Bonitz—τό ὡς. There are indications (see comment to Λ v) that a model of the heavenly spheres was on display as this lecture was delivered, and it appears that as the lecturer used the words ὡδί and ὡς (here, in this manner), he pointed to the model. This interpretation is reinforced by the observation that there is a close correspondence between πως and ὡς in this sentence and between τρόπον τινά and ὡδί in the preceding sentence (70ᵇ32).

[2] (71ª1) ταῦτα, these, i.e. the substances, should be read, not ταὐτά, the same. It is a mistake to try to make the paragraph seemingly consistent by adapting ταυτα to αἱ αὐταί.

instance water/wine; the elements or powers/flesh, man. This is the doctrine of H VI, according to which matter contains its determination within itself. But, the philosopher here continues, in another sense potentiality and actuality are not one and the same, namely if actuality is not solely found in form or determination but also in the moving cause (where it is not found in H). For in so far as the matter is not the same for different individuals their character (*eidos*) is not the same either[1] (matter determines the individual's character; see pp. 134 ff.). For instance an individual man has for his material cause the elements fire, etc., and for his formal cause species, but beyond this, there are external causes, a particular, his father, and universal causes, the sun and the ecliptic; and these causes do not coincide with matter or form or privation or specific form: they are moving causes.

This argument is an exact parallel to that of Λ IV, in that it first confirms H's theory of the oneness of potentiality and actuality but then criticizes it, if anything more sharply than does Λ IV, by reducing the importance of matter through the emphasis it lays on the external cause. It is thereby stressed that generation does not depend on the potential in matter but on the actual which is outside matter.

It is obvious that we here have to follow a severely contracted argument, condensed from an earlier, longer discussion. Two lines of thought intermingle in it and of this there are several traces. (*a*) The two sentences 71ᵃ4–7 are connected by verbal association, namely the word 'the same', but 'the same' has two quite different meanings in these two sentences; in the first place (71ᵃ4) it refers to unchanging principles, in the second (71ᵃ6) it denotes identical objects entering into different states. (*b*) The parenthesis explaining the connection between actuality and form etc. (71ᵃ7) is oddly placed. (*c*) 'In some instances' and 'in another sense' (*en eniois* and *allôs*, 71ᵃ6 and 11), do not properly correspond to each other although they are meant to in the context. (*d*) The reference to the sun and the ecliptic in 71ᵃ15 is doubly odd, first because the argument requires a reference to the individual father only, and secondly because if the sun and the ecliptic are mentioned the prime mover should also have been referred to. (Did perhaps the model available

---

[1] The second ὤν must be understood as τούτων (71ᵃ12): the first ὤν is a relative pronoun, the second demonstrative. The meaning of the sentence is: those things which do not have the same matter do not have the same character.

at this point only allow the reference to the sun etc., but not to the prime mover?)

(3) From 71ᵃ17 to the end of the chapter the teaching of the entire section is recapitulated, with the aid of tables, the equivalent of a blackboard showing columns of opposites (*systoichiai*), and a model. Let us further look (*horan dei*), the lecturer says, and understand that one can, and cannot, speak of universal principles. The point made is once again that in a broad logical sense it is possible to speak of universal principles but not in an empirical sense. For individuals differ from individuals, genera from genera, species from species. The proximate (formal and material) causes of everything, we read, are individual causes. Man does not beget man, but Peleus begets Achilles.[1] Nor do the same principles apply to all genera; these, too, differ. Indeed, within a species individuals differ from one another because each has its own matter, character and moving cause (its progenitor).

Another recapitulation now seems to follow (71ᵃ29), and it is in this passage that the use of tables and a model is most clearly discernible: the deictic 'here' (*hôdi*)[2] occurs in it four times. (It also occurs in Λ vi, 71ᵇ34 and 37.) As one searches for the principles and elements of substances and relations etc., the lecturer says, it is manifest that, comprehensively speaking, they are the same for everything but, as one considers the particular, they are not. And pointing to the tables he continues: on this column (*hôdi*) they are the same, i.e. matter, form, privation, the moving cause; also substance as the first category; further (pointing to the model) that which is actual in the ultimate sense. But on this column (*hôdi*) they are not the same, i.e. the proximate causes, which are neither generic (good/bad) nor universal opposites (form/privation), but individual opposites (based on matter); also kinds of matter.

Reconstruction of the tables

Column I: Universal	Column II: Particular
1. *B: BA*	1. *B: BA*
Father: son	Peleus: Achilles
2. Substance as such	2. Individual substance

[1] The distinction between man in general and individual man is also made in *Metaph.* Z x; compare Z xi (35ᵇ30 and 37ᵃ7).

[2] ὧδε, ὡδὶ can mean hither, e.g. in Sophocles, *O.T.* 7; 144. See Bonitz's Index for the use of the word in the Corpus.

Column I: Universal	Column II: Particular
3. Form, privation, different genera of opposites—hot and cold, black and white etc.	3. The opposites as they occur in individuals
4. Matter— the four elements	4. An individual's matter—proximate matter.

Beside the tables a model of the heavenly spheres was on display.

As has been noticed, Λ IV–V contains several anticipations of the final teaching of Λ and one may conclude that these anticipations were prompted by the presence in the lecture-room of the model and the tables, which—as one may further surmise—were not available when the Λ-course was first delivered but were constructed after Λ had been incorporated in the school programme, that is, for a re-delivery of the course.

The summing-up at the end of Λ V. The concluding sentence of Λ V refers to the discussion of the principles and their number, and to the question in what sense the principles are the same for everything and in what sense they are not. It is obvious, then, that this summary both duplicates and extends an earlier summary, that at the end of Λ II where, it seems, the discussion of the principles originally ended. It would follow that the section Λ IV–V is an addition to the original Λ-course. Moreover, it is interesting to note that the first part of the Λ V summary fully agrees with three summaries in *Physics* A (on which, as we have seen, Λ draws), namely 191ª3 and 20, and 192ᵇ2. On the other hand, its second part, that is the reference to the sameness or otherwise of the principles, has no parallel either in Λ or *Physics* A; from which one may conclude that the polemic against both a primarily logical, eidetic approach and against a strongly materialistic view, as expressed in *Metaph.* H, is peculiar to the section Λ IV–V, and also, that this section is later than Λ I–II and *Physics* A I–VII.

The section Λ IV–V is characterized first by its endeavour to put strict limits on the use of logic. Logic is here subjected to the test of the empirical and the view is expounded that principles vary even within species and that one can speak of universal principles only in a broad, ambiguous sense. It is characterized secondly by its critique of the view that determination lies chiefly in matter, and that it is possible to explain changes without full regard to the principle of the external cause. So it appears that the philosopher in this section opposes both a purely eidetic and a strictly materialistic view.

The comparative lateness of this section is confirmed by several linguistic peculiarities, especially in Λ v.[1]

Λ VI

This chapter concludes the physical course. In Λ I–II the perceptible substances were discussed; Λ VI proves that an eternal, immovable substance exists and that its nature is actuality.

By its opening statement Λ VI is connected with Λ I (69ᵃ30); by its rejection of materialism it reiterates views expressed in Λ II (71ᵇ28; 69ᵇ22 ff.). In other words, Λ VI starts where Λ II left off.

The argument in Λ VI is based on physical, more particularly, astronomical theory, as found in *Physics* Θ, in *De Caelo* and in *Gen. Corr.* There must exist something eternal and this must be a substance, the philosopher states, for otherwise, if all substances (which are primary) were perishable, everything would be perishable. But this cannot be so, for movement—that is, change—is without beginning or end (hence, the world of changing things has neither beginning nor end); nor does time begin or end, and time is either the same as movement or its affection (*pathos*). Moreover time is continuous and, hence, equals cyclical movement.

The points made so far are summary restatements of discussions contained in *Physics* Θ I, VII and VIII (see also *De Caelo*, A XII; B I). What follows is Λ's specific teaching that the original cause of all movement, though unmoved, is pure actuality. For if the moving cause were only potentially functioning, the philosopher says, movement might be interrupted; hence, it must always be actually functioning. Nor could ideas in Plato's sense be this cause, because they are static and cannot originate movement. It is at this point (71ᵇ20) that Λ begins to evolve its own notion of actuality. Actuality is the universal moving cause as such, immaterial and eternal. The moving cause has no other substance than actuality, unqualified—it is not e.g. love and strife.

---

[1] The position of ἄνευ (without) in 71ᵃ2 is unusual, as is also κάμνον for νόσος (illness) in 71ᵃ10; see Ross, *Comm.* p. 362. Further the double use of the pronoun ὄν in the conditional clause 71ᵃ12 (ὄν μὴ ... ὄν οὐ) is harsh and probably late; see p. 154 n.

After this, the flow of argument is interrupted and what has been stated so far is defended against materialists and distinguished from what Plato held (71ᵇ23 ff.). It is true that potentiality *seems* to precede actuality; yet this is impossible for then nothing might exist. And as to those who make everything emerge from chaos, they make matter move itself—which is impossible: there must be a cause, through actuality. And although Leucippus and Plato speak of eternal movement they explain neither the nature nor the cause of this movement—*neither this (circular) movement here* (pointing to the model) *nor its cause.*[1] Yet it is of the greatest importance to determine what is the first cause. And the paragraph concludes that while in one (presumably semi-popular) sense, potentiality precedes actuality, in another sense actuality is first, as has been explained, namely in this paragraph.

In the last part of this chapter (from 72ᵃ5) the philosopher first invokes the authority of Anaxagoras, Empedocles and Leucippus to reinforce his previous argument about the priority of actuality. If things always remain the same due to cyclical movement there must always be something actually functioning in the same way. Then he makes an additional point about the movement of the heavens, more particularly, the ecliptic of the sun in accordance with *Gen. Corr.* B x. For as the sun approaches the earth or recedes from it, it causes heat to increase or decrease and thus produces the changes in nature. For according to biological theory, the hot and the cold bind or dissolve the elements in compounds and thereby cause changes—generation and destruction. Hence, the philosopher continues, because there is generation and destruction there must be a second movent beside the first, one whose movement varies. Here, he says, pointing to the model, one movent must move in one way and, here, another movent in another way. The movement of the second must either be independent or be caused by the movement of the first. But, he concludes, it is best to assume that the first movent causes both its own unchanging cyclic motion

[1] 71ᵇ34. The traditional text should be read, οὐδὲ ὡδὶ οὐδὲ τὴν αἰτίαν. This text has puzzled critics and various emendations have been proposed. My translation (above, in italics) shows how I think the words should be understood. ὡδὶ also occurs twice in 71ᵇ36: 'For nothing moves by chance; there is always a cause as things are moved either by nature in *this* (*hôdi*) manner [pointing to the model or, rather, moving parts of it], down or up; or by force or reason or something else [God?] in *this* (*hôdi*) manner [again moving parts of the model], i.e. up or down against nature, or in circular motion.'

and the second movent's varied motion; that is, causes all motion. All this, he adds, agrees with what we observe (in the heavens). Should we then not be satisfied that we have discovered the true principles of all movement, all change?

Λ VI—*Conclusions.* The background of Λ VI is the same as that of Λ I–II: the physical and biological theories stated more copiously in the *Physics* and in *Gen. Corr.* But Λ goes beyond merely scientific theories. Its subject is ontological, not physical. It elaborates the notion of the highest substance as immaterial and immutable; not as potentiality and actuality, but as pure actuality. In the *Physics*, too, a perpetually functioning movent is mentioned, but there it is moving itself, not unmoved (*Phys.* 256ᵃ21; 257ᵇ7; also in *De Caelo*, 300ᵇ22);[1] and it is in Λ that this movent is explained as the unmoved primary cause of all movement, as actuality. Moreover, Λ VI, as does Λ I–II, conducts a polemic both against the Platonists and against materialists. It puts pure actuality in the place of pure form, which, it says, is static and so cannot explain the origin of motion (see also *Metaph.* A, 988ᵇ2 ff.). Equally it rejects the view that matter contains the agents of change within itself. Hence, there is a significant contrast between H's and Λ's notions of actuality. Whereas in H actuality is the determining force *within matter* (its latent form), in Λ actuality is the pure cause *outside and beyond matter*. Nevertheless, the edifice of Λ is erected on the basis of scientific doctrines, which, it seems, were widely accepted. Λ concedes that while movement is primarily caused by the first movent, the movements, i.e. changes, in nature (though occasioned by the sun's ecliptic) take place in accordance with their own, biological, laws. In short, Λ subtly reasserts a non-materialistic philosophy, on scientific foundations.

Λ VII—*the theology of* Λ

The essence of what is preserved of Peripatetic theology is found in Λ VII. Here the doctrine of the divine nature of the prime mover is stated but, it seems, incompletely; certain links are missing and questions are raised without being explicitly answered. Hence, although some further explanations of the doctrine are

---

[1] In another passage of the *Physics* the prime mover is unmoved (256ᵇ24). So while the theory of the unmoved mover is categorically maintained throughout Λ, the problem of the first cause of movement is still, or again, under discussion in the *Physics.*

added in Λ ix, the theology of Λ has given rise to various interpretations and speculations in the Middle Ages and in modern
times. It remains a subject of debate, all the more so because
it is hardly possible to supplement the argument of Λ on the basis
of other Corpus treatises. For although the Corpus contains many
echoes of the views of Λ[1] it nowhere offers a much fuller discussion
of them, with the possible exception of *Eth. Nic.* x, 7, where the joy
inherent in the actuality of contemplation is dwelt on at some length.

The doctrinal part of the chapter (72ª19–ᵇ31) is followed by a
refutation of views held by the Pythagoreans and Speusippus, and a
further characterization of the prime mover in conformity with the
teaching of *Physics* Θ x. The main doctrinal section itself is composite
in the sense that it consists of two sets of parallel passages, on the
unmoved mover (72ª24 ff. and 72ᵇ5–14) and on the best life (72ᵇ15–18
and 72ᵇ23–31), and of a third statement of the essentials of the
doctrine, this time with reference to 'tables', indicating that this third
statement was added for a re-delivery of the course (72ª30–ᵇ4).

Résumé. (1) After a recapitulation of points demonstrated in
Λ vi (71ᵇ12 ff. and 72ª7 ff.), namely that there *is* continuous cyclic
movement and that the highest heaven is eternal, the philosopher
turns to the problem of the movent. Whereas, he says, the things that
are in motion also cause motion and, therefore, are merely inter-
mediates,[2] there is something which causes motion, being itself
unmoved, and this something—he adds, repeating the results of
Λ vi—is eternal, substance, actuality. In other words, the immovable
substance for which a search is made (in Λ ii and vi) is stated to be the
original cause of all movement and change.

(2) The question now arises, though it is not put: how can
an immovable substance cause movement? The established[3]
answer comes from ethics and psychology. That which is desired
and thought (visualized) moves while remaining unmoved. And in
contrast to *De Anima* iii, 9 the philosopher emphasizes that we

---

[1] Parallels to the doctrines of Λ are found in *Phys.* A iv, 188ª9; Γ iv, 203ª30;
Θ v and x; *De Caelo*, 270ᵇ7; *Metaph.* Θ; M ix; N i–ii; *De Anima* iii, especially 3, 5
and 9; *Eth Nic.* i, 4; vii, 1153ª14; x, 1175ª15; *Eth. Eud.* i, 8, 1217ᵇi and 31.

[2] I read the traditional text, ἐπεὶ δὲ τὸ κινούμενον καὶ κινοῦν καὶ μέσον τοίνυν,
ἔστι τι ὃ οὐ κινούμενον κινεῖ. The meaning is: motion caused by motion is
derivative. Hence, original motion is caused by something unmoved.

[3] That this is the generally accepted solution to the problem is shown e.g. by
Theophr. *Metaph.* 4ᵇ22 ff. For the 'good' as motive power see also *Phys.* 192ª16;
Gen. Corr. 336ᵇ27; *De Vita et Morte*, 469ª28; *Part. An.* 687ª15; *Inc. An.* 704ᵇ15.

do not think that which we desire to be fine but desire that which we think is fine,[1] i.e. that reason precedes volition. 'Thinking is the beginning' (*archê gar hê noêsis*). However, precisely in what manner the first heaven is caused by thought and desire to circle around the unmoved mover, is not indicated (see conclusion to Λ VII, pp. 164 ff.).

(3) At this point, a demonstration of the theory expounded is given with the aid of tables. On the tables ethical concepts are juxtaposed with logical—not physical—concepts.

The mind is moved by the object of its thought, the philosopher continues, linking the coming demonstration to what has just been said, and *this* column, the column of the immutables, covers that which is intelligible by itself (i.e. requires no sense perception); and here substance is first, and among substances, simple and actual substance. The philosopher emphasizes that by simple he means homogeneous substance, not merely substance as numerically one. He goes on to say: we also find the good and that which is desired for its own sake on this column, and here each time the best in a class or what corresponds to the best, is first. And it is further clear that the end is on this column, for the end for its own sake is a subdivision of the good, whereas the end as a means to an end is not.[2] For it is the end that moves by being desired whereas that which is moved by an end, e.g. a living creature, moves other things: e.g. a man moved by the desire to be healthy exercises his limbs.

The column reconstructed
Objects of Pure Thought—Immutables

Substances—Other Categories		The Good	
Simple, actual substance	Mixed substance	That which is desirable for its own sake: the end	The best in each class, e.g. health, knowledge (see *Eth. Eud.* I, 8, 1217[b]1)

---

[1] But in *De Anima* III, 3 the same view as in Λ VII is expressed. The question of reason versus volition is left open in *Phys.* Θ IV, 253[a]15 ff.

[2] Compare *De Anima*, 415[b]2, where the two meanings of 'the end', οὗ ἕνεκα, are similarly stated. For a full and penetrating analysis of the various passages where the double οὗ ἕνεκα occurs I refer the reader to Professor K. Gaiser's paper, 'Das zweifache Telos bei Aristoteles', in Düring, *Naturphilosophie* etc. The passages discussed are: *Eth. Eud.* 1249[b]9 ff.; *De Anima*, 415[a]26 ff.; 415[b]15 ff.; *Phys.* 194[a]27 ff.; *Metaph.* Λ VII, 1071[b]1 ff.

(4) Now follows another proof to show that the movent is unmoved and actuality, after three previous proofs, one in Λ VII ($72^{a}24$) and two in Λ VI ($71^{b}3$ and 23). At this point, the theory of the unmoved mover is maintained against those who hold that the primary motion of the heaven is its own cause, i.e. that actuality is in the motion (*phora*) itself—a view preserved for us in Theophrastus's *Metaphysics* ($6^{a}5$–14; $10^{a}9$–21; see edition by Ross and Fobes, p. xxv). But, the philosopher says, if this were so it would be possible for the first heaven to change its motion, though not its substance; and only on the assumption that the prime mover is actuality and unmoved is it impossible for the motion to be other than it is; only then is the motion one by necessity. And he sums up by stating emphatically that the heaven and all nature depend on this principle or original cause.[1]

What is necessary is good, according to Λ VII. But it is conceded that necessity has several meanings (this chapter and *Metaph.* Δ, $1015^{a}26$ ff.; see also *De Interpr.* $23^{a}22$ ff.).[2] It is sometimes conceived of as connected with force, and hence, as an evil. Above all, necessity is inherent in mechanistic, materialistic views of nature, for nature as a sequence of causes and effects is nature ruled by necessity. What happens necessarily is opposite to that which is achieved by design. Necessity is said to belong to matter (*Phys.* B IX, $200^{a}1$ ff.; 14). So the Aristotelian treatises contain two sharply contrasted concepts of necessity, one teleological, the other mechanistic.

(5) The lecturer returns to the psychological, ethical theme ($72^{b}15$). In a paragraph, which is terse to the point of obscurity and understandable only in conjunction with the passage which follows, he indicates that our life, in as far as it is spent in contemplating the cosmos, is similar to the best life, though for a short time only. The divine condition equals the best life always,

---

[1] In most editions this sentence ($72^{b}13$) is separated from the preceding and shown as the opening sentence of the following paragraph, which reverts to the ethical theme of the best life and begins with the word *diagôgê*, i.e. life. Although the word *diagôgê* has been variously interpreted it can only refer to the life of man or, broadly, 'animal'; it cannot be used in connection with the heaven or even the 'star-souls'. Hence, a new paragraph begins with *diagôgê*. For the meaning of *diagôgê*, see *Republic*, 344E; *Theaetetus*, 177A; *Eth. Nic.* $1127^{b}35$; $1171^{b}13$; $1176^{b}12$ and 14; $1177^{a}9$ and 27.

[2] The concept is also used in a logical sense, i.e. as the necessity of a conclusion following from its premisses. See *Metaph.* Δ and *Organon*. (Perhaps $72^{b}11$ echoes *Phaedrus*, 245D).

whereas for us such perpetuity is unattainable. And our life of contemplation is similar to the best life because the actuality inherent in it is joyful, as is proved by the fact that waking, perceiving etc., are our most pleasant experiences.

More about the contemplative life is to follow almost immediately. Nevertheless, this paragraph stands by itself, for in it thinking is mentioned as one of the mind's activities along with others, whereas thinking as the highest actuality is the main theme of the following paragraph, which broadens out into theology.

(6) The discussion of thinking, begun earlier in this chapter (72ᵃ26–30), is resumed. Thinking in itself, the philosopher says, is thinking of that which is best in itself and (referring to the divine intellect) thinking in itself in the ultimate sense is thinking of the best in itself in the ultimate sense. There follows a statement on epistemological lines. The intellect thinks itself by partaking of the intelligible; by directly grasping its object[1] it becomes identical with it. Hence, the subject and the object of pure thought are one, for the intellect is the organ corresponding to the intelligible, that is, substance (in the sense of essence). In *De Anima* it is explained that the organ of perception by reflecting the object becomes identical with its form (II, 12, 424ᵃ17 and III, 4); similarly, the intellect is here said to be the same as the intelligible. In the context of Λ as a whole, however, this must be understood to mean that reason is both subject and object. As subject, it *thinks* order; as object, it *is* order—the cosmos. The Greek word *nous* denotes mind, intellect, reason; *noêton* that which is thought, reasoned, ordered.

Next, actuality in relation to the intellect is described. It is said to lie in the thinking of the object by the subject, but, the philosopher adds, the divine seems to belong to the act of thinking rather than to the object. And this actuality which consists in the contemplation of the ordered universe, is the most pleasant and best possible experience, enjoyed by us for some time and intermittently, but by God, even more intensely than by us, for ever. (Fuller discussions of the joy of contemplation are found in *Eth. Nic.* and *Eth. Eud.*)[2]

Finally, interpreting the actuality of reason (as the source of all movement) as life, the philosopher describes God as living and his

---

[1] For the figurative use of 'to touch' (*thigganein*), meaning immediate perception or intuition, see *Metaph.* Θ, 51ᵇ24 and Theophr. *Metaph.* 9ᵇ15.

[2] *Eth. Nic.* 1153ᵃ14; 1175ᵃ15; *Eth. Eud.* 1217ᵃ18.

actuality as the best, eternal life. Indeed, he states that perpetual actuality as such *is* God.

Here the doctrinal part of Λ VII ends. Its main teaching appears to be that the self-contemplation of the divine reason equals the highest actuality. This theory, it has always been thought, contains the essence of the Peripatetic theology. Commentators and theologians have attempted to grasp its full meaning. Does the God of Λ know the pure forms only, or is he also concerned with the lower forms of life? A close examination of the text establishes the first alternative as correct.[1] But certain other questions, too, are implicit in the brief exposition given, and the answers to these must be sought not in the Corpus but in the works of Plato. The theology of Λ is rooted in the *Timaeus*, *Phaedrus* and *Laws*; so much so that one must almost conclude that the Λ-philosopher could presuppose his students' close acquaintance with Plato's writings as he lectured to them.

He does not explain how the Deity by causing the movement of the heavens causes man to strive for the morally best. But this is explained in *Timaeus*, where Plato teaches that by thinking the harmonies of the heavens and making our understanding like to what we thus understand we rise to that goal which the gods have set before us. That is, we learn order by attuning ourselves to the order and reason of the universe (*Timaeus*, 90D). More explicitly still, Plato says in the *Laws*: 'The soul by its own motions, which are called wishes, reflections . . . joy and grief . . . love and hate etc., causes the secondary motions of the bodies, by which these are made to undergo changes; and when the soul acts in conjunction with reason it governs all things rightly and happily as a true goddess' (*Laws*, 896 ff.; translated after R. G. Bury). So, human reason by admiring and emulating the divine reason in action causes the movements of the soul and subsequently the body towards the right order.

Moreover, the concept of life and, it seems, that of the joy of contemplation are derived from Plato. When the Father perceived the created universe as a thing in motion and alive he rejoiced (*Timaeus*, 37C; see also *Phaedrus*, 245C ff.). That cyclic motion is the best and most akin to reason is stated in *Timaeus*, 34A.

Nevertheless, although the theology of Λ is based on Plato's it

[1] See Professor D. J. Allan's excellent analysis of the theology of Λ in *The Philosophy of Aristotle*, Oxford 1952, pp. 118 ff.

also differs from it in some important aspects. (*a*) The Peripatetic prime mover is unmoved whereas Plato's is in motion, moving itself. (*b*) The concept of actuality as the highest principle replaces Plato's soul as the source of motion. (*c*) Λ seems to imply that the world, as it is, is the best possible world and that it is ruled by reason; whereas Plato holds that reason is opposed by unreason, so man must be exhorted to obey reason.

It follows from these differences that Λ, however deeply affected by the thought of Plato, is not the work of a disciple of Plato's nor, as Jaeger assumed, of a comparatively young philosopher who had not yet freed himself of his master's influence; on the contrary, Λ reveals that significant philosophical developments had taken place since the time of the *Timaeus* and the *Laws*, and that certain characteristically Peripatetic concepts had since been formed. Hence, Λ is likely to be considerably later than Plato's last works.[1] Now the question of the time of Λ leads on to another problem, namely whether the theology of the Greek philosophers is purely Greek in its roots or can have taken shape only through the influence of non-Greek religious thinking. It is known that Persian, Mesopotamian or even biblical religious ideas reached Athens about the time when Plato wrote the *Timaeus* (and perhaps also *Phaedrus*), between 357 and 347 B.C.[2] (see above, p. 20), and it was at this time that the twin-concept of the God of heaven as the moral God was first understood and admired in Greece. Subsequently, the enthusiasm for Eastern religion probably subsided for a while (apparently during Alexander's campaigns when it was believed that the whole world would be Hellenized), but it was revived during the last decade or so of the fourth century prior to or coinciding with the rise of the Stoic school. It is likely, therefore, that the theology of Λ, since it significantly differs from Plato's, belongs to

---

[1] A. Mansion (while maintaining that Aristotle conceived of theology as 'first philosophy' in an early phase of his development) rightly emphasizes that some of the ontological doctrines which characterize the theology of Λ represent a move away from Plato. See 'Philosophie première, philosophie seconde et métaphysique chez Aristote' in *Revue philosophique de Louvain* 56 (1958), pp. 165 ff.; reprinted in Hager, *Metaphysik und Theologie des Aristoteles*, pp. 299 ff., especially p. 344.

[2] M. L. West in *Early Greek Philosophy and the Orient*, Oxford 1971, offers —I believe, convincing—evidence of the influence of Oriental conceptions on early Ionian thinking (see especially his chapter on Heraclitus). See also Jaeger, pp. 132 ff.

the phase of the revival of Eastern religious thought rather than to the period of its first impact. We shall return later to the question of the date and the growth of Λ, after completing the analysis of the book.

Λ VII *continued and concluded.* In the penultimate paragraph of the chapter (72^b30–73^a3) a view said to be held by the Pythagoreans and Speusippus is discussed, that the good and the perfect are not found at the beginning of things but belong to the final stage of evolution. The implication seems to be that this view contains a critique of Λ's doctrine of the actuality of the divine reason as the prime cause of all motion and generation. The critique is refuted on the grounds that the actual (man) is prior to the potential (semen). This is a refutation in general Peripatetic terms; it is not specifically related to the theological argument of Λ. The *locus classicus* for the doctrine of the priority of actuality over potentiality is *Metaph.* Θ VIII (49^b24 ff., especially 26). A fuller discussion of the views of the Pythagoreans and Speusippus is found in *Metaph.* N (1091^a33).

The final paragraph of the chapter (73^a3–13) clearly belongs to the physical, not the theological part of Λ; it is connected with Λ VI, not with Λ VII. After repeating that there exists an eternal, immovable substance, separate from perceptible substances, as has been shown, the philosopher continues that it has also been shown that this substance possesses no magnitude, no physical or logically distinguishable parts, because it functions over an infinite period; further that it can neither be affected nor changed. In other words, this substance is immaterial in every sense.

Nearly all the points made here are also made in *Physics* Θ x. There the force that moves the heavens is described as an immaterial power (*dynamis*) inherent in nature itself, and it is of great interest to find that in this paragraph of Λ VII the term 'power' (*dynamis*) occurs instead of 'actuality' (*energeia*) otherwise used throughout Λ. One may, therefore, conclude that this paragraph was composed by a lecturer who was not concerned with theology or the doctrine of actuality but with a problem of physics.

Λ VIII

After the theory of the one unmoved mover, God, has been stated powerfully in Λ VII, the question is unexpectedly posed in Λ VIII whether there is only one original mover or several. The answer is firmly in favour of the existence of several movers and, in the main part of Λ VIII, three theories about the exact number of the movers are outlined. So Λ VIII and VII contradict each other both in the letter and in the spirit of their teaching. Whereas the origin of movement is described as divine in Λ VII it is explained in purely physical, astronomical terms in Λ VIII. Moreover, the main part of the chapter differs from the rest of Λ by its style, which, in contrast to the usual extreme brevity of the book, is elaborate and even copious with features often found in treatises on astronomy and also in doxographic works. Hence, this chapter is generally regarded as inserted, without a dissenting voice, as far as I know.[1] Still, by whom it was inserted, whether by Aristotle himself or a late editor, has remained a point in dispute.[2] It is probable, however, that it was added to Λ by a lecturer who, in re-delivering the course to a new generation of students, found it necessary to satisfy their demands for scientific astronomy to supplement his onto-logical explanations of heavenly movements. To do this, the lecturer—as will soon become clear—incorporated in his course an earlier, probably independent, lecture on theories about the motions of stars, prefacing this lecture by a transitional paragraph and adding to it some comment, either his own or that of some other philosopher. As we shall see, there are some contradictions even within Λ VIII. The chapter may be divided into five parts.

Résumé. (1) (73ª14–23). The chapter begins by posing the question of the one or the several movers, also of the exact number of the movers. The term for mover used here is substance, as in the last, physical, section of Λ VII. The question of the number of the mover-substances is taken up first, polemically. The exponents of the theory of number-ideas, the lecturer says, cannot solve the problem for they have neither arrived at a consistent view (on whether numbers are infinite or limited) nor can they prove what they assert. Hence, he continues, we must argue from the basis of what we have established ourselves.

(2) (73ª23–ᵇ17). After repeating the main points made before (in Λ VI–VII), the lecturer firmly states that, since not only the first heaven moves eternally but there are also other eternal move-ments, namely of the sun, the moon and the planets, there must be

---

[1] It appears that I. Düring, in a hardly successful attempt at unifying the teaching of Λ, dissents from this view. See I. Düring, *Aristoteles. Darstel-lung und Interpretation seines Denkens*, Heidelberg 1966, pp. 214 ff.

[2] Λ VIII is discussed at length by Jaeger (pp. 345 ff.), who believes that it marks a late phase in Aristotle's development.

a corresponding number of eternal, immaterial, immovable mover-substances. So only one question remains, that of the precise number of the movements; for which an answer must be sought, not from mathematician-philosophers but from mathematician-astronomers. Accordingly, the lecturer proposes to place the views of some outstanding astronomers before his students so that they should have an initial grasp of the matter. For the rest, he says, we must both search ourselves and listen to what other researchers have to say, and if their conclusions clash with what we have stated, give further attention to both their views and ours, deciding in favour of the more stringent scientists. This is possibly an allusion to the third theory explained in this chapter, with its two, or even three versions, which are stated without a clear preference shown for any of them (74ª1 ff.). Beyond this, however, it is apparent that the lecturer doubts whether any of the theories devised so far is fully satisfactory—a doubt expressed very strongly by Theophrastus: 'The problem of the number of the spheres, and of the why of any particular number, requires a great deal more deliberation. The astronomers' work, [so far?] at any rate, is inadequate' (Theophr. *Metaph.* 5ª11).

Next the theories of Eudoxus and Callippus about the number of the spheres are delineated, followed by a Peripatetic theory, of which, as we have indicated, two or even three versions are offered.

What is common to all these theories is the assumption that the sun, the moon and the planets each move not in one, but in several spheres, shifting from one sphere to another. In this way, their complex movements which we observe are to be explained. It is further taken as certain that all heavenly bodies move in circular courses, that the circles are concentric, with the smaller running within the larger, and that the earth is the centre.

The lecturer first outlines the theory of Eudoxus, an outstanding Academic mathematician (*c.* 408–355 B.C.). Apart from the outermost, largest sphere of the highest heaven, Eudoxus assumed that three spheres belonged to the sun, three to the moon, and four to each of the five planets, Saturn, Jupiter, Mars, Venus and Mercury, and he thus arrived at a total of 27 heavenly spheres. As the spheres were thought to differ in location and size they were regarded as capable of explaining the movements of the heavenly bodies. In particular, the sun, as it changed from sphere to sphere was believed now to approach, now to recede from the earth.

Still, Eudoxus's theory was felt to be inadequate as new observations were made. In particular, it failed to explain certain retrograde motions of the planet Mars. Besides, it could only approximately account for the movements of the sun. So the theory had to be revised. This was done by the astronomer Callippus, who was about twenty or thirty years younger than Eudoxus. Callippus ascribed five spheres to the sun, five to the moon, five to each of three of the planets (Mars, Venus, Mercury) and four each to two planets (Saturn and Jupiter). His total, therefore, was 33 spheres.

In its turn, Callippus's theory was further revised by the Peripatetics themselves, but from a new viewpoint. The purpose of the Peripatetic revision was, not to account for the observable movements of the heavenly bodies with still greater accuracy, but to explain the ultimate harmony of all heavenly movements or, to show how the uniform motion of the first heaven can cause the complex movements of the sun, the moon and the planets. Hence, the Peripatetic philosopher assumed the existence of still more spheres, namely of re-agent or counteracting spheres, in addition to the main spheres. The re-agent spheres were thought to prevent the original spheres from becoming independent of each other; and so, on the basis of this revised theory, the whole cosmos could be seen as one mechanical unity.[1]

Of this Peripatetic theory at least two versions are here recorded. According to the first, there would be 55 spheres in all. According to the second, which denies re-agent spheres to the sun and the moon, there would be, the lecturer says, 47 spheres. This figure, however, is puzzling: the total should now be 49. Various explanations of the discrepancy between the figures 47 and 49 have been offered by both ancient and modern commentators, who have either held that the text is at fault and that nine (*ennea*) should be read instead of seven (*hepta*) or simply, that the lecturer in computing his figures made a mistake.[2] However there is a third possibility of explaining the total of 47. The lecturer may have

---

[1] On Greek astronomical theory see: T. Heath, *Aristarchus of Samos*, Oxford 1913; W. Burkert, *Weisheit und Wissenschaft*, Nürnberg 1962; S. Sambursky, *The Physical World of the Greeks*, London 1959, pp. 50 ff., 80 ff.; T. Heath, *Greek Astronomy*, London 1932; J. H. Dreyer, *A History of Astronomy from Thales to Kepler*, New York 1953.

[2] On how a mistake may have been caused, see Ross, *Comm. ad loc.*

had in mind yet another version of the theory involving re-agent spheres, on the basis of which 47 was the correct total. And of this version, in the highly condensed or even garbled text we read, the figure 47 would be the only remaining trace.

A concluding statement now follows ($74^{a}14$). Let it be accepted, the lecturer says, that this is the number of the spheres, and hence also of the immovable mover-substances (55 or 49?). And he adds with obvious sarcasm: 'Let others more competent than myself prove that this number (at which we have arrived scientifically) is also logically necessary.'

(3) Although the sarcasm of this remark may well have been aimed at the exponents of the theory of ideas and numbers, the challenge contained in it is taken up by a Peripatetic in the immediately following paragraph, in which it is shown that the number of heavenly motions arrived at *is* logically necessary ($74^{a}17$ ff.). The argument runs thus. If there are no heavenly motions except those relating to stars, and if stars are moved for their own sake, there cannot be more moving substances than mentioned, that is, what has been asserted about their number is based on logical necessity. In brief, since there are no motions beyond those stated there can be no more movers than has been stated. The argument continues with a negative proof. If there were further moving substances they would cause some further movements; but this cannot be, as is reasonable to conclude from the theory of movement in general. For if every movement is for the sake, not of some movement, but of a thing moved, every (primary) movement is related to a star; otherwise, that is, if movement were for movement's sake, there would be an infinite regress. So, each (primary) movement is for the sake of one of the heavenly bodies (which we observe). In brief, the number of heavenly bodies circumscribes the number of movements (=spheres), hence, of mover-substances.

(4) There now follows another logical argument, but this time one which contradicts the rest of Λ VIII ($74^{a}31$). It is now shown that it is impossible for several mover-substances to exist and that there can be only one immaterial, unmoved prime mover.

The connecting link between this paragraph and the preceding is a word—'heaven'. Manifestly, the lecturer says, there can be only one heaven, meaning that only the outermost sphere can be primarily moved. This is proved as follows: essence, pure form, is unique; it is *entelecheia*, that is, perfect independent Being (causing the original motion). Multiplicity, on the other hand, necessarily involves matter, for when (generic) form is severally impressed on matter, several instances of a genus come into being. So as regards both its form and its occurrence the prime mover is unique; it is impossible for several substances to be eternal, immaterial prime movers.

Parallels to this argument are found in *De Caelo*, 278ᵇ5 ff., where the first heaven is stated to be unique and in *Metaph.* K, 1065ᵇ21 ff., where *entelecheia* is said to exist simultaneously with motion. Essentially, however, this paragraph is related to passages like *Metaph.* Z VIII, 1034ᵃ7. There, the uniqueness of the pure generic form is similarly distinguished from the multiplicity of individuals composed of form and matter. It is clear, therefore, that this passage, in which the original thesis of Λ is re-stated against the rest of Λ VIII, has emanated from the logical 'department' of the Peripatos; probably, it was added after the completion of the chapter, and it may well be its last-written section.

(5) The final paragraph of the chapter (74ᵃ38) once more connects astronomy with religion but in a different spirit from Λ VII. It offers an interpretation of the true meaning of ancient Greek beliefs. Our forefathers, the lecturer says, regarded the stars as gods, and to the extent that they considered the forces that move the universe as transcendent they were right; for they anticipated our doctrine of primary mover-substances. The forces referred to are, no doubt, the movers of the several spheres—'star gods'. There is no suggestion in this paragraph of the God of Λ VII who in moving the heavens causes man to seek moral perfection.

Λ VIII—*conclusions.* It emerges from Theophrastus's *Metaphysics*, as well as from the present chapter, that the question of the prime mover, whether there existed only one or several, was keenly debated within the school at some time. As we have seen, Theophrastus considered all the astronomers' theories as unsatisfactory, and he criticized both opposing views. If there is only one mover—he asks—why is not all movement uniform? And if there are several movers, how can different movements all be directed towards the best end (Theophr. *Metaph.* 5ᵃ14 ff.)?

The main part of Λ VIII, section 2, in which various theories about the number of the spheres are expounded, is firmly based on the doctrine of the existence of several movers, although the possibility is not excluded that the movers are interconnected. It is this section which is stylistically distinguished (73^a23-^b18); as is also section 5 (on ancient religious beliefs). We note further that the lecture contains no deictic pronouns; hence, that it was not composed with a model in mind. These various observations make it likely that sections 2 and 5 were originally an independent work, of a comparatively early date. For although Callippus lived possibly until 320 or 315 B.C., and although some non-Callippean theories are included, the lecture may go back to 325 B.C. or to a date not much later.[1]

The remaining sections, on the other hand, are almost entirely written in the usual short-hand style of the Corpus. Moreover, the lecturer introducing the chapter is not committed to either of the alternative views, as is clear from his opening question: is there one, or are there many prime movers? By now, it seems, the debate on this issue had been going on for some time; logical arguments in favour of both views had been constructed and are incorporated in the chapter. So, the framework of the chapter—if we may call it that—is very probably a great deal later than its main part. It may be as late as *c*. 300 B.C. A linguistic observation seems to support this late dating. At the beginning of the chapter the word *apophasis* occurs in the quite unusual or even unnatural meaning of 'statement' or 'opinion'; its normal meaning is, of course, 'negation'. It is likely, therefore, that the correct reading is *apophansis* which means 'affirmative statement'. *Apophansis* is a term coined by the Stoics, whose school was founded *c*. 304 B.C.[2]

---

[1] Professor W. Theiler, however, believes Λ VIII to be the latest-composed part of Λ, assigning the chapter to *c*. 330 B.C. On the other hand, he considers Λ as a whole to be early and, in accordance with this assumption, he distinguishes between an Aristotelian *metaphysica generalis* and *metaphysica specialis*, of which the former is characterized by its connection with astronomy (Λ) and the latter by the discovery of 'intelligible norms' (Z, H). See 'Die Entstehung der Metaphysik des Aristoteles', in *Museum Helveticum* 15/2 (1958); reprinted in Hager, *Metaphysik und Theologie des Aristoteles*, pp. 266 ff., especially 272, 274, 287.

[2] There is only one other instance of ἀπόφασις in the sense of affirmative statement, in *Rhet.* A VIII, 1365^{b}26, but here, too, the correct reading may well be ἀπόφανσις. Alternatively, the transitional clause containing the word ἀπόφασις could belong, not to the lecturer, but to a late editor who no longer understood the difference between ἀπόφασις and ἀπόφανσις, in which case the opening question was originally followed directly by the reference to the exponents of the theory of ideas (73^a17).

Λ IX

This chapter returns to the subject of Λ VII, *nous*, but it would be wrong to assume that the inquiry into the problems of the mind, begun in Λ VII and interrupted by an 'interpolated' Λ VIII, is continued and taken further here. No new doctrine is stated in Λ IX, nor are the theories expounded before developed more profoundly. What we find is that the points made in Λ VII are defended against several objections and so reasserted, either explicitly or implicitly: i.e. that thought is actuality; that the subject and the object of thought are the same; that the mind thinks itself; that what the human mind enjoys for a time the divine mind enjoys eternally.[1]

Against these tenets, the following objections had been raised in the first place: that the mind is not continually active; that it is not independent in its function; that its object is not always the best.

Résumé. The mind, or reason, the lecturer says, is regarded as the most divine of all that has been discovered,[2] but how it can be that is a question which causes some discomfort. For if (at times) it thinks nothing, what is so exalted about it?[3] Also, if it thinks something but is dependent on some other agency[4] it would think only potentially and so would not be the best substance. Further, if its object is not itself but something else, does it shift from one thing to another and even dwell on some (sordid) matter?

---

[1] H.-J. Krämer, in his article 'Zur geschichtlichen Stellung der aristotelischen Metaphysik' (*Kant-Studien* 58/3, 1967), assembles evidence to prove that the theology of Λ can only be understood on the basis of an intimate connection with post-Platonic Academic thought (for Λ IX see especially p. 333 with n. 70). On the importance which Krämer attaches to Xenocrates for an understanding of the Aristotelian metaphysics, see his *Der Ursprung der Geistmetaphysik*, Amsterdam 1964/7.

[2] φαινόμενα for 'things discovered' is puzzling, but the word ἐπιφαίνεσθαι occurs with a similar meaning in *Phygn.* 809ᵃ8; see Ross, *Comm.* ad loc.

[3] It should be realized that the tone of this lecture (Λ IX) is relaxed rather than solemn, as indicated by the choice of the words 'discomfort' (*dyskolia*), 'exalted', or 'grand' (*semnon*), and perhaps also the clause 'there are things one would rather not see than see' (74ᵇ33). A similar, light tone is occasionally discernible in other parts of Λ, e.g. Λ V, where the lecturer, after stating that man is not the cause of man but Peleus the cause of Achilles, picks out an individual student to tell him: your cause is your father (71ᵃ22).

[4] The allusion is probably not to a common, or supreme, sense organ, *koinon* or *kyrion aisthêtêrion* (*De Vita et Morte*, 467ᵇ28; *De Somno*, 455ᵃ20), but any one of the sense organs, sight, hearing etc., which provide *nous* with an object; see Ross, *Comm.* ad loc.

No doubt, what is preserved in this chapter (as also in *De Anima*), is a debate between two schools of psychologists, idealistic and empiricist. The lecturer maintains the idealistic viewpoint; the objections raised are rooted in empiricist theories of cognition. That thinking is dependent on something else, namely perception, is stated in *De Anima* III, 8 (432ᵃ6); and it is, of course, the Epicurean view, too (Diog. L. x, 49 and 66). The mind is nothing actually before it thinks: this is asserted several times in *De Anima* III, 4 (429ᵃ23 and 29; 429ᵇ32).

Against these objections the idealistic doctrines of Λ VII are maintained, as they are also in *De Anima* III, 5 (where the active mind is the supreme agency perpetually functioning), and partly in III, 4 (where the mind *can* think itself, 429ᵇ23). The argument runs as follows. Manifestly, the mind always has for its object the most divine and noble. For (*a*) if it changed its object it would change for the worse; moreover, in that case, the mind would not be immutable; (*b*) if it only thought potentially, thinking would be constant effort;[1] (*c*) if the mind could think the good and the bad, its object (the good or the best) would be nobler than the mind itself. The conclusion is that the mind, if it is the supreme agency, thinks itself. Reason contemplates reason, which is the noblest object; thinking is thought of thought.

An objection now follows, which, with its corollary, is aimed at the doctrine just expounded, that thought is of itself (74ᵃ36). How can this be maintained, the critics imply, since it is apparent that all apprehension is (primarily) of something external, and only secondarily of itself? And if, accordingly, the subject and the object of thought differ, where lies the good, in the subject or the object? These objections are refuted on the grounds that a distinction must be made between the productive and the theoretical sciences. In the former, the matter may be abstracted; the latter are concerned with pure form, the *logos*. Whereas in the productive sciences (e.g. architecture), the substance or essence of a thing are the objects of thought (e.g. the idea of a house, in the mind of the architect), in the theoretical sciences the definition, or thought itself, is the sole object, and reason is concerned with reason. And with this, the second objection is also answered. As the subject and object of thought are the same the question to which of them the good belongs, does not arise.

---

[1] On effortless activity see *Metaph.* Θ, 50ᵇ24.

Once again, the criticism offered has its basis in empiricist theory, as expressed in *De Anima* III, 2, a chapter dealing with perception. In it, it is taken as certain that we primarily perceive an external object but secondarily perceive that we perceive.[1] A similar view was held about the mind as may be concluded from III, 4, where the function of the mind is described as analogous to that of the perceptive organs (429ᵃ13 ff.). According to this view, thought is primarily of forms embedded in compounds which the senses present, and only secondarily of itself. Against this, Λ IX teaches the absolute identity of reason as the subject and reason as the object, a doctrine to which parallels are found in *De Anima* III, 7 (431ᵃ1) and in the complex chapter III, 4 (430ᵃ5).

The final paragraph of the chapter (75ᵃ6 ff.) is condensed to such a degree that interpretations of it must vary. There is yet another difficulty, the lecturer says, in cases where the object of thought is composite (not necessarily a compound of matter and form). In such circumstances, the critics maintain, the mind would undergo changes as it shifts from one part to another of the compound. But, the lecturer replies, that which has no matter (even if composite) is indivisible, as is the human mind, as well as that composite entity which is the mind's object during one certain time. For its object is not the parts at one moment and another, but the whole, which is something beyond the sum of its parts, during an entire period; e.g. the object of the mind is not some part of the good at one time and some other part of the good at another time but the best as a whole during its entire time of life; while the object of thought itself, i.e. divine thought, is the best throughout eternity.

This objection, too, seems to have come from the empiricists, who hold that the mind is merely a receptive organ, which undergoes changes as it adapts itself to its varying objects (*De Anima*, 429ᵃ14 ff.). The lecturer's answer, on the other hand, is based on the following mainly eidetic views. (*a*) Even thought can be compounded (*De Anima* III, 6, 430ᵃ29); even pure form has parts (*Metaph.* Z X, 1035ᵃ9; ᵇ33). (*b*) The whole is more than its combined parts (*Metaph.* Z XVII, 1041ᵇ16 ff.). (*c*) The best (i.e. perfect virtue) is

---

[1] In *De Anima* III, 2, the problem of our awareness of our cognitive acts is discussed and it is explained that the organ responsible for such awareness is not a common or supreme organ but, in each case, one of the perceptive faculties operating in its own sphere; e.g. we know through sight that we see.

attained over a whole lifetime (*Eth. Nic.* 1, 7, 1098ᵃ18 ff.). (*d*) Indivisible[1] form is the object of thought of an indivisible mind in indivisible time (*De Anima* III, 6, 430ᵇ15).

Λ IX—*Conclusions.* Throughout this chapter, the theory of the supremacy of the mind is maintained against objections, and there is little doubt that the chapter was added to an already existing course, probably, as Λ VIII, in response to queries from students, who in this instance, were influenced by empiricist views. At the same time, one may conclude from this chapter that during the interval between the writing of Λ VII and Λ IX the cognitive faculties had been intensely studied, or even, that the problems of epistemology and psychology in general had attracted much interest both outside and within the school.

Λ X

This chapter consists of two clearly distinguishable sections, 75ᵃ11–25 and 75ᵃ25 to the end of the chapter. The first section relates to the theology of Λ VII, the second to the doctrines of the physical part of the Λ-course, Λ I–II and Λ VI.

First section. Although it had been clearly stated that the divine mind—the prime mover—rules the universe for the best, this doctrine is now made the subject of a discussion. Two critical questions relating to it are to be answered. (*a*) Does not the good of nature lie in the order of nature as a whole rather than in a separate, supreme mover? (*b*) Can the order of nature really be directed towards the common best although, admittedly, many parts of nature move, not in accordance with necessary laws, but as chance makes them? Both these questions come from scientifically oriented philosophers. The view that the good is immanent in nature has its parallel in the doctrine that movement is its own cause;[2] teleological philosophy is rejected by the Atomists as well as by Theophrastus.[3]

The lecturer answers both questions with the aid of metaphors. Where does the good of an army lie—he asks—in its organization or in the general? It lies rather in the general because it is by

---

[1] On the dispute about the indivisibility, or divisibility, of pure form, see discussion of Z X and XI, p. 99.

[2] This doctrine is stated in Theophr. *Metaph.* 10ᵃ9 ff. See also *De Caelo*, 300ᵇ22 and above pp. 162, 168 and 182.

[3] Theophr. *Metaph.* 10ᵃ22 ff.

reason of the general that the army is organized. He then points out that while one order pervades the universe it is an order which admits of differences as in a house in which free people as well as slaves and animals live. There it is the free people who strictly obey the laws whereas the others follow their own impulses. Nevertheless, each in their own way, form part of a common whole. In this metaphor, the free people may represent the heavenly bodies which move by necessity, and the slaves etc., all sublunary creatures;[1] or, as the Peripatetic philosophy permits chance to play a part beside the causal laws, the first may refer to the phenomena occurring necessarily and the second to all that which happens accidentally.

So, this section of Λ x reaffirms the teaching of Λ vii, but in a changed style. None of the essential concepts of Λ vii—God, mind or prime mover—arc referred to; instead, one finds the liberal use of political metaphor. It is likely, therefore, that this passage is rather later than Λ vii. Moreover, the concept of the free person, as the one who always acts in accordance with the law, is unusual in the Aristotelian writings;[2] it is, however, a well-known Stoic concept: 'Those who are ruled by anger, desire, or any other passion or wickedness are slaves, and those who live in accordance with the law are free.'[3]

Second section. Secondly, the physical doctrines of Λ are vigorously defended against a number of alternative views, mainly those of the Platonists. As one reads the section it appears to be episodic—a 'mosaic' according to Jaeger; still, on closer study a design emerges. As the philosopher makes his several points he broadly follows the order of the argument as developed in Λ i–ii and Λ vi. Moreover, since he amplifies his polemic by assertions paralleled in *Metaph.* A and N and also Θ, it is clear that his defence of Λ has its roots in the doxographic-critical course which formed part of the programme of the Peripatos. The doctrine underlying the entire section is that of the one moving principle, that is, of the final cause which is, at the same time, the efficient cause.

---

[1] See Ross, *Comm.* ad loc.

[2] See Bonitz's Index, s.v. ἐλεύθερος.

[3] Philo; Arnim, *SVF* iii, 87, 42. The only possible parallel to this conception that I can find in earlier philosophy occurs in *Laws* xii, 941C-942A, where Plato rules that, for crimes against the State, free citizens should be punished more severely than strangers and slaves.

(1) (75ª25). The section begins with a restatement of the theory of the substrate, which is matter (see Λ I, 69ᵇ2 and Λ II, 69ᵇ9). (A full discussion of this theory is, of course, preserved in *Physics* A.) The views of all those who make everything spring from two contraries, disregarding the substrate, are repudiated (see *Metaph.* N I, 1087ª29).[1] Nor can matter be one of the contraries, still less the bad, as Plato held (see *Metaph.* A VI, 988ª9–15; N IV, 1091ᵇ35; *Philebus*, 25E–26B). The disciples of Plato allow neither the good nor the bad to be a principle (they regard number as the ultimate principle— an untenable view). Others rightly hold that the good is a principle (Empedocles and Anaxagoras) but they cannot say in what sense it is a principle, namely as the final cause (see *Metaph.* A VII, 988ᵇ7). Of these thinkers, Empedocles confuses form and matter and absurdly makes strife, which is the same as the bad, an imperishable principle (see *Metaph.* A IV, 985ª4; VII, 988ᵇ7; Θ IX, 1051ª19). Anaxagoras makes the good the efficient cause but then the final cause, towards which the Mind moves, would be something other than the good, so there would be a contrary to the good—which is absurd (*Metaph.* A IV, 985ª19 and VII, 988ᵇ7). It is at this point that the philosopher clearly expresses the view that the efficient cause and the final cause are one. Medicine which produces health contains within itself the form of health which is its objective. And the philosopher concludes his polemic about the contraries by a summary statement. All those who have expounded theories about the contraries, he says, have failed to treat them methodically—as only the Peripatetics do.

(2) (75ᵇ13). The other thinkers cannot explain why some things are perishable and other things imperishable because they derive all from the same principles, and not from three different substances, as we do (see Λ I, 69ª29). The mythologists derive Being from not-Being, and the Eleatics regard everything as one (see *Metaph.* A V, 986ᵇ10). Moreover no one else can explain why there is perpetual generation (see *Metaph.* Λ II, 69ᵇ11 and 19; *Gen. Corr.* II, 10, 337ª17 ff.).

(2a) (75ᵇ17). Once again it is stated that two principles do not suffice, but this time it seems that the further principle which the

---

[1] It is interesting to note that the question of the 'third' is discussed with complete impartiality in *Gen. Corr.* where arguments both in favour and against the assumption of a substratum are successively stated. See *Gen. Corr.* I, 7, 324ª10 ff., especially 19.

lecturer has in mind is the moving (efficient) cause (see *Metaph.* Λ IV, 70ᵇ22 and compare *Metaph.* Λ II, 69ᵇ33). Besides, on the basis of all other views wisdom and the noblest science would have a contrary. But on the basis of our view ignorance can only relate to that which has matter, whereas that which is primary, the mind or reason, reflects reason only, and hence, has no contrary (see Λ IX; *De Anima* III, 4, 430ᵃ5 and 7, 431ᵃ17).

(3) (75ᵇ24). If only perceptibles existed, as the theologians (i.e. mythologists) and physicists hold, there would be neither an ultimate principle (of movement) nor order etc. (see Λ VI, 71ᵇ22). Forms or numbers cannot be the cause of anything, least of all of motion (see *Metaph.* A IX, 991ᵃ10 and ᵇ9). Further, the contraries cannot be moving (efficient) causes for if they were they would only operate potentially, and hence could cease to operate, in which case there could not be the eternal movement of the heavens (see Λ VI, 71ᵇ3–22).

(4) (75ᵇ34). It is impossible to explain how numbers, soul and body, and, generally, form and the compound can be one, except on the basis of our doctrine of the efficient = final cause. (Compare the somewhat different version of this doctrine in *Metaph.* H VI, 1045ᵃ7ff.; 45ᵃ31; 45ᵇ23. On the problem of the unity of number, see H III, 1044ᵃ3 ff.)

(75ᵇ37). Those who regard number as the ultimate (Speusippus), developing the different substances from numbers, make the universe incoherent and give it many governing principles (see *Metaph.* Λ VI, 72ᵃ15 ff. and *Metaph.* N III, 1090ᵇ13). Here, the lecturer adds: 'But the world will not be governed badly—"The rule of many is not good; let there be one ruler".'

It would be wrong to assume that the Homeric quotation is meant as a rebuttal of the theory of the many movers as expounded in Λ VIII. It primarily refers to the Speusippean theory of numbers just stated. But if it has a second meaning the allusion may well be to the contemporary political scene. In that case, however, it would less fit the era of Alexander than that of the wars of the diadochs, and as it has a triumphal ring one may conjecture that the reference is to Cassander who after the battle of Ipsus (301 B.C.) restored the rule of Macedonia over Greece. It would then be likely that Λ x was composed as a spirited attack on the Platonists who, following the fall of Demetrius of Phalerum (307 B.C.), may well have tried vigorously to damage or destroy the prestige of the Peripatos.

Section 2 of Λ x is in the nature of an appendix to Λ I–II and Λ VI. The views contained in it are not explicitly stated but merely referred to. In each case, with one exception, the lecturer points out the absurdities to which other theories lead, only to say that the Peripatetic philosophy has provided adequate solutions of the various problems discussed. The exception is the paragraph stating once again that two principles do not suffice, and also that there is no contrary to wisdom etc. (75^{b}17–24). Here, a proof of the Peripatetic doctrine is offered; besides, this paragraph is marked off from the rest of the section (*a*) by its use of the connecting particle 'and' (*kai*) instead of 'further' (*eti*)—which otherwise occurs throughout; (*b*) by its relation, not to Λ I–II and Λ VI, but to Λ IV and possibly Λ IX. With the exception of this paragraph, the combination of Λ I–II, Λ VI and Λ X presents the familiar pattern of a statement of doctrine followed by a polemic to defend that doctrine. Similarly Z IX is related to Z VII–VIII, Z XI to Z X, and Z XIV to Z XII. Moreover, the section is introduced by the phrase, '. . . should not remain unsaid, or undisclosed' (*dei mê lanthanein*), as is the case with other chapters, e.g. H III and IV, and Λ VIII.[1]

Book Λ—*conclusions*

Of the two courses which together form book Λ, the first course, the physical, comprises Λ I–VI and Λ x(2). Its nucleus is found in Λ I–II and Λ VI. The three kinds of substance, which are its theme, are stated in Λ I (69^{a}30), and a sentence (in the form of a question) emphatically implying that all movement and change has now been explained occurs at the end of Λ VI (72^{a}18). To this nucleus Λ III–V and Λ x(2) were added for differing reasons, as has been pointed out. It is true that the original course appears to be brief but we must bear in mind that what we read are records of lectures, which in oral delivery were, no doubt, much fuller than their preserved counterparts. In the case of Λ x(2), e.g. where we find the briefest possible allusions to Peripatetic doctrine, it is likely that the lecturer explained those doctrines in detail, and that what is recorded in this section originally occupied several teaching hours.

---

[1] By contrast the first section of Λ x is introduced by the phrase 'we must investigate' (*episkepteon*). In Λ x (1) a clear-cut question is asked and answered in detail. In Λ x (2) several objections are referred to but the answers to them are merely hinted at.

Correspondingly, Λ VII contains the nucleus of the theological course, although in this instance it is probable that the lecture was not only shortened for the record but the record itself abridged. Λ VIII, Λ IX and Λ X (1) are additions to this course—or to the whole.[1] The *Ur-Λ*, therefore, consisted of Λ I–II, Λ VI and Λ VII. One may raise the question whether perhaps the two courses were merely put together by a librarian-editor, but this possibility should be ruled out on the grounds that Λ VII is linked to Λ VI not by a stereo-typed editorial phrase but by means of a somewhat copious summing-up of the doctrines of Λ VI, that is, in a manner characteristic of a Peripatetic philosopher lecturing to his students. So it may be concluded that the *Ur-Λ* as a combined course of lectures was actually delivered at the school.

Time of Λ. On the principle that a shorter, more dogmatic version is later than a longer, fully argued one, the *Ur-Λ* follows *Physics* A I–VII and Θ I–IX, also *Metaph.* H and the main part of *Gen. Corr.* However, it precedes *Physics* A VIII–IX and Θ X (and probably also *De Caelo*).[2] The added sections of Λ, on the other hand, presuppose *Physics* A VIII–IX and Θ X; in particular, the paragraph 1073ᵃ5 ff. depends on *Physics* Θ X. It is noteworthy, too, that Anaxagoras and, to a lesser extent, Empedocles are quoted with approval in *Metaph.* H and *Ur-Λ*, but are sharply criticized in *Metaph.* A (with the exception of A III) and in Λ X(2); so it appears, as also on other grounds, that the praise of these philosophers belongs to an earlier phase than their criticism. As, no doubt, one or two decades elapsed between the composition of the original and the various added parts of Λ, the *Ur-Λ* probably falls somewhere in the middle of that fruitful period 317–307 B.C. while the remaining sections are likely to belong to a date near 300 B.C.

Not only in its theological part but also in its physical sections, Λ reflects a non-materialistic philosophy; which, with the exception of most of Λ VIII, is maintained even more strongly in the added than in the original chapters. Hence, the Λ-course may have been conceived as an antithesis to courses of an empirical, materialistic tendency, e.g. *Metaph.* H. However, the controversy did not end

---

[1] It is conceivable that the present arrangement of Λ is due to a librarian or editor. In particular, it is not unlikely that Λ VIII and X (1 and 2) were shifted from a position at the end of the physical course to their present position at the end of Λ.

[2] See below, Excursus.

there. In its turn, Λ provoked criticism within the school and new attempts to advance scientific, empirical theories. In *Metaph.* B (996ᵃ22) the concept of an unmoved mover or an unmoved absolute good is repudiated, and many severe strictures of the doctrines of Λ are found in the so-called *Metaphysics* of Theophrastus. In this work, or in the short fragment of it which has been preserved, several points are made in deliberate opposition to Λ.

Whether or not the author of this fragment is Theophrastus,[1] one cannot doubt that the work is an esoteric treatise, that is, the record of lectures delivered at the school. Its style, although a close examination may reveal some individual peculiarities, shows the characteristic brevity of the style of the Corpus. It has other features in common with some Corpus treatises, e.g. *Metaph.* B. On the whole it seems to be less dogmatic than aporetic, raising problems rather than solving them.[2] Often it is difficult to determine which is the view held by the author; while clearly inclining towards empiricism he seems to aim at offering an almost comprehensive survey of opinion.

We have mentioned before that the author of the fragment is well acquainted with the controversy of the one mover of the heavens versus many movers (see discussion of Λ vIII); also that he criticizes both views because they leave many problems unsolved. He criticizes the doctrine of the unmoved mover as not adequately supported by proof (7ᵇ15), and indeed as untenable since movement is of the essence of the universe—its life (10ᵃ13). He doubts that cyclical movement is the best (5ᵇ25 ff.) and asks how non-cyclical movement can possibly be an imitation of cyclical movement (5ᵃ17 and ᵇ20 ff.). He criticizes not only theories separating the heavenly cyclical movements from the rectilinear movements in the sublunar sphere (5ᵇ19 ff.) but also doctrines on the interconnection of heavenly movements and changes on earth, including a view—which he says is much propagated—according to which the ecliptic course of the sun is the cause of all changes (7ᵇ1 ff.). Above all,

[1] See Introduction to Ross-Fobes's edition of the *Metaphysics* of Theophrastus, pp. ix ff.

[2] Compare J. B. Skemp's analysis of Theophrastus's *Metaphysics* in 'The *Metaphysics* of Theophrastus in relation to the doctrine of *kinêsis* in Plato's later dialogues' (in Düring, *Naturphilosophie* etc.). While appreciating the critical aspects of this metaphysics, Professor Skemp also points out its underlying positive doctrines which he shows to be close to Plato's views in the *Timaeus* and *Sophist*.

he sets strict limits to a teleological explanation of the phenomena of nature, thereby revealing his scientific outlook ($10^{a}22$ to end of fragment). In short, it appears that, if Λ is an antithesis to Peripatetic materialism, Theophrastus's *Metaphysics* is the antithesis of the teleological philosophy of Λ.[1]

It is of special interest to note that Theophrastus ascribes the theory of the sun's movement as the cause of change to 'some', that is to Peripatetic philosophers who remain unnamed (not to Aristotle), although this theory is stated, or, in any case, briefly referred to, in *Gen. Corr.* B X, that is, in a work included in the Corpus and commonly regarded as a treatise by Aristotle. In general, Theophrastus's *Metaphysics* is significant both because it vividly reflects intra-school controversy and polemic and because it reveals that growing trend towards scientific empiricism which was to lead to the appointment, or election, of Strato the physicist as the next scholarch. So the date of Theophrastus's *Metaphysics* may well be the second half of the headship of Theophrastus, 300–287 B.C.

*   *   *

Excursus: The Theory of the Proper Place

The relationship of the unmoved mover to that of the proper, or natural, place (*topos oikeios*) remains a much-debated problem. According to the latter doctrine—which is mainly preserved for us in *De Caelo*, with references to it elsewhere, chiefly in *Physics, Gen. Corr.* and *De Anima*—the four elements each have their own proper place in the cosmos, which they must occupy unless they are debarred from it by force. Earth is in the centre, i.e. lowest; above it is water; above water, air; above air, fire. Two of the elements, fire and air, have an upward tendency, the other two tend downwards. There are indications that a fifth element, ether, even above fire and air, was included in the theory, or in some version of it.

[1] For a recent study of the relation of Aristotelian and Theophrastian theories about the elements and their changes, see P. Steinmetz, 'Ansatzpunkte der Elementenlehre Theophrasts im Werk des Aristoteles', in Düring, *Naturphilosophie* etc.

The theory is, it seems, of Peripatetic origin, with hardly any conception in pre-Socratic or Platonic thinking, from which it could be said to have been derived (see F. Solmsen, *Aristotle's System of the Physical World*, Ithaca University Press 1961, pp. 128 ff. and 266 ff.).

Two main problems arise: (1) Are the theories of the unmoved mover and of the proper place compatible with each other? (2) Which of the two theories belongs to an earlier phase of Peripatetic thinking?

(1) There are signs that the theory of the proper place itself underwent an evolution. Initially, it seems, it was meant to explain the cosmos as we first perceive it, with earth beneath the ocean, air above the surface of land and sea, and fiery stars highest in the heaven. But then the question was asked: if each of the elements is naturally carried to its own place, how is it that, in infinite time, the elements have not become separated from each other and are thus at rest (*Gen. Corr.* II, 10, 337ª8)? So, if the theory was to be upheld another (dynamic) dimension had to be added to it. Not only had the basic position of the elements to be explained but also the movements within them and their combinations. While the first (static) version of the theory was physical-astronomical, its second (dynamic) version has a biological basis in that the 'powers' (*dynameis*) hot and cold, dry and moist, are shown to be significant. It is at this point that the theory of the proper place is connected with that of the heavenly movements. Whereas the motion of the highest heavens is uniform and cyclical, the sun moving on its ecliptic course is at some time nearer and at some time further away from the earth, causing heat and dryness to increase or decrease, and thereby inducing changes within the elements, and hence movements on earth (*Gen. Corr.* II, 10). In this way, the theories of the prime mover and of the proper place appear to be in harmony with each other.

Still, the theory of the proper place relies heavily on the forces within matter. If it is related to doctrines of heavenly motions the connection is rather with the theory of the self-moving heaven as expressed in *Physics* Θ V (256ª21 ff.; 257ᵇ1ff.) and Θ X (267ᵇ2 ff.) than with that of the unmoved mover, in accordance with *Metaph.* Λ VI or VII. For in the theory of the proper place the changes and movements of the elements are the result of biological and mechanical causes, not of the final cause; they are not directed towards the good as their end. So even if, at some stage, the theory of the proper place related earthly to heavenly movements, basically, it is a materialistic theory, in contrast to Λ VI or VII. Besides, in *De Caelo* the heavenly sphere with its cyclical movements and the sublunar sphere where movement is rectilinear appear to be completely separated; there is no hint of their interconnection.

H. von Arnim was the first forcefully to express the view that the two theories are irreconcilable (in 'Die Entwicklung der aristotelischen Gotteslehre', *Sitzungsberichte der Akademie der Wissenschaften in Wien*, 1931). Since the elements naturally move upwards or downwards, von Arnim argues, a movement induced by an unmoved mover would be against nature, and since that which is against nature cannot precede what is natural, the doctrine of an original unmoved mover is inconceivable within the theory of the proper place. But W. K. C. Guthrie maintained against von Arnim that the doctrine of the unmoved mover was added to the doctrine of the proper place as the crowning aspect of Aristotle's philosophy of heavenly and earthly movements ('The development of Aristotle's theology', *Classical Quarterly*, 1933 and 1934).

(2) Equally, the question of the relative time of the two theories has remained controversial. Jaeger believed that Aristotle conceived the theory of the unmoved mover while he was still under Plato's influence and indeed a member of the Academy; and that he devised the theory of the proper place at a maturer stage when he had moved towards a scientific, empirical standpoint. Von Arnim, on the other hand, considers the theory of the proper place to be early and the theology of Λ as representing the final phase of Aristotle's thinking. G. A. Seeck, in a contribution to the Fourth Symposium Aristotelicum, Göteborg 1966, reasserts Jaeger's view. The theory of the proper place, he argues, has no room for an unmoved mover. As a physical theory it is complete in itself and belongs to a mature phase in Aristotle's development (see 'Leicht-schwer und der unbewegte Beweger', published in Düring, *Naturphilosophie* etc., pp. 210 ff.).

This is indeed the more probable view. While the possibility cannot be excluded that, during some period, the two theories were held within the school concurrently, they are essentially incompatible with each other. Still there is nothing to indicate that either was conceived as a direct antithesis to the other, although both theories were criticized within the school. We have seen that the theory of the unmoved mover was attacked (see above, pp. 182 ff.), and, equally, there are passages which suggest that the doctrine of the proper place, too, was criticized or even ridiculed (see *Phys.* Θ IV, 254^{b}33–256^{a}2, especially 255^{a}6 ff., a passage possibly directed against *De Caelo* IV, 3).[1] However, the general trend of thought pointed to science and empiricism, and there are signs that of the two theories that of the proper place made the more lasting impression. It was accepted as valid by Strato, albeit with important modifications (see fragments 50–3 and 73 in Wehrli's edition). On the other hand there is little evidence of the survival of the theory of the unmoved mover. Cicero certainly did not know of it as a celebrated, clearly-defined theory; on the contrary he angrily describes the theology of the Peripatetic and Academic schools as a confused mass of contradictory conceptions (*De Nat. Deorum* I, 33 ff.). In conclusion it is likely that the theory of the proper place if not in its original, at least in its dynamic-biological form, was conceived later than the doctrine of the unmoved prime mover.

---

[1] The passage occurs in a composite chapter, in which the criticism of the theory of the proper place is followed by a defence of it after the theory has been restated in the terms of potentiality and actuality (255^{a}23 ff.; 30 ff. to 256^{a}2). On this basis, the questions earlier presumed to be unanswerable are dealt with: (1) Since every movement requires a moving force, how is it that the elements move by themselves? (2) If, however, they do move by themselves, why are they not free to move in either direction, now up, now down? The answers are as follows. While it is conceded that every movement is due to a moving force, the motive power in the case of the elements is said to be a potentiality natural to them, i.e. a tendency always to move either upwards or downwards (255^{b}15 ff.). Hence the movement of an element is according to nature 'when its potentiality is turned into its own, corresponding, actuality' (255^{a}29 ff.). As a further explanation it is added that the ultimate cause of the natural movements is the creator (*ho gennêsas kai poiêsas*), who gave each of the elements its own tendency to move in one direction only (255^{b}31 ff.).

The conclusion is that the criticism of the theory of the proper place in its traditional form was made from the standpoint of a physicist, strictly applying the principle of causality to the entire inanimate world; whereas the acceptance of the theory after re-interpretation is based on a much broader concept of cause, namely one which is partly biological and partly theological, the latter going back to the myths of the *Timaeus* (39E–40D).

CHAPTER EIGHT

A Volume on Potentiality and Actuality: Metaphysics Θ

Θ is on a clearly defined theme, on one aspect of the ontological problem, potentiality and actuality. So Θ, like Z and Λ, begins with statements on Being, on substance and the other categories; but then goes on to say that there is yet another angle, from which Being can be described, namely potentiality, full actuality (*entelecheia*) and actuality (here *kata to ergon*), and that it is these concepts which are to be discussed. The following book, I, is also on one theme, the concept of the One.

The book is broadly divided into two sections: Θ I–VI and Θ VII–X. The first section contains a continuous argument of a pattern similar to that of Λ (and H), that is, it first deals with what is mainly matter (potentiality, perceptible substance) and then discusses that which is beyond matter (actuality). Within this section, the essential points are made in Θ I, possibly Θ II or V, and Θ VI; Θ III and IV were manifestly added for the purpose of refuting Sceptical critics of the theory of the potential and the actual. The chapters of the second section are apparently isolated units. While in Θ VI actuality is discussed after potentiality has been dealt with, Θ VII reverts to potentiality. Θ VIII once again dwells on actuality. Θ IX and X concentrate on more remote aspects of the theory; Θ IX(1) on the relative worth of good and bad potentiality/actuality; Θ IX(2) on actuality as involved in geometrical constructions; Θ X on the relation of the actual to truth and falsity.

The argument as developed in Θ I–VI

After stating his theme, potentiality and actuality as an aspect of Being, the lecturer says that although he will first discuss potentiality in accordance with its principal connotation, namely motion (change), not this, but another meaning of the term is most relevant for his present intention, and this meaning he will discuss later, in connection

187

with actuality.[1] This promise is fulfilled in Θ VI. Dismissing the metaphorical meanings of the term as of no interest to him (compare *Metaph.* Δ XII,), he defines all potentialities of one type, the first, as principles of change in another thing or in the thing itself *qua* other.

The question arises: which is the other—the 'most relevant meaning'? The answer is found in Θ VI ($1048^{b}9$), where potentiality and actuality are discussed, not in relation to motion or becoming, but to existence. From this standpoint potentiality is seen as matter and actuality as substance (as form or the compound). The view underlying potentiality as first defined is that every potentiality must lead to its own actuality unless there is an impediment. It is not quite clear whether this view applies equally to potentiality/actuality as defined later in Θ VI.

The lecturer goes on to explain how the principle of change works, namely both in a passive and an active manner. Potentiality is, in X, a readiness to react; in Y, a potency to cause reaction. For example, oily material is inflammable; a hot agent causes the material to burn. And when the material is on fire the active and the passive principles become one and the same (see *Gen. Corr.* I, 7; 'the patient necessarily changes into the agent', $324^{a}12$). But once the unison has taken place, i.e. when the potential has turned into the actual, the thing can no longer be acted upon by itself.[2] The lecturer adds that an incapacity corresponds to every capacity, or potency, and that it is its contrary and its privation. This statement has a bearing on what follows.

Θ II, as well as Θ V, deals with a logical difficulty. The possible is generally defined as that which admits of A and not-A. If it is possible for man to be wise it must be possible for man to be not-wise. However, this definition of the possible conflicts with the

---

[1] *Dynamis* comprises the two meanings 'potency' and 'potentiality', but according to Bonitz and Ross, 'Aristotle does not successfully preserve the distinction between the two meanings'; see Ross, *Comm.* to $1045^{b}35$ ff. The explanation for this apparent lack of clarity seems to be, that the distinction between the two meanings is valid from an eidetic standpoint only, whereas to a philosopher with a materialistic outlook 'potency' and 'potentiality' are the same.

[2] In his interesting paper, '"Action" and "passion": some philosophical reflections on *Physics* III, 3' (in Düring, *Naturphilosophie* etc.), A. Edel analyses the serious difficulties implicit in the theory of the unity of agent and patient, as expounded in *Metaph.* Θ, *Physics* and *De Anima*, and explains that these difficulties arise because Aristotle approaches the problem on two levels: (*a*) an observational (epistemological) level; (*b*) a physiological level. Edel concludes his article by suggesting a solution, albeit within narrow limits.

basic theory of Θ, namely that every potentiality must lead to its own actuality, and to nothing else. To deal with this difficulty, both Θ II and Θ V distinguish between two kinds of potencies, rational and non-reasoning, of which the first belongs to living, rational beings, the second to inanimate things. Now, rational potencies, the lecturer in Θ II says, admit of A and not-A; a physician is capable of producing both health or illness, as he wishes; but non-reasoning potencies necessarily produce one thing only; the hot can only produce heat, not cold. So, in a biological sense, the theory of the potential turning into the actual is upheld; at the same time, it is shown that there is an area to which the definition of the possible applies. The *logos* transcends the physical necessity although, of course, A and its contrary, health and illness, must remain within the same genus, state of health. In Θ V, however, an attempt is made to maintain the theory fully. There the philosopher says that although rational potencies are productive of A and not-A, something superior to the mere potency, namely desire or choice, directs a rational being so that it can act in one way only. Thus it is shown that the actualization even of rational potency is strictly subjected to necessity; and on this note the discussion of potentiality seems to end.[1]

Θ VI explains actuality—what it is and of what kind it is. That is, its full meaning is to be made clear. And pointing out that 'potential', too, not only applies to that which is capable of causing motion and being moved, but is also used in other senses, the lecturer now says (contradicting Θ I, 46ᵃ2–4; see above, p. 188) that he *has* discussed these other senses. Next, the promised explanation is given, through a number of examples which, it seems, cover the principal meanings of both potentiality and actuality. The examples (with the potential first preceding, then following the actual) are given as follows: a piece of wood—a figure carved out of it; a whole divisible into halves—a half of this whole; a knowledgeable person not applying his knowledge—applying his knowledge; (the actual first from now on)[2] the building of a house—ability to build; waking—sleeping; seeing—not seeing while possessing sight;

---

[1] It is of interest to note that according to *De Interpr.* even some non-reasoning potencies admit of two contraries; but no example is given (23ᵃ3).

[2] There seems to be a break at this point. The passage 48ᵃ36–ᵇ9 may well be a doublet of 48ᵃ31–6, for the example of matter compared with the finished work is repeated, as is also the reference to 'the analogous'.

an object carved out of wood—the wood; a finished object—unworked material. While it would be impossible, the lecturer implies, to give examples for every nuance in the meaning of the two terms, the illustrations given broadly cover the whole range of their meanings (*to analogon*). The principal of these are capacity of change in things, and capacity of coming-to-be in matter. As he puts it himself, summing up: the relationship of the actual to the potential is either that of motion (change) to the capacity to move (change), or that of substance (the compound) to mere matter. With this, it may be inferred, all that the lecturer regards as essential has been said.

The last two paragraphs of Θ VI are almost in the nature of annotations; two special points are made. In the first of these paragraphs we find a remark explaining in what sense the potential and the actual apply to the infinite and the void. As regards existence, the lecturer says, these remain potentialities; they never actually exist. They are actualities only to knowledge; they exist only as concepts in the minds of scientists. The purpose of this paragraph appears to be, to reaffirm the Peripatetic doctrines of the infinite and the void against (possible) attempts at undermining them by falsely applying to them the concepts of the potential and the actual (compare with this passage *Phys.* Γ IV–VIII; Δ VI–IX; *Gen. Corr.* 320ᵇ28 and 326ᵇ31).[1]

Finally, a distinction between movement and actuality is introduced (1048ᵇ18 to the end of Θ VI).[2] Movement, the lecturer says, such as learning, building, walking, has a limit, but no end within itself; actuality, such as living (well) or thinking, has an end in itself. On this basis, there is a difference between the present and perfect tenses of verbs of movement, but not of verbs signifying actuality. A man builds a house; when he has reached the limit, i.e. done the work, he has built the house. A man walks; when he has reached his goal, he has walked. But man lives, not to achieve something outside living, but in order to live; life is the end of living. Similarly, thinking is the end of thinking. The perfect

---

[1] See also Ross, *Comm.* ad loc. on the Aristotelian theories of the infinite and the void.

[2] See. J. L. Ackrill, 'Aristotle's distinction between *energeia* and *kinêsis*', in Bambrough, *New Essays* etc. Ackrill, in a full discussion of this passage, analyses the (linguistic) difficulty involved in the manner in which the distinction between actuality and movement is made, and rightly points out that the teaching of Θ VI is very different from that of *De Anima*, 417ᵇ8.

tenses 'I have lived', 'I have thought', do not mean, as in verbs of movement, that a task has been accomplished. (The perfect tenses of the Greek verbs *zên*, to live, and *noein*, to think, must not be construed to mean that life, or thought, has come to an end: they are *perfecta praesentia* signifying continuity.)

There are other passages in which movement and actuality are *not* distinguished (especially *Metaph.* K, 65ᵇ15; compare 66ᵃ26). Nor does it appear that the distinction is envisaged in the first paragraph of Θ VI (48ᵃ25–ᵇ9). By differentiating between movement and actuality the author of the passage reveals his teleological, eidetic standpoint; whereas, when actuality is equated with movement, the principle of which may inhere in matter, a materialistic view is indicated. In yet another passage, the end (*telos*) is said to be in the product of the action as well as in the action, or actuality, itself (in the *noêton* as in *noein*; Θ VIII, 50ᵃ3).

There can be little doubt that the last paragraph of Θ VI is an addition to the original chapter. Besides, it consists of two parallel statements, repeating the same points (48ᵇ18–27 and 48ᵇ29–35). In the first statement, the term 'action' (*praxis*) is used opposite 'movement', instead of 'actuality' (*energeia*); in the second, actuality is the term employed. One may infer that the second statement was put in to make quite clear that it is actuality which is discussed in relation to movement. In Jaeger's edition the whole paragraph is bracketed off, on the grounds of its very harsh and obscure language and the corruption of the text. But there is no special reason for singling out this paragraph as spurious. Harsh and obscure diction is also found in Θ II and Θ VII, each time towards the end of these chapters, where, as in Θ VI, close parallels occur (46ᵇ15–28; 49ᵃ18—ᵇ2). Each of these passages was probably added for a re-delivery of the course, by philosophers living at the turn of the fourth and third centuries B.C.; this also applies to Θ IX and X, and possibly even Θ VII and VIII.

The chapter closes with a sentence marking the end of the inquiry into actuality, and of the course.

Θ III and IV are clearly inserted chapters. This follows for Θ III from the fact that the chapter deals with actuality as well as potentiality, although it is said in Θ VI that the discussion of actuality is now to begin. Θ III is a polemical chapter designed to refute a Sceptical objection, namely that there is no possible or potential; that what is not actually, is not; i.e. that the word 'potential' is meaningless. Against this criticism the lecturer points out that if the potential is denied, generation and movement (change) are inexplicable; also that without potentiality there would only be Being and not-Being, but no transition between them and no evolution. The refuted view is ascribed to the Megaric school, but this raises problems. The Megaric school flourished in Plato's time; hence, its original members could not have been acquainted with the Peripatetic concepts of the potential and the actual. The allusion can, therefore, only be to a later, Sceptical, school, which, in fact, grew out of the Megaric school. Indeed, Sceptics generally made the theory of the potential and actual one of their favourite butts (see Sext. Emp. *Outlines* II, 225).

The chapter also contains a reference to Protagoras's theory that nothing exists unless it is perceived. Against this the lecturer once more proves that there must be something between Being and not-Being, for otherwise a man would either see or be blind whereas, in fact, a man may possess sight without actually seeing.

In the last paragraph of Θ III an attempt is made to ascertain the original meanings of the terms actuality (*energeia*) and full actuality (*entelecheia*); the lecturer adds that actuality is mostly considered to be movement—a statement which is at variance with Θ VI (48^{b}9 and ^{b}34 ff.) and, of course, with Λ, where the highest actuality is described as unmoved. It appears that the lecturer is mainly concerned with psychology. Distinguishing between two classes of not-Being, absolute not-Being and not-Being = potential Being, he says that movement does not apply to either class but that that which may come to be may be the object of thought and desire.

Θ IV (1)—to 47^{b}14—takes up a point already made in Θ III (47^{a}11 ff.); it conducts a polemic against those who deny that there are instances of the impossible. This denial once more implies the view that there is nothing between Being and not-Being; hence, that that which does not exist actually does not exist potentially either. For a thing that is considered possible, say the Sceptics emanating from the Megaric school, may or may not be, that is, at some future time it either will or will not exist, and for that which will not exist it is impossible to exist.

We learn from the *Topics* that the denial of the impossible was used as an eristic device by the Sophists (159^{a}1 ff.); the present passage shows that the distinction between the actual and the potential was rejected on this basis. Against this rejection it is pointed out in Θ IV that there is a difference between that which will not, and that which cannot, be, that is, between a contingent not-A and a necessary not-A. For example, it is not sufficient to say that the diagonal will not be measured; the truth is that it cannot be measured. By implication there is a difference between judging that AB is not true and that AB is impossible. It follows that the actual and the potential do not coincide. For while there are things which can never be, there are also those which exist not actually but potentially, that is, are not now but will be at some other time.[1]

Θ IV(2), starting 'at the same time, it is also clear ...' (*hama de dêlon ...*), offers several examples of syllogisms, which are designed to show that from problematic premisses problematic conclusions follow. In this paragraph, which has a close parallel in *An. Pr.* A XIII, especially 34^{a}5 ff., the theme of Θ, actuality and potentiality, is altogether lost sight of. So, whereas Θ IV(1) appears to be a direct continuation of Θ III and may well belong to a lecturer re-delivering the Θ-course, Θ IV(2) is more likely to have been added to the volume by a librarian-editor, who selected the passage from a purely logical course because it deals, if not with the potential, at least with the possible.

The remaining chapters of Θ

Θ VII (on potentiality) and Θ VIII (on actuality) form an unequal and contradictory pair. The teaching of Θ VII is scientific, materialistic; that of Θ VIII is eidetic. Both chapters seem to be independent units because, first, they each start with a clearly-defined question or thesis and conclude by stating that the question has been answered or the thesis proved; and, secondly, they resume an inquiry which, according to Θ VI (48^{b}9 and 35), has been completed.

Θ VII(1) deals with a specific aspect of the theory of the potential. It asks: at what stage can it be said of a something that it potentially exists? The answer is: in the phase of proximate matter—although the term is not used. For earth is not yet potentially man. Semen is, and even semen only under certain conditions. It is then explained, in the remainder of the section, which conditions must be fulfilled if one is to speak of a potentially existing something; and it is of interest to note that the explanation given covers both natural

---

[1] At the beginning of Θ IV (47^{b}3) I read, following Alexander as understood by Bonitz: εἰ δ'ἐστὶ τὸ εἰρήμενον δυνατὸν ἧ ἀκολουθεῖ ἐνέργεια — 'if the possible referred to occurs only in so far as an actuality follows [it]'.

generation and artificial production. First, everything that comes to be from a certain material must already exist in this material; for example, if a man is to be restored to health he must have basic health in him. Secondly, there must be nothing outside or within the matter preventing its transformation into a determinate something. For example, a house exists potentially if (*a*) someone decides to build it without anything external hindering him, (*b*) if nothing in the matter hinders the building, that is, if there is nothing to be added to the material, or to be taken away from it, or to be changed about it. Similarly, semen both by a principle working within it, and by obtaining the necessary conditions in another medium, reaches the stage when it is potentially a man. Similarly, too, earth has to change into bronze by its own principle and under favourable conditions before it is potentially a statue.

The main points made in this chapter are that it is proximate matter that changes into an actual something and that matter has a principle of movement within itself. It is, then, clear that Θ VII offers a materialistic version of the theory of potentiality and actuality, a version akin to that of *Metaph.* H VI, which teaches that whatever exists actually also exists potentially, and even that the actual and the potential are one and the same. The version of Θ VII is also comparable to the doctrine of the proper place according to which the elements move by themselves if their natural tendencies are not impeded (see *Gen. Corr.* I, 6, 323ª1 ff., especially 10, where the doctrine of the proper place is treated in connection with the theory of action and passion as discussed in Θ I).

The question, which is prior, the actual or the potential, is not asked in this chapter, but the obvious inference from its teaching is that either the actual and the potential coexist simultaneously or even, in contrast to Θ VIII, that the potential is prior to the actual.

Further, as in other scientifically oriented sections, *artistic creation is here described as a case of generation.* This is clear from the example of the architect, for from his decision, as the moving principle, the building of the house necessarily follows if there is no hindrance. Conversely, in eidetic sections, *natural generation is treated as an instance of purposive production.*

Θ VII(2), 49ª18 ff., offers a linguistic confirmation of the theory just expounded. There is, of course, evidence throughout the Corpus of the importance attached to linguistic observations. Not only is it true to say that Greek thought was influenced by the grammar and character of the Greek language: philosophers certainly believed that insights could be gained by an analysis of language; that language was a means of proving or disproving doctrines. Besides, Sophists had long been used to exploiting language for eristic purposes.

How is it that the matter of which something consists is described not by a noun denoting substance but by an adjective which denotes quality? For instance, a box is not wood, but wooden. This question had been discussed elsewhere (see *Phys.* H, 245^{b}9 ff.; *Metaph.* Z, 1033^{a}7 ff.). An explanation was offered, namely that the matter which changes disappears in the change. The present section raises the same question once more, but in a way adapted to the theory of ☉ VII(1): how is it that the potentially existing something is described by an adjective?

The lecturer begins by pointing out that what has been described as matter proves to be a quality—wooden, not wood. He goes on to say that the same applies to a whole process of generation and regeneration; wood is not earth but earthen, earth not air but airy, air not fire but fiery; and generally, in each case, the latter term (the adjective) always expresses the potential. But, he explains, when we arrive at a kind of matter that can no longer be described with reference to something else (*kat' allo*), that is, of which no quality derived from some other matter can be predicated, we have reached ultimate matter, which is not a determinate something. So where there is no further matter there is no further quality; that is, matter and quality fully correspond to each other. Therefore the potential is expressed by adjectives as well as by nouns; and from qualities as well as from matter the actual can be seen to emerge.

Now that the linguistic point has been made in physical terms it is made once more in terms of logic (49^{a}27 ff.). Accordingly, the philosopher now speaks of the substratum and attributes, and apparently continuing the argument explains that, in a proposition, the subject (the substratum) either is, or is not, a determinate something (substance). When it is, the predicate is an attribute (*pathos*), e.g. white or cultured. On the other hand, when the predicate is a form or an individual, the ultimate subject[1] is matter, or material substance. It is then clear, once again, that an adjective and the matter or the affection (*pathos*) to which this adjective refers

---

[1] *To eschaton* (49^{a}34): the ultimate; that is, the subject of the last proposition in a series of propositions.

fully correspond to each other because, in propositions, either of them can form the complement of a substance.

However, the philosopher wishes to make one other point, namely that in a sense, affections are comparable to matter. For this reason he concludes by saying that it is right that adjectives should refer to both matter and affections because both matter and affections are indefinite (of any matter many things can be formed; an affection applies to many things): in other words, affections contain the potential as does matter.

With this statement Θ VII(2) ends. There follows the final sentence of the chapter which, however, refers to Θ VII(1) only. From this it is to be inferred that Θ VII(2) is an added section. And indeed, one finds harsh and obscure language and textual uncertainty in this section as much as in the last paragraph of Θ VI (48ᵇ18 ff.; see above, p. 191). Obscurity and textual variants occur especially in the logical part of the argument, which may well have been superadded to the earlier, physical, part. For the link between the two parts is formed by verbal association: 'this thing here' (*todi*, 49ᵃ24) and 'a particular thing' (*tode ti*, 49ᵃ28); and it is not unlikely that the words 'not being a particular thing' (*ou tode ti ousa*, 49ᵃ27), which are bare of meaning, were deliberately inserted by the author of the logical argument for the purpose of providing a connecting point for his own demonstration.

Θ VIII, which is decidedly eidetic-teleological, appears to be a rejoinder, not to Θ VII (with which it has little direct connection) but to the Θ-course (mainly Θ I and VI). This is apparent (*a*) from the fact that Θ VIII deliberately rectifies the opening definition of potentiality as given in Θ I;[1] (*b*) because Θ VIII reverses the teaching of the original Θ-course by its doctrine of the priority of actuality over potentiality.

Moreover, Θ VIII is a much-revised chapter, for the order of discussion as stated at the beginning is not observed in the discussion itself; whereas actuality was to be examined according to *logos*, substance and time, it is in fact investigated according to *logos* and time, with substance following. Besides there are at least two sections on substance, expressing slightly divergent views. With the discussion of actuality under those three heads the main part of the chapter is completed (50ᵇ6). There follows an added section,

[1] Similarly Λ IV (70ᵇ22 ff.) rectifies the opening statement of the theme of Λ (69ᵃ30 ff.).

containing several further observations which have a bearing on the doctrine of the chapter.

Θ VIII teaches that the movent is not a principle potentially inherent in matter, as claimed in Θ I; it is the actual—form or substance. For the actual is the end towards which the potential moves, it is the condition of generation and existence. Hence, the actual precedes the potential.

Résumé. After an allusion to a discussion of the several meanings of 'prior', the lecturer begins his inquiry by redrafting the definition of potentiality as given in Θ I. Potentiality, he says, is not merely a principle, inherent in a thing, of producing change in another thing or in itself *qua* other (i.e. as if it were acting on itself from without). In other words it is not merely a potency to produce a specific change in specific matter. Rather, it must be understood in a wider sense, as any principle of motion or rest in general, that is, as nature changing itself. With this, nature is conceived in one sense as altogether indeterminate and in another sense as self-determining. And the lecturer proceeds to state his thesis, that, within nature, the actual is prior to the potential, in *logos* and substance always, in time sometimes.

In *logos* it is prior because the knowledge of the potential is merely a regress from the knowledge of the actual; we cannot define and know a potential X unless we have previously defined and known the actual X.

In time, it is prior in the sense that form, i.e. species, precedes all generation. It is, however, posterior in another sense: an individual is preceded by semen, corn by seed, seeing by the capacity to see. This exposition appears to be evenly balanced. But evidently two views were held on the relation of actuality to time, for the philosopher goes on to say that even in time a potential individual is preceded by an actual individual, son by father, a student of the arts by a teacher of the arts; and that, as a result, in general the potential is always preceded by an actually existing proximate movent.[1]

The reasoning in this paragraph is imprecise, according to Ross.[2] Altogether it is worth noticing that eidetic passages are frequently less closely argued than scientifically oriented passages.

---

[1] Θ IX returns to this problem, but there only the first of the two views is stated.

[2] Ross, *Comm.* II, p. 260.

Further, it is clear that *logos* can be juxtaposed with time, or with substance, but when time and substance are juxtaposed there must be overlaps, as this passage shows. So one has to infer an early conflation of two versions, resulting in an analysis of the problem of priority in this chapter not under two, but three heads— *logos*, time (generation) and substance.

There follows a defence of the thesis of the priority of actuality against a Sophistical objection (48^{b}27 ff.), namely that one can never learn a skill, because if one possesses and exercises it one does not have to learn it, and if one does not possess it one cannot exercise, hence not learn the skill. No one can build who has not built. The basis of this objection is the Peripatetic doctrine that in form the actual and the potential are the same; from which it is concluded that there can be no development from the potential to the actual. This appears to be a Megaric argument.

However, the philosopher replies by pointing out that the movement of an entity is preceded by the movement of a part of that entity, as demonstrated in *Physics* (Z VI); analogously, that a learner is likely to possess some knowledge or special skill, which will enable him to acquire the whole of that knowledge or skill. It follows, once again, that actuality is prior to potentiality in generation, that is, in time. It is interesting to note that this whole argument is introduced by an obviously frequently repeated general statement on generation, as found at the beginning of both *Metaph.* Z VII and VIII; from which it may be concluded that the objection dealt with here was expressly directed at Peripatetic teaching.

At this point, the discussion of substance begins, introduced— as if it were an afterthought—by the words 'but indeed also as regards substance' (*alla mên kai ousiai ge*, 50^{a}4). Repeating some of the examples given before under the heading 'time', the philosopher first states that, though not in generation, the actual is prior in form, that is, substance: adult precedes child; man, having the form, precedes his semen which does not have it. Secondly, he expounds the view which is the main distinguishing mark of this chapter, namely a strictly teleological conception of nature. Whatever comes to be, he says, does so by moving towards an end; hence, the purpose (*to hou heneka*) or the end (*telos*) is the moving principle; and the end is actuality. In short, the efficient cause is here submerged in the final cause. There are parallels to this passage in

the ethical writings: 'The good itself is the end' (*Eth. Eud.* 1218ᵇ12).
The actuality as the end is said to be the moving principle of such
ethical action as loving, and also of producing works of art (*Mag.
Mor.* 1211ᵇ27–33). Analogously, according to Θ VIII, the end is
the moving principle of generation (see also *Part. An.* 639ᵇ15 ff.).

The end pre-exists. For, the philosopher continues, it is for the
sake of the end, the actuality, that the capacity is acquired. We have
sight in order to see; we acquire the skill of building and of thinking,
in order to build and to think.[1] The first of these examples contradicts an assertion made earlier in this chapter, that the capacity
of sight precedes the actuality of seeing (49ᵇ20 ff.)—a more natural
assumption, which is here abandoned on the basis of a fully
developed teleology.

Further (thirdly?), matter only exists potentially *because* it can
be formed; and it is formed matter which exists actually, and is the
end, and hence, the moving principle of generation. Similarly,
there are cases where the movement, the action, is itself the end;
flute-playing is the end of flute-playing. And this is why teachers
want to show their pupils performing, as does nature; for the
proof of the capacity to see is seeing. Otherwise, if pupils did not
exhibit their knowledge one would be reminded of Pauson's
Hermes, who from one angle, is hidden in his case, but from another
is plainly visible.[2] The action, *ergon*, is the end; and adding an
etymological analysis the lecturer points out that, for this very
reason, the term 'actuality' (*energeia*), is derived from the word
'action' (*ergon*); also that the meaning of 'actuality' leads on to that of
final or 'end-actuality' (*entelecheia*, a word derived from 'end'—
telos).

Now, retrospectively (or belatedly) the philosopher explains in
general terms that, in some cases, the activity itself is the 'ultimate'
(*eschaton*) and, in other cases, the activity as well as its result, the
product. The act of seeing is the ultimate end of sight; but both the
building of a house and the house itself are the ends of architecture.
The lecturer concludes that, in the second case, the end is more

---

[1] The clause which follows (50ª14 ff.) is difficult; see Ross, *Comm.* ad loc. I
offer this explanation. People do not think in order to acquire the skill of thinking,
except those who practise (thinking), but they only think like this (ὡδί—pointing
to the tables showing concepts and their opposites, universals and particulars
etc.), or they think about subjects on which one need not seriously reflect.

[2] Nothing very definite is known about Pauson's Hermes.

decidedly in the actual product, the house, than in the potential, the capacity for building, because the action and its results are correlated. The house goes up as the work proceeds.

There follows a parallel passage on activity and its result (50ª30 ff.), but the view now expressed partly diverges from the previous doctrine just stated. The philosopher no longer holds that actuality ultimately resides in the activity; on the contrary, he teaches that it resides in the agent, the subject. Where there is a product—an object—actuality belongs to it; on the other hand, where the activity is all, actuality is in the agent. In the case of seeing, or thinking, it is in the one who sees, or thinks; as regards living the actuality is in the soul; as regards a happy life it is in the (right kind of) soul. The significance of this explanation clearly emerges from the conclusion: actuality belongs to substance, that is, form.

Manifestly, this second passage on activity and the product is even more markedly influenced by ethical thinking than the first passage, with its references to the activity of the soul and to the happy life. For comparison I quote from *Eth. Eud.*: 'The soul has an action peculiar to itself. It is directed towards the good as its end' (1219ª5 ff.; see also *Mag. Mor.* 1211ᵇ27–33). One might even discern an affinity to Stoic thinking in this passage although it would be very difficult to decide which of the two schools, the Peripatetic or the Stoic, influenced the other.

The paragraph ends with a summary which seems to belong to the first passage on action and the product rather than to the second. From this argument, the philosopher says, it is evident that actuality is prior to potentiality in substance, and—he adds—as we have said before (where?), in point of time one actuality is always preceded by another until we come to the original movent in each case. The second part of this summary points to a lost argument, perhaps on the lines of Λ VIII.

Here, the main part of Θ VIII ends (50ᵇ6). The final section of the chapter still deals with actuality and potentiality but in a strictly scientific—physical and biological—context. The priority of actuality over potentiality is no longer debated; only the priority of eternal over perishable substances is referred to. Three points are made, and the section closes with a critique of the theory of ideas.

(1) Nothing eternal exists potentially. Of this assertion a proof

is offered, which recalls the proofs of the same doctrine in Λ VI (71ᵇ12–23) but, in comparison with Λ, one which is almost pedantically elaborate. The gist of the proof is that all that is potential may, or may not, come to be. Hence, that which is eternal cannot be potential, for it always is. This paragraph also deals with imperishable substances which are not absolutely immutable, such as the sun and the planets. Of these, in contrast to the first heaven, it is admitted that they contain matter, not indeed matter subject to generation and destruction but liable to changes in quality and place.[1]

This last section of the chapter is introduced by the phrase 'but indeed also in a more important sense' (is actuality prior to potentiality). The form of the Greek phrase used here[2] is, no doubt, late (mid-Hellenistic); still, it is not to be concluded that the whole section is late. The probability is rather that the entire introductory clause, 'but indeed also in a more important sense, for eternal things are prior in substance to perishable things', was added by a librarian-editor who attempted to fit lecture records together in order to make up a more or less homogeneous volume.

Paragraphs 2 and 3 deal with forces in sublunar nature and explain which of these are actualities and which potentialities. In contrast to the preceding paragraph, all the points are here made with the utmost brevity.

(2) The continuous movement of the four (perishable) elements, fire, air etc., is compared to the continuous movement of the eternal bodies. This comparison is probably based on the theory of the proper place, for it is explained that the elements have a moving force within themselves, and this drives each of them in one direction only, fire and air upwards, water and earth downwards; hence, they are actualities. In *De Caelo*, too, the movements of the elements, with their lightness or heaviness respectively, are discussed in terms of the actual and the potential (311ᵃ1 ff.).

(3) Whereas the elements are actualities, the other powers, both the rational and the non-rational ones, are not, because they *all* admit of two opposite effects; the latter through their absence or presence. Cold by its absence allows warmth to take its place (see *Phys.* 251ᵃ31).[3] This theory is at variance with both Θ II and V. It

---

[1] ποθὲν ποί, from where and where to (50ᵇ21), probably refers to the ecliptic of the sun and the varied courses of the planets.

[2] κυριωτέρως.

[3] See Ross, *Comm. ad loc.*

is true, Θ II admits that a rational power, e.g. medicine, can produce either of two contraries, health or illness, but in both Θ II and V non-rational powers can lead to one, necessary, result only. It follows that Θ VIII cannot refer to Θ II or V, and that the phrase 'from what has been explained before' (*ex hôn diôristai*) alludes to a lost version on the subject of the powers—a conclusion strengthened by the fact that the terms 'contradiction' (*antiphasis*) and 'presence/not-presence' (*tôi pareinai kai mê*) do not occur in Θ II and V. These are logical terms characteristic of the present section, which is fully in line with logical thinking; it allows no exception at all to the rule that the possible, according to its definition, always admits of two contraries. Moreover, the notion of the presence or absence of a power is obviously based on the Platonic theory of opposites changing into opposites; whereas according to Peripatetic doctrine as expressed in *Physics* A, opposites do not change into each other and it is only the substrate which undergoes change.

Still, the last paragraph of this section is devoted to a critique of the theory of ideas. If ideas existed separately, the philosopher says, as though they were entities of nature, that is, substances, e.g. the ideas of knowledge or of movement, then something more real than the real, more knowledgeable than knowledge, more mobile than movement, would exist. For in that case the ideas would be existing actually while that which is real would exist only potentially—a view which (this is implied) is patently absurd. This is a new, special version of the critique of the theory of ideas, from which it is possible to infer that at the time of this critique some Platonists, here described as the people who 'deal in words', already knew of the Peripatetic concepts of actuality and potentiality, and that they had adapted them for use in their own arguments.

The chapter closes with a summary sentence which obviously refers to the main part of the chapter only (up to 50ᵇ6). Moreover, the summary plainly shows, as does the opening statement of Θ VIII to which it corresponds, that the analyses offered in this chapter were meant to counter and amend the teaching of the Θ-course (Θ I and VI) and, in particular, to rectify the definition of potentiality as given in Θ I: 'Potency ⟨inherent in a thing⟩ is a principle of effecting a change in another thing or in itself *qua* other' (46ª10). For the philosopher says here: 'It has become evident that actuality is prior to potentiality and to every principle of change.' In other words, the philosopher claims to have shown that potencies do not initiate changes by themselves, but each depend for their functioning on an actuality existing prior to the potency; whether this actuality be movement, or form and substance.

Θ VIII—*conclusions.* Θ VIII is closer to those chapters of Λ which deal with the unmoved mover than is the rest of book Θ. For like Λ VI and VII, Θ VIII dwells on purpose: on actuality as its own end; on the actuality of the heavenly bodies; on the happy life. It is true, the mind (*nous*), which is of such great importance to Λ, is not discussed in Θ VIII. On the other hand, Peripatetic teleology as applied to nature and the universe is nowhere, not even in Λ, so powerfully stated as here—a fact which has made Θ VIII a famous chapter; only in the ethical writings is a comparable teleological philosophy found.[1]

So, by maintaining the doctrine of the priority of the actual over the potential, of form or the spirit over matter, with hardly any reservations, Θ VIII takes its stand at one end of the Peripatetic spectrum. It is worth recalling that the opposite doctrine, that of the priority of the potential over the actual, has also found expression in the Aristotelian treatises. 'That which exists potentially, not actually, must be prior in Being' (*Gen. Corr.* 317ᵇ17). 'Matter, as part of a whole-to-be-created, pre-exists' (*Metaph.* Z VII, 1033ᵃ1). 'Some things are prior potentially, some actually' (*Metaph.* Δ, 1019ᵃ7). Akin to this latter doctrine is the view that the potential and the actual exist simultaneously (*Phys.* Δ, 213ᵃ6 and *Metaph.* H VI, 1045ᵇ21).

Probable time of Θ VIII. The main part of Θ VIII must be later than the Θ-course, which it criticizes, and so may well belong to the last decade of the fourth century B.C. On the other hand, it is likely that the final section of the chapter (from 50ᵇ6) is earlier in origin than the main part, although it was probably attached to it at quite a late date.

Θ IX contains two unrelated observations on aspects of the theory of the actual and potential: the first, on the actuality of the good and the bad; the second, on the actuality of knowledge, in particular, geometrical knowledge.

The main thesis of the first section (51ᵃ4–21) appears to be that

---

[1] The final cause (*heneka tinos*) is also given great prominence in the opening chapter of *Part. An.* where its importance is compared with that of necessity (*anagkê,* 639ᵇ11 ff.; 642ᵃ2 ff.).

only the good is a principle, not the bad. This doctrine is opposed to the Platonic teaching that both the good and the bad are principles,[1] and the section has been interpreted as a critique of Platonism.

The argument begins with the assertion that an actuality relating to matters of relevance (*spoudaia*) is better and worthier than the corresponding potentiality. The proof of this is that a potentiality embraces A and its opposite, health and illness, at the same time; whereas an actuality is one thing only at one time. It follows that the actuality is better; in other words, the concept of the better, or best, implies actual existence. Vice versa, a bad actuality is worse than the corresponding potentiality; the actually existing bad is worse than the potentially bad. Now, the lecturer continues, it is obvious that the actually existing bad always attaches to a particular something, because, being destructive, it presupposes its contrary, the good; and hence, is posterior by nature[2] to potentiality which comprises the good and the bad. The conclusion is, that the bad exists only in the region of the perishable, not of the eternal substances; so only the good can belong to that which is primary actuality, hence, a principle.

Although this section is directed against a tenet of Platonism, it is Platonic in spirit. Its conceptions are akin to those of Λ VI and VII, and of Θ VIII. Indeed, its relation to Θ VIII is quite close. While it is not a continuation of the argument of Θ VIII(2) (50ᵇ6–28), it follows a similar line of thought. It stresses the superiority of the actual, and it discusses the relation of perishable to eternal substance. In addition, the doctrine of the 'possible', strictly according to the definition of the 'possible', is that of Θ VIII, 50ᵇ31 (see p. 201). Moreover, one finds parallels to this section, as well as to Θ VIII, in the ethical treatises. 'A [good] deed (*ergon*) is better than the corresponding inclination (*hexis*)' (*Eth. Eud.* 1219ᵃ8). In Θ IX we read that the actually existing good is better than that which is potentially good (or bad).

---

[1] See *Rep.* 476A (402C); *Theaet.* 176E; *Laws*, 896E; 898C. Compare *Metaph.* 988ᵃ14; 1075ᵃ35; 1091ᵇ31.

[2] ὕστερον τῇ φύσει: the actual bad, being the contrary of the good, is by nature posterior to the potential (bad). Compare *Cat.* 14ᵇ12 ff. In the case of two opposites, of which the existence of one excludes the existence of the other, that which is the condition of the other's existence may well be said to be *naturally prior* to the other.

The argument of Θ IX(1) has been criticized as containing one or several fallacies by Bonitz,[1] and indeed, it is not easy to be sure of its cogency. But the argument is, no doubt, contracted, with the result that some important tenets are not stated but merely implied: (1) that eternal substances are purely actual; (2) that pure actuality is the cause of all movement; (3) that the bad, or destructive, presupposes the good of which it is the contrary. We have noticed before that eidetic passages are often not quite rigorously argued, one of the probable reasons being that Platonizing arguments were particularly well known to students, so lecturers felt inclined to omit much that it would otherwise be necessary to state expressly.

The second part of Θ IX, in which cognition (*noêsis*) and, in particular, the discovery of geometrical truths is discussed, also contains serious difficulties, though mainly in relation to the geometrical proofs given;[2] philosophically, it is comparatively easy to follow. Geometrical theorems, the lecturer begins, are discovered by being actualized as constructions. One finds them by dividing a given figure; so long as the figure is undivided, the theorem, or truth, only exists potentially. Two propositions are given as examples: (1) the angles in a triangle equal two right angles; (2) the angle in a semicircle is always a right angle. It is shown that one arrives at each of these theorems by constructing the relevant figures; whereby it is proved that a potential truth is discovered by an actual construction, and hence that (in the field of geometry or learning) actuality is cognition, or knowledge.[3] The lecturer concludes by saying that, whereas the actuality of knowledge is prior to the fact capable of being known, the potentially known particular fact is prior to actual knowledge in becoming (*genesis*). The implication seems to be that form or species is prior to its particular instances but particular instances exist prior to their being known.

A similar assertion about the priority of the actual in one sense and

---

[1] Bonitz argues that the actual existence of evil must precede its potentiality, i.e. the ability of choosing it. But according to Θ IX, evil, which is destructive of the good, presupposes the good. Hence only the actually good precedes the potentially good, whereas the actually bad is posterior to its potentiality, which is the existence of the good.

[2] On this I refer the reader to Ross, *Comm.*

[3] I read the traditional text, νόησις ἡ ἐνέργεια.

of the potential in another sense is made in Θ VIII (49ᵇ18 ff.) where it is explained that, as form, an actual *A* precedes a potential *A* whereas when *A* is a particular the potential is prior to the actual. Further, the notion of knowledge as an actuality is contained in Θ VIII (49ᵇ27–50ª23) as it is in Θ IX. So, affinity to Θ VIII is evident throughout Θ IX; hence, it is likely that the two sections of Θ IX were taken from the same collection of lecture records as the two sections of Θ VIII: Θ IX(2) from the part of the collection which included Θ VIII(1), and Θ IX(1) from the part to which Θ VIII(2) belonged.

Θ X is devoted to logical problems: (1) the truth or falsity of propositions referring to composite objects; (2) the immediate cognition or non-cognition of indivisible entities.

The chapter is almost like a mosaic. All the various tenets contained in it are, if not taken from other treatises, at least paralleled in them—in *Categories*, *De Interpr.*, *Metaph.* Γ, E, Z and H, and in *De Anima* III. Still, as it is more closely related to the logical treatises than to ontological (*Metaph.* E, Z, H) or epistemological (*De Anima*), it is likely to stem from the logical 'department' of the Peripatos, where at a certain stage the concepts of the actual and potential had been incorporated in logical doctrine.

The chapter is divided into two sections, 51ª34–ᵇ33 and 51ᵇ33–52ª11. The first deals with the two problems referred to at some length; in the second, the points made before are restated in a concise form and, in addition, it is explained why propositions about immutable entities must always be either true or false.

Θ X (1*a*). The discussion in this part (to 51ᵇ17) is based on the following tenets: (1) When *A* has the attribute *B* a composite, unitary entity *AB* exists. When *A* is separated from *B* no entity *AB* exists. (2) If a composite entity exists, to affirm *AB* is true, to deny *AB* is false. If no entity exists, to affirm *AB* is false, to deny *AB* is true.

Résumé. The lecture begins with a reference to the various uses of the word 'Being', not only in relation to the categories and potentiality and actuality, but also truth and falsehood. This kind of introduction to a course of lectures frequently occurs in the *Metaphysics*: i.e. Θ I; E II and IV; Z I. However, the emphasis placed here on truth and falsehood as the most important aspects in the use of the word 'Being' (i.e. 'to be' used as the copula) is in direct contradiction to E IV (1027^{b}31).[1] Next, after a brief explanation of the relation of true and false propositions to existing and non-existing things, as in E IV (1027^{b}18, the 'basic tenets'; see above), the special question of this part of the chapter is posed: *when* does truth, or falsehood, occur? In other words is a proposition always true, or always false, or are there some propositions which are sometimes true and sometimes false? The answer is that as there are things that are always unified and cannot be divided, but others that can be unified or divided, so there are propositions which are always true or false but also propositions which are sometimes true and sometimes false (see also *De Interpr.* 21^{b}13). However, before this answer is given, it is stressed that the truth of a statement is not the cause of the existence of a thing, or fact, but, on the contrary, the existence of the thing is the cause of the truth of the statement. This view is also, and more fully, expressed in *Cat.* 14^{b}18. It probably implies the rebuttal of a Sophistical argument arising from the convertibility of terms in some propositions. It is a fallacy to assume, the lecturer points out, that when two things depend on each other (e.g. the truth of a statement and the corresponding fact), they cause each other. On the contrary, if *B* (the fact) is the cause of *A* (the statement), *A* cannot be the cause of *B* (see *An. Post.* 78^{a}27 ff.; 98^{a}35 ff.; *Soph. El.* 167^{b}1 ff.).

The argument in this section is interrupted by the sentence 'to exist means to be unified, that is, a unity, and not to exist means not to be unified, but to be a plurality' (51^{b}11–13), for the point made in the preceding clause, namely that there are things which are sometimes unified and sometimes divided, is not referred to in this sentence but taken up in the following one. Hence, an emendation of the passage has been attempted by Bonitz; but it is considered unnecessary by Ross. One does, of course, find many similar instances of arguments disturbed by parenthetical observations, but when it is realized that the treatises we read are, in fact, highly compressed lecture records this is not surprising. For although,

---

[1] The phrase 'Being in the most important sense' is therefore deleted by Ross. But it is upheld by Jaeger—rightly I believe—although it means a contradiction between this chapter, in which the most important meaning of Being is derived from its use as the copula, and E IV, in which a different meaning of Being (e.g. essence) is described as *the* relevant one. To explain this contradiction, one may assume that Being was investigated from different standpoints in the different departments of the school and that, naturally, in each department, its own aspect was considered particularly significant.

on the whole, the recording technique developed within the Peripatos deserves the greatest admiration, it is unavoidable that, occasionally, it should prove slightly inadequate to the task at hand.

Θ x(1*b*) (51ᵇ17–33). Secondly, the question is asked: what do existence and non-existence, truth and falsity mean with regard to incomposite entities such as points, lines and forms?[1] Answering the question, the lecturer states that neither the former criteria of existence and non-existence, i.e. unification or separation, nor the former notions of truth and falsity now apply; instead, one must speak of 'touching', i.e. immediate comprehension (*thigein*) or non-comprehension respectively, and use the term 'to assert' (*phanai*), not 'to affirm' (*kataphanai*), where incomposite entities are concerned. For, the lecturer adds, error, i.e. falsity, is impossible with regard to essences, except accidentally (*kata sumbebêkos*; see below). And this, he continues, applies to incomposite substances, too, that is, to the eternal substances, the first heaven etc., as in Λ vi–vii, Θ viii (1050ᵇ6–28) and *De Caelo*. For Being itself is neither generated nor does it perish, and these substances exist, not potentially, but actually, that is eternally, as essences; hence, one cannot err about them but only think, or not think, them. However, he adds, certain inquiries are being made (by Peripatetic physicists), to find out whether these substances are, or are not, of some particular nature.

One finds this doctrine of the immediate comprehension of essences, or points touching on it, stated in several other treatises: *Cat.* 2ᵃ8; *Metaph.* E iv, 1027ᵇ28; Z xvii, 1041ᵇ9; H iii, 1043ᵇ25. More copiously than elsewhere it is discussed, from an epistemological standpoint, in *De Anima* iii, 6—a notoriously difficult chapter; in which, moreover, it is treated in a similar context to that of Θ x, that is, in connection with actuality and potentiality, and with time (see conclusion to Θ x). The word 'to touch' (*thigein*) in the sense of 'to grasp directly' is also found in Λ vii, 1072ᵇ21.

The distinction between 'assertion' and 'affirmation' (*phasis, kataphasis*) equally occurs in *De Interpr.* 16ᵇ27 and 17ᵃ17, but not in *De Interpr.* 21ᵇ20, nor in *De Anima* iii, 6 and 7, 430ᵇ27 and 432ᵃ10, nor in *Metaph.* Γ, 1008ᵃ34. It seems to follow that the clear distinction between 'assertion' and 'affirmation' was only made in

[1] See *De Anima* iii, 6, 430ᵇ7 ff.; also *Metaph.* H iv.

strictly logical discussions but not in ontological or epistemological analyses.

The clause 'it is impossible to be deceived about essences except accidentally' (51ᵇ25) is very difficult to interpret. Rightly rejecting Alexander's and Bonitz's explanation, which was based on an artificial construction of the phrase 'not to be deceived' (*ouk apatethênai*), Ross explains that while there can be no error about simple terms denoting essences, these, nevertheless, comprise genus and diffcrentiae, hence, are complex in this sense; so it is possible to err about them 'accidentally'.

Another conceivable explanation, based on *De Interpr.* 23ᵇ15, is this: since an essence is only known as itself, a proposition asserting that an essence *X* equals its negative opposite *Y* can only be an accidental—or inferential—proposition, which may, or may not, be true. For instance in essence the good is good; hence, the proposition 'the good is not-bad' is an accidental (inferential) proposition.[1]

Also, the clause 'however, inquiries are being made' etc. (51ᵇ33) presents difficulties and has been much discussed, frequently in connection with the clause about error in accidentals.[2] However, the most natural explanation seems to be that the clause refers to questions investigated in the *Physics, De Caelo,* and also in Θ VIII. Do the external substances consist of fire, or ether? Do they contain an admixture of matter (50ᵇ22)? Or are they pure objects of thought (*noêta*)?

Θ x(2) (51ᵇ33 ff.). There follows a very concise restatement of the teaching offered in the main part of the chapter. If there is anything new in this second statement it is the emphasis placed on the distinction between non-cognition absolutely and non-cognition which is potential cognition. As for the relation of existence to truth and non-existence to falsity, the lecturer says, truth in the sense of a true proposition refers to a unitary something, that is, to an *AB* consisting of unified components; whereas, if components are not unified, a proposition affirming the existence of *AB* is false. For, he adds, if a unity exists it exists in this way, that is as *AB*; and if it does not exist in this way it does not exist at all. In

---

[1] Since essence is grasped directly all inferred attributes must be accidental attributes. It follows that *kata to symbebêkos* covers the meaning 'by inference'. Compare Bonitz's Index, s.v. *symbainein* (3*b*), and see p. 123, n. 4.

[2] See Ross, *Comm.* ad loc.

another sense, truth means the thinking of the things themselves[1] (essences), and in respect of these falsity or error are not possible, only non-cognition; non-cognition, however, which is not, like blindness, the total absence of the (cognitive) faculty, but such as may turn into cognition.

The final observation of the chapter (52ᵃ4 ff.) is again concerned with the relation of truth to time, as is the first (51ᵇ5 ff.). As before, the analysis is based on a close correspondence of the kind of object involved and the knowledge of it. Statements about unchangeable objects, the lecturer says, cannot contain an error with regard to time, that is, such statements cannot be sometimes true and sometimes false. For instance if one accepts that the triangle remains unchanged one will also accept that it always contains two right angles. Only about the different members of an (immutable) species is it possible to have two views and hence to err. For instance one may believe that no even number is a prime number, or that some even numbers are and some are not. But about a single member of an immutable species it is not possible to have two views or to err even in this sense. One cannot hold that it is a something A at one time and a something B at another time, but as it remains the same always, one's statement about it is always either true or false.

Θ x—*Conclusions.* The chapter ends without a closing summary; from which one may conclude that the set of lectures to which it belonged, was cut short by a librarian-editor, for inclusion in book Θ. On the other hand, the opening paragraph of Θ x, which is characteristic of a new start, clearly marks the beginning of this set. The question has been asked: how does Θ x, which deals with logical problems, fit into book Θ?[2] The reason for its inclusion seems to be that the course, to which Θ x belonged, not only dealt with the relation of truth to existence, but also to actual and potential existence. This aspect of its theme is in evidence in each section of Θ x; moreover, it is prominent in two passages to which Θ x is closely related, *De Anima* III, 6 and *De Interpr.* 21ᵇ12 ff. As to the time of Θ x, this chapter may well be the latest-composed of the book (after 290 B.C.?) for the following reasons. It treats somewhat specialized problems, and nearly all of it is paralleled

---

[1] αὐτά (sc. τὰ ὄντα) should be read with E and J, not ταῦτα; compare τὸ ὄν αὐτό (51ᵇ29). The two meanings of 'truth' referred to before are here juxtaposed as follows: . . . μὲν . . . ἀληθὲς (51ᵇ34)—τὸ δὲ ἀληθὲς (52ᵃ1).

[2] See Ross, *Comm.* p. 274.

in other treatises, of which many may well be regarded as late. Moreover, the feminine form *synthetai*, which is used here, also occurs in *De Anima* II, I (*synthetê*) and in *Physics* Θ IX, probably late passages, whereas in *Metaph.* H III (1043ª30) the form *synthetos* (with *ousia*) is used.

Book Θ—*conclusions*

It has emerged that Θ consists of several treatises, that is, sets of lectures, or parts of them, on the subject of actuality and potentiality —concepts which had become important for Peripatetic thinking, and in the light of which some principal doctrines of the school, including the doctrine of immanent substance, were re-discussed. Θ starts with a basic course of a structure similar to that of Λ; it appears, however, that some original parts of this course are lost and that some new parts were added. The basic course is followed in the volume by four shorter, partly incomplete, sets of lectures. The philosophy of the book is by no means unitary. Whereas the basic course, to which only Θ I and VI belong with certainty, is influenced by scientific thinking (as is also Θ VII) and, therefore, is more akin to *Metaph.* H than Λ, Θ VIII is strongly eidetic, hence, close to Λ.

Within the basic course, Θ I deals with potentiality and Θ VI with actuality. Θ III and IV are manifestly inserted chapters (see p. 191). But the question arises: does either Θ II or Θ V belong to the original, basic course? That they cannot both belong to it is certain. They are not complementary to each other but contain alternative versions of an inquiry into the same dilemma: how can the logical doctrine that the possible always admits of *A* and its contrary be reconciled with the physical-biological doctrine that every potency necessarily leads to one actuality only? Of the two chapters, Θ II attempts more strictly to uphold the logical rule, and so stands nearer to Θ III and IV, while Θ V, introducing a psychological aspect, is more closely related to Θ I and VI. But even so it is hardly likely that Θ V belongs to the original course, because what is required for it is not an inquiry into this special dilemma but a discussion of the potential, not solely in the sense of movement, but also in the sense of matter and substance. This is indicated in Θ VI, and indeed it is stated there that such a discussion had been included: 'We have discussed these senses as well' (48ª30). Nor is it likely that Θ VII, which returns to the theme of potentiality, is part of the original course. For Θ VII deals with potentiality in one particular sense, namely as proximate matter, and there is nothing in the section on actuality, Θ VI, to correspond to an analysis of such a specialized kind.

There are some further indications of the loss of passages relevant to the subject of Θ. (1) Θ VIII says that in the world of perishable things all potencies admit of A and its contrary, 'as has been explained before' (50^b30-2). But this view is at variance with the theories stated in both Θ II and Θ V, from which it follows that the reference can only be to a lost passage, not to Θ as it stands. (2) Further, we read in Θ VIII: 'As regards time, one actuality is always preceded by another until the original movent in each case is reached, "as we have said before"' (50^b2 ff.). But no such doctrine is stated in Θ (it might have been suppressed at the beginning of Θ VIII, 49^b10 ff., where, as we saw, two or more versions are conflated); so, once again, the reference points to a lost paragraph.

These three instances of false reference strengthen the conclusion reached already, that several treatises, or records of lectures, on the topic of actuality and potentiality existed at one time, and that Θ is made up of parts of them. There are two possible explanations of the manner in which Θ reached its present form. Either the volume we read was assembled by a librarian-editor at the school or in one of the great libraries during the Hellenistic era; or, several volumes on the subject were compiled at that time, and it was Andronicus of Rhodes who, drawing on all or some of them, arranged the Θ we know in the second part of the first century B.C.

SELECT BIBLIOGRAPHY

1. *Some nineteenth-century works*
Bonitz, H. *Observationes criticae in Aristotelis libros metaphysicos*, Berlin 1842.
Aristotelische Schriften, vols. 1–5, Vienna 1862–7.
Gomperz, T. *Griechische Denker*, 4 vols., Leipzig 1893–1902. Translated by L. Magnus and G. G. Berrie under the title *Greek Thinkers*, London 1901–12.
Windelband, W. *Geschichte der alten Philosophie*, Nördlingen 1888. Translated by H. E. Cushman under the title *History of Ancient Philosophy*, London and Cambridge (Mass.) 1900.
Zeller, E. *Die Philosophie der Griechen*, vols. 1–3, Tübingen 1844–52. *Aristoteles und die alten Peripatetiker*, Leipzig 1879. Translated by Costelloe and Muirhead under the title *Aristotle and the Earlier Peripatetics*, London 1897. (This work is also quoted as *Die Philosophie der Griechen, in ihrer geschichtlichen Entwicklung dargestellt*, vol. II, 2, Leipzig 1879.)
Grundriss der Geschichte der griechischen Philosophie, Berlin 1883. Translated by L. R. Palmer under the title *Outlines of the History of Greek Philosophy*, London 1931.

2. *Some general works*
Ackrill, J. L. *Aristotle*, London 1971.
Allan, D. J. *Aristotle*, London 1952.
Düring, I. *Aristoteles. Darstellung und Interpretation seines Denkens*, Heidelberg 1966.
Jaeger, W. W. *Aristoteles. Grundlegung einer Geschichte seiner Entwicklung*, Berlin 1923. Translated by R. Robinson under the title *Aristotle: Fundamentals of the History of his Development*, Oxford 1934 and 1948.
Lloyd, G. E. R. *Aristotle: The Growth and Structure of his Thought*, London 1968.
Mure, G. R. G. *Aristotle*, London 1932.
Randall, J. H. Jr. *Aristotle*, New York 1960.
Robin, L. *Aristote*, Paris 1944.
Ross, W. D. *Aristotle*, London 1923.
Taylor, A. E. *Aristotle*, 1912.

3. *Life of Aristotle and history of the Aristotelian books*
Bignone, E. *L'Aristotele perduto e la formazione filosofica di Epicuro*, Florence 1935.
Düring, I. *Aristotle in the Ancient Biographical Tradition*, Göteborg 1957.
Moraux, P. *Les Listes anciennes des ouvrages d'Aristote*, Louvain 1951.

4. *The Metaphysics*
Aubenque, P. *Le Problème de l'être chez Aristote*, Paris 1962 (3rd edition 1972).
Cherniss, H. F. *Aristotle's Criticism of Pre-Socratic Philosophy*, Baltimore 1935.
Aristotle's Criticism of Plato and the Academy, Baltimore 1944.
Happ, H. *Hyle. Studien zum aristotelischen Materie-Begriff*, Berlin-New York 1971.
Jaeger, W. W. *Studien zur Enstehungsgeschichte der Metaphysik des Aristoteles*, Berlin 1912.
Oggione, E. *La filosofia prima di Aristotele*, Milan 1931.
Owens, J. *The Doctrine of Being in the Aristotelian Metaphysics*, revised edition, Toronto 1963.
Van der Meulen, J. *Aristoteles. Die Mitte in seinem Denken*, Meisenheim 1951.

5. *Editions and commentaries*
(*a*) *Works of Aristotle*
Apostle, H. G. (ed.) *Metaphysics*, translated into English with a commentary and glossary, University of Indiana Press 1967.
Bekker, I. (ed.) *Aristotelis Opera*, Berlin 1831.
Bonitz, H. (ed.) *Metaphysics*, with a commentary, 2 vols., Bonn 1848–1849.
Jaeger, W. W. (ed.) *Metaphysics*, Oxford 1957.
Ross, W. D. (ed.) *Metaphysics*, with a commentary, 2 vols., Oxford 1924 and 1953.
Schwegler, A. *Metaphysics*, with a German translation and commentary, 4 vols., Tübingen 1847–8.

(*b*) *Ancient commentators*
The Royal Academy, Berlin (eds.) *Commentaria in Aristotelem Graeca (CIAG)*, 23 vols., Berlin 1882–1909.

(c) Peripatetic philosophers
Wehrli, F. (ed.) *Die Schule des Aristoteles. Texte und Kommentar*,
10 parts, Basel–Stuttgart 1944–59.

(d) The Stoa
Arnim, H. von (ed.) *Stoicorum Veterum Fragmenta (SVF)*, 4 vols.,
Leipzig 1905.

6. *Selected articles and collections*
Ackrill, J. L. 'Aristotle's distinction between *energeia* and *kinêsis*', in
Bambrough, *New Essays* etc.
Arnim, H. von 'Die Entwicklung der aristotelischen Gotteslehre',
Sitzungsberichte der Akademie der Wissenschaften in Wien, phil.-
hist. Klasse, vol. 212 (1931), pp. 3–80. Reprinted in Hager,
Metaphysik und Theologie etc.
Bambrough, R. (ed.) *New Essays on Plato and Aristotle*, London
1965.
Berti, E. 'Physique et métaphysique selon Aristote', in Düring,
Naturphilosophie etc.
Chroust, A.-H. 'Aristotle and Athens: some comments on
Aristotle's sojourns in Athens', in *Laval théologique et philosophique*
22, 2 (1966), pp. 186–96.
Cook Wilson, J. 'On the structure of the seventh book of the
Nicomachean Ethics, chapters I–IX', *Göttinger Gelehrter Anzeiger*,
1880 (1).
Copi, I. M. 'Essence and accident', *Journal of Philosophy* 51 (1954),
pp. 706–19. Reprinted in Moravcsik, *Aristotle* etc.
Dirlmeier, F. 'Aristoteles', *Jahrbuch für das Bistum Mainz* 5 (1950),
pp. 161 ff.
'Zum gegenwärtigen Stand der Aristoteles-Forschung', *Wiener
Studien* 76 (1963), pp. 52 ff.
Düring, I. (ed.) *Naturphilosophie bei Aristoteles und Theophrast*,
Verhandlungen des 4, Symposium Aristotelicum veranstaltet in
Göteborg, Heidelberg 1969.
Flashar, H. 'Die Kritik der platonischen Ideenlehre in der Ethik
des Aristoteles', *Synusia*, Festgabe für Wolfgang Schadewaldt,
1965, pp. 223 ff.
Fritz, K. von 'Das *apeiron* bei Aristoteles', in Düring, *Natur-
philosophie* etc.

Furley, D. 'Aristotle and the Atomists on infinity', in Düring, *Naturphilosophie* etc.

Gaiser, K. 'Das zweifache Telos bei Aristoteles', in Düring, *Naturphilosophie* etc.

Gigon, O. 'Interpretationen zu den antiken Aristoteles-Viten', *Museum Helveticum* 15 (1958), pp. 147–93.

Guthrie, W. K. C. 'The development of Aristotle's theology', *Classical Quarterly* 27 (1933), pp. 162–71, and 28 (1934), pp. 90–8. Translated into German by M. Schönherr and reprinted in Hager, *Metaphysik und Theologie* etc.

Hager, F.-P. (ed.) *Metaphysik und Theologie des Aristoteles*, Wege der Forschung, vol. 206, Darmstadt 1969.

Krämer, H. J. 'Zur geschichtlichen Stellung der aristotelischen Metaphysik', *Kant-Studien* 58/3 (1967), pp. 313–54.

Mackinnon, D. M. 'Aristotle's conception of substance', in Bambrough, *New Essays* etc.

Mansion, A. 'L'Objet de la science philosophique suprême d'après Aristote', *Mélanges Diès* 1956, pp. 151–68.

'Philosophie première, philosophie seconde et métaphysique chez Aristote', *Revue philosophique Louvain* 56 (1958), pp. 165–221. Translated into German by H.-L. Heuss and reprinted in Hager, *Metaphysik und Theologie* etc.

Mansion, S. 'Les Apories de la métaphysique d'Aristote', *Recueil d'études offert à A. Mansion*, Louvain 1955, pp. 141–79. Translated into German by M. Roth and reprinted in Hager, *Metaphysik und Theologie* etc.

Moravcsik (ed.) *Aristotle—A Collection of Critical Essays*, London 1968.

Oehler, K. 'Die systematische Integration der aristotelischen Metaphysik', in Düring, *Naturphilosophie* etc.

Owen, G. E. L. '*Tithenai ta phainomena*', Symposium Aristotelicum, Louvain 1961. Reprinted in Moravcsik, *Aristotle* etc.

'The Platonism of Aristotle', Dawes Hicks Lecture on Philosophy, *Proceedings of the British Academy* 51, London 1965.

'Aristotle on the snares of ontology', in Bambrough, *New Essays* etc.

Owens, J. 'The Aristotelian argument for the material principle of bodies', in Düring, *Naturphilosophie* etc.

Patzig, G. 'Theologie und Ontologie in der "Metaphysik" des Aristoteles', *Kant-Studien* 52/2 (1960–1), pp. 185 ff.

Theiler, W. 'Die Entstehung der Metaphysik des Aristoteles', *Museum Helveticum* 15, 2 (1958), pp. 85–105. Reprinted in Hager, *Metaphysik und Theologie* etc.

Wilpert, P. 'Zur Interpretation von Metaphysik Z 15', *Archiv für Geschichte der Philosophie* 42 (1960), pp. 130–58. Reprinted in Hager, *Metaphysik und Theologie* etc.

Woods, J. 'Problems in *Metaphysics* Z, chapter 13', in Moravcsik, *Aristotle* etc.

INDEX OF PASSAGES QUOTED IN TEXT

GENERAL INDEX

15